Heijder has taken a completely new and 21st-century approach to the study of the 19th-century genius Beethoven. The book is exciting, convincing and well-founded. We regard this text as an asset that not only conveys the drawbacks associated with Asperger syndrome, but demonstrates its positive aspects, as well.

AALTJE VAN ZWEDEN, *Papageno Foundation*
JAAP VAN ZWEDEN, *Music Director of the New York Philharmonic*

A fascinating view on the life of a genius. I thoroughly enjoyed reading this in-depth study on Beethoven's nature.

JANINE JANSEN, *violinist*

To truly understand how a genius phenomenon functions is often an enormous and nearly impossible task. It is clear that Mr. Heijder has come close to unlocking one of the key aspects to understanding Beethoven's inner world: one cannot help, but be convinced that, indeed, Beethoven had Asperger syndrome. In this wonderfully written book, the author only uses the most relevant and direct references and one forms a very rounded understanding of the numerous effects the Asperger syndrome had on Beethoven's creativity and on his life, many of which were positive. I find this book to be an invaluable contribution to a new, much broader awareness of the complex, eccentric and captivating genius that Beethoven was.

ALEXANDER GAVRYLYUK, *pianist*

Beethoven is an undisputed genius. This book investigates his social behaviour and personality, which clearly gives evidence of him having Asperger syndrome. It sheds light on a subject that has often, mistakenly, negative connotations. The human condition is immensely complex. We develop expectations and stigmas towards those who don't fit in society. This book opens up discussion for how did this serve him in his genius. Did it perhaps give him limitations or in fact play a part in his incredible ability to express human emotions such as joy or suffering through music?

CANDIDA THOMPSON, *violinist, artistic director of Amsterdam Sinfonietta*

According to writer Heijder, there is an immediate linkage between the constitution of the personality Beethoven and the genius Beethoven, without that Heijder is tempted to only label Beethoven. The latter is not possible anyhow, as the genius Beethoven surpasses any single label. However, the endeavor to link the diagnostic concept of Asperger syndrome with this genius in order to understand Beethoven better, provides us with an extraordinary insight into the personality Beethoven and therewith the creator Beethoven. This book contains a very interesting thesis about a composer whose authentic compositions are so unique and overarching. The book is highly recommended for anyone who is fascinated by this exceptional composer.

ISABELLE VAN KEULEN, *violinist*

This truly inspiring book makes clear to me that Asperger syndrome played a crucial role in enabling Beethoven to write his groundbreaking music. It provides me with a deeper understanding of Beethoven, both the person and his music.

FRANK PETER ZIMMERMANN, *violinist*

This is the best exposition of high functioning autism (Asperger syndrome) that I have ever read. It's truly a, "page-turner," and I could not put it down. There is an absolutely convincing portrait of Beethoven's Asperger syndrome. There's an enormous amount in this book about autistic creativity. There are utterly fascinating portraits of those people around Beethoven and his unempathic relationship with them. This book would be fascinating to all professionals working with persons with Asperger syndrome, including psychiatrists, psychologists and therapists as well as to anybody with an interest in music and creativity. Finally, it is excellently written, and the lay public would get enormous satisfaction from reading it. I can fully recommend it.

MICHAEL FITZGERALD, author of *The Genesis of Artistic Creativity - Asperger's Syndrome and the Arts*

In this outstanding book, the writer, who is an asperger himself, makes a very convincing case that Beethoven had Asperger syndrome. The author even concludes that the asperger strengths have clearly enhanced Beethoven's talent.

DICK SWAAB, author of *We are our Brains*

This book brings us closer to the person Beethoven than ever before and thereby it brings us closer to his music.

JAN WILLEM DE VRIEND, *conductor*

When conducting a diagnostic assessment for Asperger's syndrome, the diagnostician seeks information on the person's developmental history and profile of abilities. Walter Heijder has collated information on Beethoven's life that is valuable source material for a specialist in diagnosing Asperger's syndrome. As I read the descriptions of Beethoven by his contemporaries and Beethoven's own words, they resonated with the descriptions of family members and friends of the clients that I see, their personal histories, and the descriptive text for the diagnostic criteria for Asperger's syndrome. One of the characteristics of Asperger's syndrome is to create and escape into alternative worlds and for Beethoven, this was the world of music. Another characteristic is to have difficulty converting thoughts and emotions into conversational speech. However, those who have Asperger's syndrome can have a remarkable ability and eloquence expressing their thoughts and feelings through music. Beethoven expresses his inner world through his music.

TONY ATTWOOD, author of *The Complete Guide to Asperger's Syndrome*

Beethoven: The Asperger Connection

Walter Heijder

Ludwig Publishers, Amsterdam

ISBN 9781086315899
Cover Design: PHprojecten
General Support: De Boekenfluisteraar
Editing: Book Helpline

Front cover: Beethoven bust by Hugo Hagen

Published by Ludwig Publishers, Amsterdam
First edition

The illustrations in this book are taken from various sources.

Dedicated to Eva

Many aspergers lack common sense. Much of what governs our social interactions is intuitive, and something that is expected to be known almost without explicit training. It is difficult to define 'common sense.' Even so, most people, even school-age children have an inkling of what is inferred by the term. Aspergers are so severely handicapped in this domain that they may themselves feel that they do not know 'how to live.' They appear lost and forlorn. It is usually only toward the end of the pre-adolescent period that it becomes obvious that aspergers are so totally lacking in common sense. [...] It is important to distinguish between having a hobby/interest on the one hand and the kind of obsessive pursuit of narrow interests which is the rule in Asperger syndrome on the other.[1]

CHRISTOPHER GILLBERG

On the other side of the misery of his training, there was the ecstasy of music itself. When he escaped from his father's regime and found better teachers and discovered his own ambitions, the teenage Beethoven still sought solitude, hours when he could be alone with music and pore over his own creations. Even though he was performing constantly in public, the rest of the world and everybody in it could not reach him in that solitude.

Music was the one extraordinary thing in a sea of the disappointing and ordinary. Reared as he was in a relentless discipline, instinctively responsive to music as he was, the boy never truly learned to understand the world outside music. Nobody ever really demanded that of him until, disastrously, near the end of his life. Nor did he ever really understand love. He could perceive the world and other people only through the prism of his own consciousness, judging them in the unforgiving terms he judged himself.

Otherwise Beethoven had little grasp of the world at all. In childhood he did not truly comprehend the independent existence of other people. He never really did. He reached maturity knowing all about music, from writing notes to selling them, but otherwise he did not know how to live in the world. In the ideals he lived by in his solitude, instead of human beings there would be an exalted abstraction: Humanity.[2]

JAN SWAFFORD

TABLE OF CONTENTS

PREFACE

Ludwig van Beethoven was clearly one of the greatest composers of all time. His symphonies, concertos, chamber music, piano music, and not to mention the *Missa Solemnis*, are masterpieces that have been played and analyzed around the world for two centuries. But what about the man behind the music? Countless biographies exist describing the minutiae of his life and of his music. But none of the biographers to date have been able to come up with a reasonably cohesive understanding of the man of genius. Beethoven himself has remained "a mystery."

Several years ago, I was approached by a man who said he thought he had a clue to understanding Beethoven from a new perspective. Walter Heijder came to my office in London and sat with me for hours showing me the results of his research. I was overwhelmed by the thoroughness of his investigative style and much impressed by the high quality of his research.

When I now hold Heijder's book about Beethoven in my hands, I am no less impressed. The book is beautifully written, and, despite the fact that it is packed with historical references, easily accessible. If you have the slightest interest in Beethoven, it makes for compulsive reading.

Heijder gives a detailed and vivid account of Beethoven as he comes across in correspondence and as seen through the eyes of others. You come away convinced that Beethoven must have been somebody who would have met the diagnostic criteria for the syndrome, had they existed in Beethoven's lifetime.

This is a book of high scientific quality, and, perhaps surprisingly, a very enjoyable read.

Christopher Gillberg

INTRODUCTION

Wednesday, 4 March 1807, was a bright spring day in Vienna; only the temperature still indicated winter. The thirty-six-year-old composer Ludwig van Beethoven was at the zenith of his career. The previous year, he had finished his Fourth Piano Concerto, his Third Symphony had been published and his Violin Concerto had had its first performance. But that very morning, bachelor Beethoven had other things on his mind. He fancied a short trip together with a nice woman and immediately thought of the engaging twenty-one-year-old Marie Bigot. Marie Bigot had moved from Switzerland to Vienna together with her husband, the forty-year-old Paul Bigot. She was a gifted pianist and had been introduced to both Salieri and Haydn; the latter is reported to have praised her playing. She received piano lessons from Beethoven and amazed him with her sight-reading of the rain-damaged autograph of his Piano Sonata Opus 57 (*Appassionata*). Halfway, Beethoven said, "That is not exactly the character I wanted to give this piece; but go right on. If it is not wholly mine it is something better."[3]

Marie Bigot (1786–1820)

That very morning, in March 1807, Beethoven wrote a letter that was delivered right away.

> *My dear, honored Marie!*
> *The weather is so divinely beautiful – and who knows whether it will be so tomorrow? I therefore propose to come and fetch you today about twelve noon for a drive. As [Paul] Bigot is probably already out, we cannot of course take him with us – but to give it up entirely on that account, even Bigot himself*

would not make such a demand. Only the mornings are now best. Why not seize the moment, which passes away so quickly. It would be quite unlike Marie, who is so enlightened and well-bred, if for the sake of mere scruples she would wish to deprive me of the very great pleasure. Whatever reasons you might assign for not accepting my proposal, I should ascribe it entirely to the little confidence which you place in my character – and should never believe that you entertain true friendship for me. Wrap up [little] Caroline in swaddling-clothes from head to foot, so that nothing may happen to her. Answer me, my dear Marie, whether you can. I do not ask you whether you are willing – for the latter would only bring a declaration to my detriment – so only answer in [one of] two words: yes or no. Farewell, and arrange that the selfish pleasure may be granted to me of sharing with two persons in whom I take so great interest, the cheerful enjoyment of bright beautiful nature.
Your friend and admirer, Ludwig van Beethoven[4]

This letter shows social awkwardness. It was written even though Beethoven had been told by Paul Bigot that he did not wish Marie to go out with Beethoven alone. Paul Bigot obviously disliked the idea that his much younger wife was seen in public with the famous composer Beethoven when he himself was absent. It also seems to elude Beethoven that his style of writing can easily be misunderstood.

To the astonishment of Beethoven, the invitation was declined and even worse: the letter was not well received at all. Here is the beginning of his next letter to Marie and Paul Bigot, written two days later:

Dear Marie, Dear Bigot,
Only with the deepest regret am I forced to perceive that the purest, most innocent, feelings can often be misconstrued. As you have received me so kindly, it never occurred to me to explain it otherwise than that you bestow on me your friendship. You must think me very vain or small-minded if you suppose that the civility itself of such excellent persons as you are could lead me to believe that – I had at once won your affection. Besides, it is one of my first principles never to stand in other than friendly relationship with the wife of another man.[5]

This kind of strange behavior on the part of Beethoven has caused some consternation. The Flemish conductor and musicologist Jan Caeyers called Beethoven (in his book *Beethoven – a biography* (2010)) *socially impaired*[6] and an *egocentric person.*[7] These exact descriptions are used as criteria to diagnose someone with Asperger syndrome.

The Austrian pediatrician Hans Asperger (1906–1980) described in 1944, a psychiatric syndrome that he called "autistic psychopathy." His article was, during his lifetime, ignored outside central Europe. But in 1981, Lorna Wing, a British autism expert, published a paper in which she introduced the term *Asperger syndrome*, because, in her opinion, the terminology "autistic psychopathy" was not appropriate anymore. Hans Asperger indicated his patients in a direct way: "autistic psychopaths." From 1981 on, the indication became indirect: "people with Asperger syndrome."

In 1991, the first book about Asperger syndrome was published (*Autism and Asperger syndrome*), including the English translation of Hans Asperger's original text. It took six years before the second book was published, but then the publishing rush started: during the first decade of the twenty-first century, hundreds of books were published about this intriguing syndrome.

Hans Asperger and Lorna Wing did not provide any diagnostic criteria for the syndrome. The Swedish professor Christopher Gillberg deserves the credit for creating these diagnostic criteria, which were published in *Autism and Asperger syndrome* (1991) and in his own book *A Guide to Asperger Syndrome* (2002).[8] The first and most important criterion is called: *Social impairment (extreme egocentricity)*.

In Hans Asperger's original article, only children are described. In Gillberg's book and most other books about Asperger syndrome, the emphasis is on children. However, children become adults and that is true for children with Asperger syndrome as well. The first author to systematically describe how Asperger syndrome manifests itself in adulthood was Ashley Stanford in her book *Asperger Syndrome and Long-Term Relationships* (2003). She wrote this book after she discovered that her husband had Asperger syndrome.

Over the course of time, the need was felt to indicate the people in question (again) with direct terminology, primarily when it became generally accepted that this syndrome can be more like a temperament or a personality type than a disorder. The most popular indication became "Aspie". Ashley Stanford uses this wording consistently. But in my opinion, this is too informal and I prefer the phrasing *asperger*. I will use this phrasing also as an adjective, for example, the asperger man, analogous to the lesbian woman.

I will frequently quote from the texts of Asperger, Gillberg, and Stanford. For the sake of legibility, I will replace the phrasings "autistic psychopaths," "person with Asperger syndrome" and "Aspie" with "asperger." The endnotes always inform about the original phrasing.

I will also frequently quote from books about Beethoven. Next to the biography of Caeyers, I will use *The Beethoven Compendium* (1991) because of the excellent chapter *Beethoven as an individual* by Anne-Louise Coldicott, and *Beethoven: Anguish and Triumph* by Jan Swafford (2014), which is the best English Beethoven biography I know.

I quote from the work of others because I am struck by the similarity between the wording of Beethoven experts and the wording of asperger experts.

For example:

> *An almost pathological need to always tell the truth is striking in many cases. The child does not appear to understand 'self-evident' social rules, and cannot be persuaded to keeping his thoughts ('truths') to him/herself.*[9]
> CHRISTOPHER GILLBERG

> *Blatant honesty is a common asperger trait*[10]
> ASHLEY STANFORD

Compare this with the following two quotes:

> *Beethoven did not mince his words.*[11]
> JAN CAEYERS

> *As a young man, Beethoven was frank to the point of rudeness.*[12]
> ANNE-LOUISE COLDICOTT

I am not the first to write about Beethoven and Asperger syndrome. In *The Genesis of Artistic Creativity - Asperger's Syndrome and the Arts* (2005) Irish professor Michael Fitzgerald devotes ten pages to this subject. In his analyses he used only one (secondary) source, an American biography. Although Fitzgerald gathered a lot of useful information from that source, for example regarding Beethoven's social behavior and his narrow interest, what he writes about Beethoven's speech, language and humor is very limited due to the absence of German sources. The reason why I do not mention his book throughout my book is simply because I wanted to start my study from the original sources rather than to build on someone else's shoulders. Yet, Fitzgerald and I value each other's work greatly. His respect for my book is expressed in his recommendation.

This book consists of five chapters. In the first three chapters, I introduce a number of people who were important in Beethoven's life. For easy reference, I divide them into two groups: men (chapter two) and women (chapter three). Beethoven's family relationships are so interwoven that I will deal with them in a separate section (chapter one).

The purpose of the first three chapters is to provide a lively description of Beethoven as a man, especially in his contact with other people. This implies descriptions will go beyond social impairment, although that is the heart of the matter. However, all the presented "social" material will be compared in chapter four with that specific feature of Asperger syndrome. In that chapter, I will also investigate whether Beethoven showed any of the other features of Asperger syndrome. Finally, in chapter five, I will compare Beethoven's behavior with the diagnostic criteria of Asperger syndrome. I will also compare my findings with two other attempts to provide a framework with regard to Beethoven's particular behavior. I will conclude with an essay about the connection between Beethoven's Asperger syndrome and his genius.

I know there are many people who will read about Beethoven and Asperger syndrome with an open mind. There are some who are critical about the post-mortem diagnoses of mental conditions of historical people. Regarding this, Gillberg writes:

> *The lives and personalities of a number of famous people – philosophers, composers, scientists and painters – have been described in sufficient detail to allow well-founded speculation that they might have had the typical features of Asperger syndrome.*[13]

On the same page, Gillberg writes:

> *Maybe one could even speculate that historic progress has quite often been made by people with autism spectrum conditions. The perseverance, drive for perfection, good concrete intelligence, ability to disregard social conventions, and not worry too much about other people's opinions or critiques, could all be seen as advantageous, maybe even a prerequisite for certain forms of new thinking and creativity.*[14]

With these thoughts in mind, I like to portray Beethoven as a person.

CHAPTER

1

"This horrible family that has been thrust upon me"

FAMILY MEMBERS IN BEETHOVEN'S LIFE

Indeed, their behavior in the social group is the clearest sign of their disorder and the source of conflicts from earliest childhood. These conflicts are especially pronounced in the smallest social unit, that is, the family.[15]
HANS ASPERGER

It is in his relationships with members of his family that Beethoven's lack of [social] *insight is most apparent; and it is here too that his inner conflicts led him to cause the most distress both to them and to himself.*[16]
ANNE-LOUISE COLDICOTT

In 1733, the court of Bonn employed Ludwig van Beethoven, a Flemish immigrant, as a musician. He would become the grandfather of Ludwig van Beethoven, one of the most famous composers of all time. As a musician, Ludwig senior was very competent and highly respected. In 1761, he was appointed *Kapellmeister*, meaning he was in charge of the music-making at the court.

Ludwig senior and his wife had one surviving child, their son Johann. Johann became a tenor at the court and taught singing and keyboard. He could also play the violin. In 1767, Johann married the young widow Maria Magdalena Keverich. Together, they had seven children. Their firstborn died a week after birth and a year later, in December 1770, their second child was born and named after his grandfather Ludwig.

Ludwig van Beethoven senior died in December 1773, too early to witness the budding talent of his grandson, who received his first music lessons the next year from his father. Johann could be harsh and severe. There are reports of the small boy standing on a footstool in front of the piano, weeping. There are also reports of physical violence and shutting the child up in the cellar.

Johann must have realized that he was not the best teacher for his son Ludwig and he organized lessons by others. The first teacher was over seventy and the lessons did not last long. The second teacher was a member of a theatrical company, who lodged with the Beethoven family. He encouraged young Ludwig to improvise, a skill that in the years before had been discouraged by his father. From him, Ludwig learned to have faith in the power of his imagination, an essential trait for the rest of his career. But this teacher also frequented taverns with Johann, returning late at night. They would drag Ludwig to the piano and force him to play, which he did, in tears.

The composer Christian Neefe came to Bonn in October 1779 to join a theatrical company as its *Kapellmeister*. He became the most important music teacher of the teenage Beethoven, whose father had taken him out of school around 1781, to prepare him for a career as a musician. In 1782, Neefe became the court organist, with Beethoven as his assistant, first unofficially and, from 1784, officially.

During the following years, Beethoven developed into a skilled and powerful pianist and some of his compositions were published. He also became a member of the court orchestra, playing the viola. His talent as a musician was noted by many people.

In the spring of 1787, Beethoven traveled to Vienna to study with Mozart. Although Beethoven and Mozart did meet, Beethoven did not become Mozart's student and left Vienna after two weeks. Back home, he found that his mother was gravely ill with advanced tuberculosis. She died in July. Beethoven had been greatly attached to his mother and always spoke highly of her throughout his life.

However, Beethoven hardly mentioned his father, who was an alcoholic. In

1784, his father's voice was described as "very stale," which was the beginning of the end of his career as a court musician. A few years later, he tried to con the next of kin of the deceased First Minister. He counterfeited a signature on a document, claiming some valuable property belonged to him. What followed was exposure and humiliation, although no legal action was taken against the son of the former *Kapellmeister*.

That Johann was still paid by the court was more charity than salary. He drank increasingly and behaved in an undignified manner. On one occasion Ludwig – in fact, the head of the household – had to intervene with the police to prevent his father from being taken into custody.

In 1789, Ludwig petitioned the court to have half his father's salary paid to him. The request was granted. Johann died in December 1792. His employer wrote to a friend that the revenues from the liquor tax had suffered a loss in Beethoven's death.

The month before his father passed away, Ludwig moved to Vienna to receive instruction from Haydn, who was at that time (after the death of Mozart in December 1791) indisputably the most important composer alive. Before Beethoven left Bonn, his friends gave him a *Stammbuch* (album) with farewell greetings. The most notable entry was by his patron Count Waldstein:

Dear Beethoven! You are now going to Vienna in fulfillment of a wish that has been long frustrated. Mozart's Genius is still in mourning and weeps for the death of its pupil. It found a refuge with the inexhaustible Haydn but no occupation; through him it wishes to form a union with another. Through uninterrupted diligence you will receive the spirit of Mozart from the hands of Haydn.[17]

HELENE VON BREUNING

In moments of stress it is not uncommon for aspergers to react with panic, 'hysteria', primitive reactions, fear, rage or childish tantrums. Such reactions may border on, or indeed sometimes develop into, confusion states, during which it is quite impossible to reason with the affected individual or even to establish any form of 'contact'.[18]
CHRISTOPHER GILLBERG

Beethoven was of good will, but sometimes it became too much for him and he lost control of himself. What followed were outbursts of pent-up frustration and distress, a pattern of behavior we will come across later in his life. Helene Breuning was acquainted with these kinds of eruptions, knew how to interpret them and realized that one must be able to live with the dark side of Beethoven's genius to profit from his light side. But above all, she was able to gain control over this phenomenon by giving it a name: his raptus.[19]
JAN CAEYERS

There is one person who does not belong to the Beethoven family (not even related by marriage) but still deserves to be mentioned in this section because she played the role of Beethoven's mother after Maria Magdalena died. And she played that role very well.

Helene Breuning lost her husband (a senior court official) during the fire of Bonn's palace in January 1777. The couple already had four children: Eleonore, Christoph, Stephan, and Lorenz. Ludwig was introduced to the Breuning family in the early eighties, to teach piano to Eleonore and Lorenz. During those years, he became more or less part of the Breuning family, sometimes even staying the night.

After her husband's death, Helene Breuning had turned her home into a kind of cultural salon, with a relaxed atmosphere, where literature was read, poems were cited and music was played. It was a place where Ludwig felt very much at home. As well as Ludwig's cultural education, Helene Breuning also invested in his social education. She gave him some basic instructions with regard to etiquette and tried to teach him to avoid expressing provocative thoughts. As a friend later wrote, Helene Breuning had considerable influence over the often offensive, unkind young man.

One of the issues was the keeping of teaching appointments. Ludwig disliked teaching (unless the pupil was of the fair sex), but Helene was of the opinion that one should stick to one's appointments. So, it could happen that Ludwig had to go to such an appointment, but went *ut iniquae mentis asellus*[20] (like a moody donkey).

Helene von Breuning (1750–1838)

Before he reached the doorstep of the house where he had to teach, he would rush back and promise Helene to teach two hours the next day. But today teaching was impossible for him, so he claimed. If Beethoven was in such a mood (or worse) and it was difficult for him to interact properly with his social environment, Helene would say, "Today he has another raptus."[21]

The Latin word *raptus* refers to a state of being carried away by overwhelming emotion. By giving it a name, Helene was able to get control over this phenomenon; but even more important, Ludwig himself was able to gain more self-control. For the rest of his life, he used this terminology when mood swings overwhelmed him.

CASPER CARL VAN BEETHOVEN

Ludwig had two brothers who survived childhood: Casper Carl and Nikolaus Johann. Casper Carl moved to Vienna in 1794 and Nikolaus Johann followed the next year. Casper Carl was active as a musician: teaching, assisting Ludwig and occasionally composing. In 1800, he became a clerk in the Department of Finance but continued to assist Beethoven in dealings with publishers until 1806, the year that he announced to his brother he intended to marry Johanna Reiss, whose hallmark seemed to be dishonesty. Already as a teenager, Johanna had accused the housekeeper of the family of stealing something she had taken herself.

Ludwig endeavored to prevent the marriage, but failed: Casper Carl married Johanna in May 1806. In September, their son Karl was born. From the beginning, Ludwig disliked his sister-in-law. As the years progressed, dislike became disgust.

In 1812, a friend asked Johanna to look after an expensive pearl necklace. Johanna hid the necklace and reported it stolen. The police were not stupid and arrested Johanna, who was sentenced to a year's imprisonment, which was later reduced to one month's house arrest. So, from that year on, Johanna had a criminal record.

In 1813, Casper Carl became seriously ill with tuberculosis. His condition was so bad that he feared he would soon be dead. In April, he made a declaration in which he requested his brother Ludwig to undertake sole guardianship of his son Karl, in the event of his death. But Casper Carl did not die that year; on the contrary, his health improved over the next months.

JOHANNA VAN BEETHOVEN:
THE CASE BEETHOVEN VERSUS BEETHOVEN

The Asperger's first impression of new information is extremely important since they tend to stick with their first belief. The asperger may lack the cognitive flexibility to change the initial impression.[22]
ASHLEY STANFORD

For well and ill, what Beethoven had been in his teens had not fundamentally changed. He had never grown into social maturity. He was not able to understand anything through another person's eyes, could see the world only through his own lens. When he made up his mind about a person or an issue, that was that, unless he could be persuaded that he had misjudged. There was no possible way Johanna could convince him he had misjudged her, so that

was that. Just as in his music he demanded that the material must submit to his will, in his personal life he demanded that the world submit to his convictions about how things ought to be.[23]
JAN SWAFFORD

Johanna was subjected to separation from her son and public denigration of her character, penalties out of all proportion to her wrongdoings. That Beethoven could inflict so much suffering and yet remain convinced that he was right cannot be sufficiently explained either by his lack of regard for other people's feelings or by his own conviction that his actions were dictated by duty.[24]
ANNE-LOUISE COLDICOTT

The prelude to the case of Ludwig van Beethoven versus Johanna van Beethoven started on 14 November 1815. The very day that Casper Carl, dying, made his will. About his son Karl, he wrote, "Along with my wife I appoint my brother Ludwig van Beethoven co-guardian." When Ludwig read the will, he insisted this sentence be changed. Later he wrote about that day and the will, "I came upon it by chance. If what I had seen was really to be the original text, then passages had to be deleted. This I had my brother make since I did not wish to be bound up in this with such a bad woman in a matter of such importance as the education of the child." After a discussion between the brothers, the sentence read, "~~Along with my wife~~ I appoint my brother Ludwig van Beethoven ~~co~~-guardian."

After Ludwig had left, it was Johanna's turn to put pressure on Casper Carl. So Casper Carl added a codicil to the will.

Codicil to my Will
Since I have observed that my brother, Herr Ludwig van Beethoven, desires after my eventual death to take wholly to himself my son Karl, and wholly to withdraw him from the supervision and training of his mother, and further, since the best of harmony does not exist between my brother and my wife, I have found it necessary to add to my will that I by no means desire that my son Karl be taken away from his mother, but that he shall always and so long as his future destiny remain with his mother, to which end she as well as my brother shall direct the guardianship over my son Karl. Only through harmony can the purpose that I had in appointing my brother guardian of my son be attained, for the welfare of my child, I recommend compliance to my wife and more moderation to my brother. God permit the two of them to be harmonious for the welfare of my child. This is the last wish of the dying husband and brother.
Vienna, 14 November 1815
Carl van Beethoven[25]

Casper Carl van Beethoven died the next day. One week later, Johanna was appointed as Karl's guardian and Ludwig was appointed associate guardian.

The case of Beethoven versus Beethoven started on 28 November, 1815, the very day Ludwig appealed to the *Landrecht* (the upper court) to exclude Johanna from Karl's guardianship. Ludwig's strategy was to make clear that the codicil was written under pressure by a woman who had a criminal record. Such a woman was unfit to bring up a child, so Ludwig argued.

On 9 January 1816, the *Landrecht* settled Karl's guardianship in Ludwig's favor and ten days later, Ludwig was legally appointed Karl's sole guardian. On 2 February, Karl was removed from his mother and placed in a boarding school run by Giannatasio del Rio. Johanna made repeated attempts to visit Karl, one time even disguising herself as a man. When Ludwig discovered this, he warned the headmaster about Johanna, writing, "Last night that Queen of the Night was at the Artists' Ball until 3 am, exposing not only her mental but also her bodily nakedness. It was whispered that she was willing to hire herself for twenty gulden! Oh horrible!"[26] There is no source to confirm this allegation. Ludwig went back to court to make sure that Johanna could not see her son. The court stipulated that Johanna could see her son during his leisure time, but only with the consent of Ludwig.

In September 1816, Karl underwent a hernia operation, after which he needed to wear a truss. During his convalescence, he stayed with his uncle in his summer residence in Baden. The reason Karl had to go to a boarding school in the first place was that it was clear to Ludwig that his apartment in Vienna was not suited to accommodate a child. But it took Ludwig until September 1816 before he started making plans to have Karl live with him, and consulting other people about domestic arrangements. However, for Ludwig, one important thing could already be organized. Ludwig wanted Karl van Beethoven to become a musician and so he arranged piano lessons with the best piano teacher of that time, Carl Czerny.

It was in January 1818 that Ludwig finally took Karl out of Giannatasio's boarding school (where he had been for almost two years) and they started to live together in Vienna. Lessons were provided by a private tutor. In May, Ludwig and Karl moved to a small town outside Vienna for the summer months; Karl was taught for a month by the village priest.

In the fall of 1818, Johanna appealed twice to the *Landrecht* to reconsider their decision. She argued that Ludwig was doing a bad job as a guardian and that his deafness had increased. Ludwig denied any problems regarding his hearing and health in general and the appeals were dismissed.

On 3 December, Karl ran away to his mother. The next morning Ludwig demanded Johanna return Karl to him. She promised to do so the same evening. Ludwig called the police, who persuaded her to hand Karl over right away and brought him to Giannatasio's boarding school.

These events were justification for Johanna to appeal to the *Landrecht* and on 11 December the court hearings took place. First, Karl was interviewed. He stated he admired his uncle. When asked whether his uncle had ever mistreated him, he replied that he had only once: after the police had returned him from his mother, his uncle had tried to throttle him.

Then it was Johanna's turn, she reasoned that her son disliked living with his uncle and that he, therefore, had run away and had come to her. Her lawyer stated that the Beethoven brothers were more enemies than friends. He added that Johanna van Beethoven's son, Karl, could not be allowed to remain under the sole influence of his uncle and guardian, because of the danger of physical suffering and moral ruin.

Then, Johanna continued and said she had heard that Ludwig intended to send Karl to a private school outside Vienna. She thought it more appropriate to send Karl to a local school. She knew that a place was available.

The third person to be interviewed was Ludwig. He stated that there were too many pupils at the local school and the supervision would be insufficient. Then he was asked what his plans were regarding Karl's education. It seems Ludwig was not prepared for this question and wanted to make clear he wanted the best of the best for Karl. So, he first talked about the boarding school and then about a private school in another town. To clarify his best intentions he added that he, of course, would send Karl to the *Theresianum Academy* "if he were but of noble birth."

To understand the devastating impact of those last seven words, it is important to realize that Vienna, at that time, was a class society. The noblemen (like barons, counts, and dukes) had their own layer in society: the upper layer. In German, the word "von" indicated that someone was a nobleman. One could be of noble birth or become a nobleman during one's lifetime, like Johann von Goethe. However, the Dutch word "van" (as in Vincent van Gogh) does not indicate nobility.

When Ludwig van Beethoven arrived in Vienna in 1792, he was soon embraced by the noble class. He became completely used to the assumption that he was a nobleman himself and it was too convenient for him to disavow it. The explicit separation between the nobility and the common man required that in Vienna the nobility had their own school (the *Theresianum Academy*) and their own court, the *Landrecht*. Common people had to appeal to the lower court, the *Magistrat*.

When during the court interview it became clear that Ludwig was not a nobleman, the *Landrecht* did not hesitate to transfer the case to the *Magistrat*. In January 1819, the *Magistrat* forced Ludwig to relinquish his role and find another guardian, while Karl temporarily returned to his mother. Now, it was Ludwig's turn to write several letters to the court, requesting reconsideration of the case. His protests were either rejected or he received no answer at all. In the year 1819, it was not clear to Karl who his guardian was (the one who had been appointed in March, resigned during the summer; after which, Johanna was appointed guardian, together with a co-guardian), and it was not clear which was his school (Ludwig wanted to send him to Landshut in Bavaria, but a passport was refused; then he was sent to another institute in Vienna).

In the fall of 1819, Ludwig took on a new legal counselor, who gave him brilliant advice. Together they wrote a long memorandum including information about Johanna, the *Magistrat*, Karl, his school reports, Ludwig's activities on his behalf, and Karl's property. They used the opportunity to describe Johanna as an evil and immoral woman, with a criminal record, with no serious education, unsuited anyway to raise a child. The brilliant move was to submit the document not to the *Magistrat* but to the Court of Appeal, the highest court in the country.

The strategy worked out perfectly. In April 1820, the Court of Appeal ruled in Ludwig's favor; Ludwig was appointed guardian, together with a co-guardian. As the verdict of the Court of Appeal is a final one, Johanna had lost absolutely. She turned to the Emperor for help, but to no avail. After a legal battle of four-and-a-half years, Karl finally completely belonged to Ludwig.

KARL VAN BEETHOVEN

Based on clinical work there can be no doubt that aspergers find it tiresome and strenuous to reflect about other people's thoughts and feelings. It would not occur to them intuitively to consider other people's perspectives or to go outside their own circumscribed egocentric vantage point.[27]
CHRISTOPHER GILLBERG

Here [in his dealings with his nephew Karl] *was the clearest example of Beethoven's inability to comprehend another person's feelings.*[28]
ANNE-LOUISE COLDICOTT

Now his human incapacities, the worst of himself – his solipsism, suspicion, hotheadedness, and misanthropy – became his worst enemies, whether he was dealing with servants, with Karl, or with Karl's teachers. He was terrible at dealing with people in general, [...] and terrible at dealing with the rest of life outside music. Now, starting with a young boy and his mother, he had no choice but to deal with people all the time, had to cope with the lives and needs of other people whom he could not begin to understand. He did it all badly.[29]
JAN SWAFFORD

In 1823, Ludwig took Karl from the institute he had entered four years earlier and took him into his apartment. From the piano lessons with Carl Czerny and his successor Joseph Czerny (not related), it had become clear that Karl had no musical talent whatsoever. Ludwig agreed that Karl should, therefore, achieve the next best thing a human being could in life, he would become a scientist. So, Karl entered university to study philosophy and languages. But there he did not find his calling either.

In June 1824, Karl informed Ludwig that he wanted to become a soldier. Ludwig was furious and did not give his consent. However, he allowed Karl to leave university the next year and enter the Polytechnic Institute to study commerce.

In May 1825, Ludwig moved to Baden – his summer residence that year. His nephew remained in Vienna and visited his uncle on Sundays. For Karl, it was a problem that Ludwig always tried to control everything he did. Arguments could arise at any moment. Ludwig wrote Karl dozens of letters, full of requests and advice, but also full of criticism and accusations. Below are two excerpts of letters Ludwig wrote to Karl in May 1825.

Although I have been informed by somebody that again there have been secret meetings between you and your mother, until now I have only suspected it. Have I once more to suffer the most abominable ingratitude?! No, if the tie between us is to be broken, let it be so, but you will be hated by all impartial people who hear about it.[30]

Moderation is necessary for the young, and you do not seem to have paid enough attention to this, since you had money without my knowing it, and without my knowing from whom. Nice goings-on. To go to the theater is not advisable just yet, on account of its great distraction, so I think. The 5 fl. laid out by Dr. Reissig, I shall pay off punctually every month – and that is done with. Spoiled as you have been, it would do you no harm at last to study simplicity and truth, for my heart has suffered too much through your crafty behavior toward me, and it is difficult to forget and even if I, like a yoke-ox, drag along without murmuring, yet if you behave toward others in the same manner, it will never win for you people who love you. God is my witness, I dream only of being completely removed from you and that wretched brother [Nikolaus Johann] and this horrible family that has been thrust upon me. May God grant my wishes. For I can no longer trust you.
Unfortunately, your Father
or, better still, not your Father[31]

One day in the spring of 1826, Karl asked his uncle for money. Ludwig went to the lodgings where Karl was staying and wanted to see the receipt of payment to the landlord for the rent of the previous month. Karl stated he had already given it to him. Ludwig said he had not. Karl searched his room, but the receipt was not to be found. Then Ludwig wanted to know how Karl spent his money. Karl denied having big expenses. A big argument followed. Ludwig did not mind that it was witnessed by other people.

When Ludwig returned to Karl's place a couple of days later, Karl said, "You consider it insolence if, after you have upbraided me for hours undeservedly, this time at least, I cannot turn from my bitter feeling of pain to jocularity. I am not so frivolous as you think. I can assure you that since the scene on Sunday in the presence of this fellow, I have been so depressed that the people in the house noticed it. The receipt for the 80 florins, which were paid in May I now positively know, after a search at home, that I gave to you, as I already said on Sunday; it must and no doubt will be found."[32]

Then Karl told Ludwig to go away because he wanted to study for the next exam. Ludwig remarked that Karl always seemed to be busy when his uncle was near, but otherwise would do nothing useful. Karl contradicted it and stated that

Ludwig believed every malicious gossip about him. A big argument followed again, this time with physical violence and uncle and nephew were separated by someone who heard the shouting. It was not the first time that there was physical violence between uncle and nephew. But it was the last argument between uncle and nephew as far as Karl was concerned. After more than ten years of Ludwig van Beethoven in his life, Karl had had enough.

Nephew Karl van Beethoven (1806–1858)

The next day Ludwig wrote to Karl:

> *Since you at least have followed my advice, all is forgiven and forgotten, more about it when I see you. I have calmed down now. Do not think that any other thought weighs with me than that of your well-being. Judge my actions from this – do not take a step, which may bring you into trouble and may shorten my life. I only got to sleep about 3 o'clock, for I was coughing the whole night. I embrace you heartily, and am sure that you will soon misunderstand me no longer, thus do I also judge your behavior of yesterday. I expect you without fail today at one o'clock; give me no more trouble and anxiety, meanwhile, farewell. Your true and faithful father.*
> *[PS] We are alone, I would not let H. come on that account, all the more as I wish that nothing be said about yesterday, come then. Let my poor heart bleed no longer.*[33]

But Karl had already made up his mind. He bought a pistol but it was discovered by his landlord, who took it away and informed Ludwig that Karl intended to shoot himself. That pistol was safely locked away. On Saturday, 5 August, Karl pawned his watch, bought two more pistols and quickly took a coach to Baden, where he and his uncle had spent many days during several summers. There he checked in for the night. The next day, he walked to a ruin on a wooded slope near Baden. There, using the two pistols, he aimed at his head and fired.

The first bullet missed completely. The second bullet made a hideous wound but did not penetrate the skull. When later that day Karl was found, he was conscious. He asked to be taken to his mother.

Ludwig was distraught. When he entered the room in Johanna's house where his nephew lay, Karl pleaded with him not to plague him with reproaches and lamentation. After Ludwig had left, Karl said he desired never to see his uncle again, because he had enough of being blamed for everything.

The doctor who attended Karl made sure that he was admitted to hospital the next day. But this was not only a medical case; it was a legal case as well, for at that time, to attempt suicide was a crime. So, the case was reported to the criminal court and Karl received religious instruction from a priest with regard to the wrong that he had done. Only if the magistrate was convinced that Karl was morally corrected, could he be released.

When Ludwig told other people about what happened, he stressed the disgrace it had caused him. He told a doctor in the hospital that he did not want to see his nephew. Karl did not deserve that, for "he caused me too much trouble."

Ironically. Karl, as a would-be suicide, could not return to Vienna, where he was very well-known. For, in fact, he now had a criminal record. The best option in this situation for him was to join the army. But first, the wound had to heal and his hair would have to grow more to cover the scar. The question of where he could stay in the meantime was answered when he and Ludwig received an offer they could not refuse. The offer came from Ludwig's brother, Nikolaus Johann van Beethoven.

NIKOLAUS JOHANN VAN BEETHOVEN

After his move to Vienna in 1795, Nikolaus Johann soon found employment as a pharmacist's assistant and in 1808 he moved to Linz to take over a pharmacy. The French armies that wandered through the region in subsequent years were hated by the local people, but Nikolaus Johann saw a business opportunity: an army needs a lot of medication and Nikolaus Johann could provide that. This business was not good for his standing in the neighborhood, but it yielded him a lot of money. By 1819, he was rich enough to buy a country estate in Gneixendorf (near Krems, some thirty miles west of Vienna).

In 1812, Johann started a relationship with his housekeeper, Therese Obermayer, who had an illegitimate child from a previous relationship. As soon as Ludwig became aware of this, he rushed to Linz to put an end to the affair. Ludwig talked first with his brother, then with the local bishop, then with the local magistrate and finally with the local police. He demanded that Therese leave Linz. But none of the people he spoke to agreed with him. His actions were counter-productive: Johann and Therese married in November.

Over the next ten years, Nikolaus Johann and Ludwig seem to have had little contact. From 1822 on, however, Ludwig used Nikolaus Johann as a business adviser. The tone of the many letters from that year on is mostly kind, but what caused some tension was the difference in net worth between the two brothers and the unwillingness of Nikolaus Johann to help his brother if Ludwig requested a loan from him. Ludwig complained sometimes about the "loveless behavior"[34] of Nikolaus Johann and called him a "pseudo-brother."[35]

In September 1826, Nikolaus Johann invited his brother and nephew to come to his estate in Gneixendorf. On 29 September, Ludwig and Karl arrived there, three days after Karl had left the hospital, with permission from the *Magistrat*. The visit was intended to last for two weeks but extended to two months.

The wealthy "pseudo-brother" Nikolaus Johann played his role well, by charging his brother a small rent. The first month (October), however, was rather relaxed for all people involved, including Therese van Beethoven. Ludwig did not show the same kind of disgust as with his other sister-in-law.

One day, Johann took Ludwig with him to visit a local official to discuss business. Nikolaus Johann took the seat that Ludwig refused, preferring to remain standing next to the door. The meeting took a while, but Ludwig remained standing. When the Beethoven brothers left, the official bowed several times. Afterward, he asked his clerk if he knew who the man who remained standing was. The clerk answered that, because the official had shown a lot of respect, the standing man must have been someone important. "Otherwise, I should take him for a dumbass."[36]

Brother Nikolaus Johann (1776–1848)

In November, Ludwig began to behave more and more like a dumbass. He withdrew from the others, refusing to eat with them. The weather in November was getting colder and Ludwig lapsed into his old habit of controlling everything Karl did. Karl disapproved of this and said, "You ask me why I do not talk...Because I have had enough...Yours is the right to command, and I must endure it all...I can only regret that I can give no answer to anything you have said today since I know of nothing better to do than listen and to remain silent as is my duty. You must not consider this insolent."[37]

This was not enough to deter Ludwig. In despair, Karl said, "But I beg of you once more not to torment me as you are doing; you might regret it, for I can endure much, but too much I cannot endure. You treated your brother in the same way today without cause. You must remember that other people are also human beings."[38]

On the night of 1 December, the two Beethoven brothers had a big argument. Ludwig demanded that in his will Nikolaus Johann should make Karl his heir. Ludwig abhorred the very thought that Beethoven money would go to Therese and her illegitimate daughter. But Nikolaus Johann refused. The argument lasted for hours. Early in the morning, Ludwig was so angry that he wanted to depart right away, taking Karl with him. It was very cold and Nikolaus Johann, although agitated, did not want his brother and nephew to travel to Vienna in these circumstances. He hoped to deter Ludwig by stating that the only vehicle available was an open-top cart. But a little later Ludwig and Karl were on their way. They drove all day and stayed the night in a tavern, in an unheated room. On the afternoon of 2 December, uncle and nephew arrived in Vienna. Ludwig was shivering from fever. He was very ill.

Karl stayed with his uncle for another month. On 2 January 1827, he left Vienna for Iglau (today Jihlava in the Czech Republic) to eventually join the army. Their parting would turn out to be final: they would never see each other again.

CHAPTER

2

"I do not deserve your friendship"

MEN IN BEETHOVEN'S LIFE

The egocentricity usually makes it hard to find real friends.[39]
CHRISTOPHER GILLBERG

For Beethoven it was difficult to make friends.[40]
JAN CAEYERS

*Rarely was he able to sustain a friendship; most were marred either by trivial
misunderstandings or by bitter quarrels.*[41]
ANNE-LOUISE COLDICOTT

*Over and over again I read in the literature that, despite appearances, aspergers don't
intend to inflict hurt on others.*[42]
ASHLEY STANFORD

*There is no record that he ever deliberately set out to hurt or betray a friend, though
he fought with most of the friends he ever had.*[43]
JAN SWAFFORD

In Beethoven's life, many men played an important role. The contacts range from lifelong friends to brief business-like relationships. In most cases, the contacts were intense. A selection of these men follows in the chronological order of the time of the chief point of contact. The men will be presented separately. That does not mean that there are no connections between them; these connections certainly existed and will be apparent.

FRANZ WEGELER

Wegeler got to know Beethoven around 1783 and they became close friends. It was Wegeler who introduced Beethoven to the Breuning family. He studied medicine and was appointed professor of medicine at the University of Bonn in 1789. In October 1794, the French army marched in Bonn and Wegeler moved to Vienna, together with Lorenz von Breuning, who studied medicine. At that time Beethoven had already lived for two years in Vienna, so the friendship was renewed. The piano lessons with Lorenz also resumed.

The first (surviving) letter from Beethoven to Wegeler dates from the few years they both lived in Vienna and shows there was a ripple in their friendship.

My dearest, my best one!
What a horrible picture you have shown to me of myself. Oh, I admit that I
do not deserve your friendship. You are so noble, so kindly disposed; and now
for the first time I do not dare to compare myself with you; I have fallen far
beneath you. Alas! For eight weeks I have given pain to my best, my noblest
friend. You believe I have ceased to be kind-hearted. No, thank heaven, for
what made me behave to you like that was not intentional, thought-out malice
on my part, but my unpardonable thoughtlessness, which prevented me from
seeing the matter in the right light. I am thoroughly ashamed for your sake,
also for mine. I scarcely venture to beg you to restore your friendship. Ah,
Wegeler! My only consolation is that you knew me almost from my childhood,
but oh, let me say it myself: I was really always of good disposition, and in
my dealings always strove to be upright and honest; how, otherwise, could you
have loved me! Could I, then, in so short a time have suddenly changed so
terribly, so greatly to my disadvantage? Impossible that these feelings for what
is great and good should all of a sudden become extinct! No, Wegeler, dear
and best one. Venture once again to come to the arms of your Beethoven. Trust
to the good qualities which you formerly found in him. I will vouch for it that
the pure temple of holy friendship which you will erect on them will forever

stand firm; no chance event, no storm will be able to shake its foundations. Firm–eternal–our friendship–forgiveness–forgetting–revival of dying, sinking friendship. Oh, Wegeler, do not cast off this hand of reconciliation; place your hand in mine. O God. But no more! I myself come to you and throw myself in your arms, and court for the lost friend, and you will give yourself to me (full of contrition), who loves and ever will be mindful of you.
Beethoven.
[PS] *I have just received your letter on my return home.*[44]

Franz Wegeler (1765–1848)

The cause of this letter is unknown but it is clear that the friendship was indeed restored, without long-term negative consequences. In 1796, Wegeler returned to Bonn; later he moved to Koblenz. In March 1802, Wegeler married Eleonore von Breuning, also called Lorchen.

In October 1797, Lorenz von Breuning returned to Bonn too. In his farewell letter, Beethoven wrote that he would never forget the time they spent together, both in Bonn and in Vienna. "Continue to be my friend and you will find me ever the same." Back in Bonn, Lorenz von Breuning died from meningitis in April 1798.

The next (surviving) letter from Beethoven to Wegeler, an elaborate one, dates from 29 June 1801, when Wegeler had already been back in Bonn for five years. Beethoven wrote that he values the friendship with Wegeler a lot, that he, Beethoven, is unforgivably negligent in maintaining their friendship, that he wishes to visit Wegeler and greet father Rhine, that he is doing well as a man and as an artist, and that as a composer, there is more demand than he can supply. But then Beethoven writes about a serious problem that has shown up:

But that jealous demon, my wretched health, has put a nasty spoke in my wheel; and it amounts to this, that for the last three years my hearing has become weaker and weaker. The trouble is supposed to have been caused by the condition of my abdomen, which, as you know, was wretched even before I left Bonn, but has become worse in Vienna where I have been constantly afflicted with diarrhea and have been suffering in consequence from an extraordinary debility. [Doctor] Frank tried to tone up my constitution with strengthening medicines and my hearing with almond oil. His treatment had no effect, my deafness became even worse and my abdomen continued to be in the same state as before. Such was my condition until fall of last year; and sometimes I gave way to despair. Then a medical ass advised me to take cold baths to improve my condition. A more sensible doctor, however, prescribed the usual tepid baths in the Danube. The result was miraculous; and my inside improved. But my deafness persisted or, I should say, became even worse. During this last winter I was truly wretched, for I had really dreadful attacks of colic and again relapsed completely into my former condition. And thus, I remained until about four weeks ago when I went to see [Doctor] Vering. For I began to think that my condition demanded the attention of a surgeon as well; and, in any case, I had confidence in him. Well, he succeeded in checking almost completely this violent diarrhea. He prescribed tepid baths in the Danube, to which I had always to add a bottle of strengthening ingredients. He ordered no medicines until about four days ago when he prescribed pills for my stomach and an infusion for my ear. As a result, I have been feeling, I may say, stronger and better; but my ears continue to hum and buzz day and night. I must confess that I lead a miserable life. For almost two years I have ceased to attend any social functions, just because I find it impossible to say to people: I am deaf. If I had any other profession, I might be able to cope with my infirmity; but, in my profession, it is a terrible handicap. And if my enemies, of whom I have a fair number, were to hear about it, what would they say? In order to give you some idea of this strange deafness, let me tell you that in the theater I have to place myself quite close to the orchestra in order to understand what the actor is saying, and that, at a distance, I cannot hear the high notes of instruments or voices. As for the spoken voice, it is surprising that some people have never noticed my deafness; but since I have always been liable to fits of absentmindedness, they attribute my hardness of hearing to that. Sometimes too I can scarcely hear a person who speaks softly; I can hear sounds, it is true, but cannot make out the words. But if anyone shouts, I can't bear it. Heaven alone knows what is to become of me. Vering tells me that my hearing will certainly improve, although my deafness may not be completely cured. Already I have often cursed my Creator and my existence. Plutarch has shown me the path of resignation. If it is at all possible, I will bid defiance to my fate, though I feel that as long as I live there will be moments when I shall be God's most unhappy creature. I beg you not to say anything about my condition to anyone, not even to Lorchen; I am only telling you this as a secret; but I should like you to correspond with Vering about it. If my trouble persists, I will visit you next spring. You will rent a house for me in some beautiful part of the country and then for six months I will lead a peasant's life. Perhaps that will make a difference. Resignation, what a wretched resource! Yet it is all that is left to me.[45]

Beethoven continued the letter by begging Wegeler to send him the portrait of his grandfather "as soon as possible." When he came to the end of the letter, he asked Wegeler to mention him to Helene Breuning and to tell her that he still occasionally has a *raptus*.

On 16 November 1801, Beethoven again wrote an elaborate letter to Wegeler, in which he again complained about his emerging deafness and the consequences thereof:

You would find it hard to believe what an empty, sad life I have had for the last two years. My poor hearing haunted me everywhere like a ghost; and I avoided all human society. I seemed to be a misanthrope and yet I am far from being one.[46]

The next letter to Wegeler seems to be from 2 May 1810. The serious problem is still there.

Yet I would be happy, perhaps one of the happiest of men, if the demon had not settled in my ears. If I had not read somewhere that man must not voluntarily part with his life as long as he can still perform a good deed, I would long ago have ceased to be—and, indeed, by my own hand. Oh, life is so beautiful, but for me it is poisoned forever.[47]

But the object of this letter was a request. Beethoven asked Wegeler to send a copy of his baptismal certificate to Vienna. Again, he pressed him to do this "soon;" similarly as the portrait of his grandfather had to be sent "as soon as possible."

Although they never saw each other again, the friendship did not fade, as letters from December 1826 and February 1827 show.

JOSEPH HAYDN

The skills that a child acquires grow out of a tension between two opposite poles; one is spontaneous production, the other imitation of adult knowledge and skills. They have to balance each other if the achievement is to be of value. When original ideas are lacking achievement is an empty shell: what has been learnt is merely a superficial and mechanical copy. Asperger intelligence is characterized by precisely the opposite of this problem. Asperger children are able to produce original ideas. Indeed, they can only be original, and mechanical learning is hard for them. They are simply not set to assimilate and learn an adult's knowledge. Just as, in general, somebody's good and bad sides are inextricably linked, so the special abilities and disabilities of aspergers are interwoven.[48]
HANS ASPERGER

To all and sundry for the rest of his life, he would declare he had learned nothing from Haydn, nothing from anybody but himself, and from studying the music of the masters.[49]
JAN SWAFFORD

Besides Mozart, Haydn is regarded as the most important composer of the second half of the eighteenth century. He spent much of his career as a court musician for the wealthy Esterházy family at their remote estate south of Vienna. When he retired in 1790, he was allowed to travel to London. Both on his journey to and from London he stayed in Bonn. On at least one of these occasions, he met with the young Beethoven, who showed him a cantata he had composed, which impressed Haydn. In November 1792, Beethoven moved to Vienna to study with Haydn. The lessons lasted until January 1794, when Haydn left once again for London.

After Haydn's departure, Beethoven started composing three piano trios, which would be published in 1795 as his Opus 1. When Haydn returned in August, he praised the piano trios but advised not to publish the third one. Beethoven was surprised and irritated because he thought the third to be the best one. His impression was that Haydn was envious and jealous. But Haydn only advised against publishing because he thought the public would not understand and appreciate the work. On the contrary, it quickly became popular.

Beethoven did dedicate his next work to Haydn: the three piano sonatas (Opus 2). Haydn felt honored but requested that Beethoven write "pupil of Haydn" on the title page of his first published works. Beethoven refused because, stating that, although he had received lessons from Haydn, he had learned nothing from him.

Joseph Haydn (1732–1809)

The relations between Beethoven and Haydn were variable. In December 1795, Haydn gave a concert during which Beethoven had the honor to perform his Second Piano Concerto. But that does not alter the fact that, behind his back, Haydn referred to Beethoven as the "Grand Mogul," meaning a "big shot" or at least someone who thinks he is.

In March 1808, Haydn's seventy-sixth birthday was celebrated in a grand manner with a spectacular festive concert. Beethoven walked forward, got down on his knees and kissed Haydn's hands with tears in his eyes. That was a big sign of respect towards the man whose shadow Beethoven could still feel at certain moments. The year before, the Esterházy family had ordered Beethoven to write a Mass. Beethoven hardly had any experience in the genre and was aware that the principal was used to "the inimitable masterpieces of the great Haydn." Later in his life, Beethoven spoke only positively about Haydn, calling him "a great man."

KARL VON LICHNOWSKY

During the period in which Lichnowsky studied law (in Leipzig and Göttingen), he developed a serious interest in music. When he returned to his birthplace of Vienna, this prince took piano lessons from Mozart. He married Countess Christiane Thun-Hohenstein and together they belonged to the most important nobility of Vienna. Because the noblemen did not have to work – the longer one could sleep in, the higher one's social status – they had time for hobbies and one of those hobbies was music. Several noblemen had their own pianists, set of chamber musicians or even a whole orchestra, and quite a few private concerts were given.

In 1789, Lichnowsky organized a concert tour for Mozart to Prague, Dresden, Leipzig, and Berlin. Lichnowsky joined Mozart during the tour, which was not beneficial to their relationship. However, the all-time low point in their relationship was two years later when Lichnowsky sued Mozart because of debts. Lichnowsky won the court case in November. Mozart died the next month.

The Lichnowskys were distantly related to Count Waldstein and thus it came about that Beethoven's first housing in Vienna was an attic room in Lichnowsky's large house. Lichnowsky became his patron and through him, Beethoven could perform at salon soirees, which became an increasing success. It took Lichnowsky until October 1794 before he realized that he had a genius like Mozart in his attic, and Beethoven was allowed to move to the first floor, where Lichnowsky himself lived. At that time, Beethoven had become Vienna's supreme pianist. His way of playing was highly praised; he was not. One woman observed, "His entire deportment showed no signs of exterior polish. On the contrary, he was lacking in manners in both demeanor and behavior."[50]

In 1795, the prince was instrumental in securing Beethoven's first public performance. In the *Burgtheater*, Beethoven played his Second Piano Concerto, which was repeated the next evening. On the third night, Beethoven performed a Mozart piano concerto. Thus, his name became known outside of the nobility.

Each Friday, a concert took place at Lichnowsky's place and several of Beethoven's compositions were first performed at these occasions. This applied to the Piano Trio's Opus 1, dedicated to the prince, who helped subsidize the publication. Beethoven later also dedicated other works to Lichnowsky, including two piano sonatas (Opus 13 (*Pathétique*) and Opus 26) and the Second Symphony.

The mark Karl von Lichnowsky left on Beethoven and his career was massive and Beethoven recognized that. But there was also a dark side; Beethoven perceived Count Lichnowsky's protection as oppressive. That included the influence of Countess Christiane, who behaved like a mother, although she was Beethoven's senior by only five and a half years. This resulted in a kind of game: As

Lichnowsky came closer, Beethoven became more distant. The prince ordered that in case he and Beethoven would call a staff member at the same time, Beethoven should be attended first. Beethoven reacted by hiring his own attendant. The Prince invited Beethoven to ride his horses. Beethoven reacted by buying his own horse. Both impulsive acts were brash, financially speaking. In May 1795, Beethoven decided to move to a house nearby.

Karl von Lichnowsky (1756–1814)

In the first half of 1796, Count Lichnowsky organized a concert tour for Beethoven to Prague, Dresden, Leipzig, and Berlin, indeed the same route as Mozart in 1789. The tour turned out to be a big success. Beethoven's name was already established in Prague and he was warmly welcomed there. Lichnowsky was clever enough not to accompany Beethoven beyond Prague, in order to avoid the mistake he had made seven years before, being too close to a genius for too long a time. The climax of the tour was in Berlin, where Beethoven was welcomed by the King of Prussia, Friedrich Wilhelm II. Here, Beethoven wrote the Cello Sonatas No. 1 and No. 2, Opus 5, dedicated to the King, who was a cellist himself.

In those times in Vienna, one of the favorite aristocratic entertainments was the piano duel between two piano players, who might be accompanied by players of other instruments. The musicians had to play and the audience chose the winner by their applause. The most famous duel until then was the one between Mozart and Clementi in December 1781. After a lot of music, the emperor called it a draw.

Beethoven disliked such showcase events. That did not deter him from winning, because he disliked losing even more. Especially the contest in 1800 against the brilliant virtuoso Daniel Steibelt from Berlin, which fired his imagination. The first encounter had been a clear victory for Steibelt. However, a week later there was a rematch. Steibelt began with an improvisation that was well-prepared. He used a theme of Beethoven's from the first contest. This provocation annoyed Beethoven to a high degree. When it was his turn, Beethoven rushed to the piano. On his way, he took the cello part of Steibelt's quintet and placed it upside-down on the piano stand. With only one finger Beethoven started to play the "theme." Then he improvised like never before. Before he finished, Steibelt had left the room. From that day on, Steibelt only wanted to perform when he got the affirmation that Beethoven would not appear.

For many years, Lichnowsky was very important to Beethoven. For example, from 1800 on, Lichnowsky provided Beethoven with a basic income. In August 1806, Lichnowsky took Beethoven to his castle near Troppau (today Opava in the Czech Republic). There, Beethoven could compose without interruption. In September, they visited another nobleman living nearby: Count Oppersdorff, who had his own orchestra, which had rehearsed Beethoven's Second Symphony. Beethoven was so pleased with the performance of this music and liked the count so much, that he dedicated his next, nearly finished Fourth Symphony to Oppersdorff, who had, of course, to pay for it.

In October, the weather was often rather bad. The staff of the castle thought Beethoven to be very strange, because he walked for hours in the park, without a coat, even if it did thunder or storm. Beethoven alternated this with sitting in his room for days, without speaking to anybody.

Prince Lichnowsky was on friendly terms with a French general, who was a music lover. He promised the general to introduce him to Beethoven and to arrange that he could enjoy Beethoven's piano playing. So, Prince Lichnowsky organized a big concert, where Beethoven should play some of his newest compositions. However, since Napoleon had declared himself emperor of France (1804), Beethoven had been in a Francophobic mood. So, Beethoven told Prince Lichnowsky that he would not play that very evening. Prince Lichnowsky was convinced that Beethoven would give in.

The soiree was attended by many noblemen and, of course, by the French general. When the musical part was about to start, Prince Lichnowsky sent several times for Beethoven. Every time, however, his staff would return with the message that Beethoven refused to come. Eventually, Prince Lichnowsky sent his highest staff member, who returned with the message that Beethoven had secretly left the building. Beethoven had left a note, stating that he would not play in front of enemies of his fatherland.

Outside it poured, but that did not deter Beethoven walking the five miles to Troppau in the dark. Beethoven was so upset that he did not notice that his luggage had become soaked, including the autograph of the Piano Sonata Opus 57 (*Appassionata*), from which Marie Bigot later played sight-reading. In his apartment in Vienna, Beethoven had a marble bust of Lichnowsky. Back home later that week, Beethoven shattered it.

As a kind of farewell letter, Beethoven wrote to Prince Lichnowsky, "Prince, what you are, you are by accident of birth. What I am, I am through myself. There have been and will always be thousands of princes. There is only one Beethoven."[51]

KARL AMENDA

Karl Amenda was born in Courland (the western part of today's Latvia). As a child, he learned to play the violin. He studied theology and music in Jena (Germany) and spent two years as a music teacher in Lausanne (Switzerland). In the spring of 1798, he arrived in Vienna and found employment in the household of Prince Lobkowitz (see later); next, he was hired by Mozart's widow Constanze as a tutor for her sons.

Karl Amenda (1771–1838)

During his stay in Vienna, he became extremely friendly with Beethoven; they frequently played music together. But then, Amenda's brother died and Amenda decided to accept the custody of his brother's children and to return to Courland in the summer of 1799. As a farewell gift, Beethoven presented him with a copy of his First String Quartet (Opus 18/1). On the copy, Beethoven wrote:

Dear Amenda,
Accept this quartet as a small remembrance of our friendship, and as often as you
play it, think of the days we spent together, and at the same time of the genuine
affection which I felt toward you, and which I shall ever continue to feel.
Your sincere and warm friend, Ludwig van Beethoven[52]

Amenda and Beethoven stayed in written contact. In their letters, the focus is very much on the friendship itself. That is also true in Beethoven's letter of 1 July 1801. Here is the beginning:

My Dear, My Good Amenda, My Heartily Beloved Friend,
With deep emotion, with mixed pain and pleasure, did I receive and read
your last letter. To what can I compare your fidelity, your attachment to me?
Oh! How pleasant it is that you have always remained so kind to me; yes, I
also know that you, of all men, are the most trustworthy. You are no Viennese
friend; no, you are one of those such as my native country produces. How often
do I wish you were with me, for your Beethoven is most unhappy and at strife
with nature and the Creator. The latter I have often cursed for exposing His
creatures to the smallest chance, so that frequently the richest buds are thereby
crushed and destroyed. Only think that the noblest part of me, my sense of
hearing, has become very weak. Already when you were with me, I noted traces
of it, and I said nothing. Now it has become worse, and it remains to be seen
whether it can ever be healed. The primal cause of it is the state of my bowels.
So far as the latter are concerned, I am almost well, but I much fear that my
hearing will not improve; maladies of that kind are most difficult of all to
cure.[53]

In the remainder of the letter, Beethoven wrote that he is compelled to lead a sad life, that as a musician and especially as a composer he is doing well and that "one of the friends of my youth" has moved to Vienna. He wished he could visit Amenda but does not see much chance of undertaking any longer journeys on account of his bad hearing, unless Amenda would accompany him. Beethoven asked Amenda to maintain strict silence on the subject of his hearing problems. In the last paragraph, he asked Amenda not to pass on the String Quartet, as he had completely revised it in the meantime. He promised to send Amenda a copy of the new version.

The letter was written two days after the lengthy letter to Franz Wegeler, making

Amenda the second person (apart from physicians) whom Beethoven entrusted with his increasing deafness.

Amenda became a pastor and he stayed in Courland for the rest of his life, together with his wife and their five children. He and Beethoven continued to write each other and regarded each other as close friends.

IGNAZ SCHUPPANZIGH

The teacher at school may be told that she has a foul breath, is ignorant, or that she has ill-fitting clothes. Alternatively, she may be 'complimented' on having such a nice bra. All these things may well be 'true.' The problem is that the asperger child does not understand social rules, cannot judge the situation, and is unable to conclude that 'certain things you just do not say in certain settings.'[54]
CHRISTOPHER GILLBERG

Beethoven teased Schuppanzigh endlessly about his weight and his love of a good time.[55]
JAN SWAFFORD

Ignaz Schuppanzigh (1776–1830)

Ignaz Schuppanzigh was a famous Viennese violist who was very much sought after by the nobility. For years, he was the leader of Prince Lichnowsky's string quartet. Schuppanzigh was a champion of Beethoven's music and was the leader in performances of the Ninth Symphony and many of the late quartets. It is clear that Beethoven thought very highly of Schuppanzigh as a musician. Schuppanzigh was a torchbearer at Beethoven's funeral.

Schuppanzigh was grossly overweight, which earned him the Beethoven nickname *Falstaff*. Beethoven wrote the thirty-second choral piece *Lob auf den Dicken* (*Praise to the fat man*), especially for him:

Schuppanzigh is a scoundrel
Who doesn't know him,
the fat sour-belly
the conceited ass's head?
Oh scoundrel Schuppanzigh
Oh donkey Schuppanzigh
We all agree
that you are the biggest ass
Oh ass, hi hi ha[56]

NIKOLAUS ZMESKALL

… approaches others only to have own needs met.[57]
CHRISTOPHER GILLBERG

In the case of Zmeskall one can simply speak about shameless contempt and abuse of trust.[58]
JAN CAEYERS

Nikolaus Zmeskall was an official in the Hungarian Chancellery, who (as long as the gout allowed it) was a capable cellist. He was a lover of Beethoven's music and a lot of Beethoven's music was played during the chamber music soirees at his home. He met Beethoven in his first year in Vienna and became a good acquaintance, supporting Beethoven by doing odd jobs like finding servants, buying mirrors and cut quill pens. Beethoven – ten years Zmeskall's junior – addressed him informally as "Cheapest Baron" or "Music Count" or "dearest scavenger of a Baron."

In April 1809, a private concert took place at Zmeskall's house. One of Beethoven's Piano Trios (Opus 70) was on the program and Zmeskall was practicing the cello part. However, two days before the concert, Zmeskall received a note from Beethoven, informing him that he would be replaced by a professional cellist.

Zmeskall bit his lip and resigned himself to his submissive role.

In his letter to Amenda of July 1801 – where Beethoven disclosed his hearing problem – Beethoven wrote about Schuppanzigh and Zmeskall, "What a sad life I am now compelled to lead; I must avoid all that is near and dear to me, and then to be among such wretched egoists such as Zmeskall, Schuppanzigh, etc. […] Zmeskall is and remains too weak for friendship. I consider him and Schuppanzigh merely as instruments on which I play when I feel inclined; but they can never be in true sympathy with me; I value them merely for what they can do for me."[59]

Nikolaus Zmeskall (1759–1833)

FERDINAND RIES

The pianist and composer Ferdinand Ries received his first musical instructions from his father in Bonn. As a child, he lost the sight in one eye because of smallpox. In 1800, he went to Munich, where he earned some money by copying music. In 1801, he moved to Vienna, armed with a letter of introduction from his father to Beethoven.

His father, the violinist Franz Ries, had been a colleague and friend of Johann van Beethoven. After Beethoven's mother had died in 1787, Franz had been of great practical help to him. Also, when Beethoven moved to Vienna and Johann died (1792), Franz Ries took care of Beethoven's two brothers. So, Beethoven owed Franz Ries a lot of gratitude.

Ferdinand Ries (1784–1838)

When Ferdinand Ries arrived in Vienna with the letter from his father, he was hailed by Beethoven and they soon established amicable contact. Due to the piano lessons he had received, Ries did some duties for Beethoven as a secretary and copyist. When Beethoven realized that Ries was short of cash, he first gave him money himself and later arranged employment for him as a pianist for noblemen, like Prince Lichnowsky.

During the next summer (1802), Beethoven lived in one of the villages outside Vienna, so Ries' piano lessons involved hikes in the countryside and woods.

During such a hike, Ries drew Beethoven's attention to the beautiful sound of a flute, played by a shepherd. Beethoven listened carefully for a long time but denied hearing any music, after which he became very silent and grave. Ries had already been told by others about Beethoven's beginning deafness and the fact that Beethoven seemed to talk about it with no one.

Because Ries spent many hours with Beethoven, he witnessed many events. One time, Beethoven was playing the piano part in his quintet for piano and wind instruments. Suddenly, without warning, Beethoven started to improvise an elaborate cadence. The other musicians did not know when to enter again and for several minutes, they were ready to restart with their part but had to wait because the creativity of Beethoven had not diminished. After the concert, the musicians were irritated. However, the audience was delighted.

Another time, it was Beethoven's turn to get irritated. During another private concert, Beethoven was playing a piano duet with Ries. In the doorway, a young count was talking with a beautiful lady. Repeated requests for silence by Beethoven were in vain. All of a sudden, Beethoven forced Ries to quit playing and shouted, "I will not play for such pigs." All the attempts by the audience to get the concert to restart were in vain. Beethoven even forbade Ries to continue playing. So, the remainder of that evening, no piano music was heard anymore, to the dissatisfaction of the audience.

One time, Ries was having dinner with Beethoven in a restaurant and Beethoven was served a different dish than he had ordered. When he complained, the waiter did not react as suited Beethoven. So Beethoven took the plate and threw it right into the waiter's face. Because he had his hands full, the waiter could not defend himself. He wanted to talk or shout but was prevented by the sauce running into his mouth. The other guests had to laugh and finally Beethoven himself could not talk anymore for laughter because of the highly entertaining exhibition of the waiter.

In the years 1803 and 1804, Beethoven worked on the composition of a piano sonata (Opus 53, dedicated to Count Waldstein in 1805). The second part of this piano sonata was an andante, which – according to a friend of Beethoven – made the sonata too long. Beethoven agreed – after becoming furious – and replaced the andante, publishing it separately.

When Beethoven had finished composing this andante, he played it for Ferdinand Ries, who liked it so much that he asked for a repeat, which he received. On his way home, Ries visited Karl von Lichnowsky and told him about Beethoven's new composition. Lichnowsky asked Ries to play it and the more Ries tried, the more he remembered, so by the time he left, Lichnowsky was able to play the beginning of it.

The next morning, Lichnowsky went to Beethoven and told him, he (Lichnowsky) had composed something himself and asked if Beethoven was in the mood to listen to it. Beethoven was not. This did not deter Lichnowsky. He placed himself at the piano and started playing the first bars of the Andante. Beethoven became furious and decided *never* to play the piano again when Ries was around. Sometimes Beethoven reconsidered a decision he'd once made, but this time he adhered to his resolution.

In 1805, Beethoven worked on his only opera *Leonore* (which is now referred to as *Fidelio*). One morning, he was having breakfast with Prince Lichnowsky and several of his friends. These friends were interested in the opera and asked Beethoven if he could play parts of it on his piano. Beethoven agreed and the party went to his apartment. But before he started to play, Beethoven demanded that Ries should leave. The appeals of the other persons present were to no avail. With tears in his eyes, Ries left. Karl von Lichnowsky followed Ries and suggested Ries should stay in the next room, so he could still hear the music. Pride made this impossible for Ries and he left the apartment. Lichnowsky went back to the audience and expressed anger at Beethoven and declared that it was appreciation of his work that was at the root of this situation. The result was that Beethoven did not play at all that morning.

Ries made his public debut at a concert in 1804, on which occasion he played the solo part of Beethoven's Third Piano Concerto. In the fall of 1805, he returned to Bonn where he was due to be conscripted into the French army. However, he was unsuitable for service because of his poor eyesight. Thereupon, he tried his luck as a musician in Paris, but with little success. In August 1808, he moved back to Vienna and the friendly contact with Beethoven was rekindled.

In the fall of 1808, Beethoven received an invitation to become the *Kapellmeister* of the royal orchestra in Kassel (Westphalia). On the one hand, this was an attractive position for Beethoven. He would have a secure income, would conduct the orchestra, but would also have ample time to compose. On the other hand, the King was not interested in music at all; he only wanted to have big names at his court. For Beethoven as a composer, such an environment was not stimulating.

Beethoven was inclined to accept the invitation and a contract was made. However, a counter-proposal was made by three highly placed Viennese music lovers who were dismayed at the prospect of his imminent departure and guaranteed him an annual income for the rest of his life, in return for his promise to stay in Vienna or in another city within the Austrian crown lands.

Ries knew about the Westphalian invitation, but was unaware of the Viennese proposal, as he himself had received an invitation to become the Westphalian *Kapellmeister* (with less payment). The messenger stated that Beethoven would not accept the invitation. Highly confused, Ries rushed to Beethoven for consultation. However, Ries was not permitted entrance to Beethoven's apartment and letters stayed unanswered for three weeks. When Ries came across Beethoven in the city, he immediately started to talk about the matter, but Beethoven only said, "So you do think you can get a job that was offered to me?" and walked on, leaving the flabbergasted Ries on the spot.

The next morning, Ries went to Beethoven's apartment, determined not to be sent away like he had been the last three weeks. Beethoven's attendant stated that Beethoven was not at home, even though Ries heard the sound of a piano. Ries demanded access, but the attendant barred the doorway. Ries became angry and knocked the attendant down. Beethoven was not so deaf as to miss the noise and appeared. Raising his voice, Ries explained his view of the situation. Beethoven said, "I did not know that. I was told that you had been trying to obtain that post behind my back." The friendship was restored. Beethoven did not sign the Westphalian contract and stayed in Vienna. For Ries, it was too late; he did not obtain the post of *Kapellmeister*.

Between 1809 and 1813, Ries was on tour in Germany, Scandinavia, and Russia. In 1813, he settled in London, where the most successful time of his life started. He married and became a member of the new Philharmonic Society, ensuring him of a prominent position in the English music scene. Next to being a sought-after pianist, conductor, and composer, Ries was the highly respected intermediary between the music scene and Beethoven. For instance, in June 1817, Ries wrote a letter to Beethoven on behalf of the Philharmonic Society, inviting him to come to England and to compose two symphonies that would be performed in London. Beethoven was positive about the proposal but asked for more money. The Philharmonic Society thought their proposal generous enough and did not accept Beethoven's demands; therefore, Beethoven did not travel to London.

In London, Ries earned so much money that in 1824 he could afford to retire. He moved near Bonn and stayed active as a musician in Germany. In May 1825, he successfully conducted the new Ninth Symphony of Beethoven in Aachen. In 1827, he moved to Frankfurt. In 1836, he received a request from Wegeler to co-author a book about Beethoven. In this book, *Biographische Notizen über Ludwig van Beethoven* (English edition: *Beethoven remembered*), Wegeler and Ries wrote down their recollections of Beethoven and provided some important letters written by him. The book was published in 1838 and became an instant success. It contributed to a large degree toward the positive image of Beethoven.

However, Ries did not live to enjoy the success of the book, for he died a few months before it came off the press.

STEPHAN VON BREUNING

The stress that provokes these kinds of reactions [leading to confusion states] *may be perceived by other people as very mild.*[60]
CHRISTOPHER GILLBERG

Beethoven's reaction to a violent quarrel with Breuning [in 1804] was totally out of proportion to the quarrel itself.[61]
ANNE-LOUISE COLDICOTT

Stephan von Breuning studied law and settled in Vienna in 1801. He made a career at the war ministry. In his letter to Amenda of 1 July 1801, Beethoven referred to Stephan von Breuning as "one of the friends of my youth." In his letter of two days earlier to Wegeler, Beethoven wrote:

Stephan von Breuning is now here, and we are together almost daily. It does me good to revive the old feelings of friendship. He is really a good, noble young fellow, who knows a thing or two, and whose heart, as with all of us more or less, is sound.[62]

Stephan von Breuning (1774–1827)

In the spring of 1804, Beethoven moved to *Das Rote Haus (The Red House)*, a large apartment complex where Breuning was also living. He appears to have left his new rooms almost immediately in order to stay in Breuning's apartment but did not cancel the lease of his own apartment. Over dinner, the visiting Casper Carl van Beethoven, provoking, as usual, blamed the oversight on Breuning. Beethoven tried to defuse the situation by jokingly blaming it on Ries, but Breuning boiled over, jumped up, and shouted that he would send for the janitor on the spot. Beethoven also stood up, sending his chair flying, bolted from the house and left for the village of Baden.

From Baden, Beethoven wrote a letter; not to Breuning, but to Ries. He explained to Ries what had happened and requested him to tell Breuning that it was never his (Beethoven's) intention to blame him (Breuning) for not canceling the lease. About Breuning himself, Beethoven wrote:

> *I have nothing more to say to Breuning. His thoughts and actions prove that there should never have been a friendly relationship between us and will certainly never be again.*[63]

Some days later, Beethoven explained his views in another letter to Ries. Here is the beginning:

> *The affair with Breuning will probably have surprised you. But, dear friend, believe me, my sudden rage was merely an explosion resulting from several previous unpleasant incidents with him. I have the gift of being able to conceal and control my sensitivity about very many things. But if I happen to be irritated at a time when I am more liable to fly into a temper than usual, then I erupt more violently than anyone else. Breuning certainly has many excellent qualities, but he thinks himself quite faultless; whereas the very defects that he discovers in others are those which he has himself to the highest degree. From my childhood, I have always despised his petty mind. More or less, I had a foreboding that something would happen between us, for our modes of thinking, acting, and feeling are entirely opposite. And yet, I believed that these difficulties might be overcome, but experience has disproved this. So now I want no more of his friendship! I have only found two friends in the world with whom I never had a misunderstanding; but what men these were! One is dead, the other still lives. Although for almost six years we have not seen each other, yet I know that I still hold the first place in his heart, as he does in mine. The true basis of friendship is to be found in sympathy of heart and soul. I only wish you would read the letter I have written to Breuning, also his to me. No, nevermore will he occupy the place in my heart which he once held.*

A man who can attribute to his friend such base thoughts, and likewise act in such a base manner towards him, does not deserve my friendship.[64]

However, a few months later, Beethoven sent a portrait of himself to Breuning, accompanied by a letter.

Behind this painting, my good dear Stephan, be forever hidden what had occurred between us for some time. I know, I have torn your heart apart; but the emotion within me, which you must certainly have detected, has punished me sufficiently for doing so. It was not malice which was surging in me against you, no, because in that case, I would no longer have been worthy of your friendship. It was passion within me and within you; but mistrust was aroused in me against you. Men came between us who are never worthy of you and me; for a long time, my portrait was meant to become yours, to whom could I give it with the warmest heart but to you, faithful, good, noble Stephan. Forgive me, if I have hurt you, I suffered just as much. When I no longer saw you beside me, for such a long time, only then did I realize fully how dear you were to my heart, how dear you always will be.
Yours
Do fly into my arms again, as in former days[65]

The friends made up. In 1806, Breuning revised the text of Beethoven's only opera *Leonore* for the second version of the opera and in 1808, Beethoven dedicated his Violin Concerto to him. The friendship lasted for years, but came to an abrupt (if temporary) end in 1815, when Breuning did something terrible, at least in Beethoven's uncompromising opinion: Breuning dissuaded Beethoven from assuming the guardianship of his nephew Karl. The first record of any contact between Breuning and Beethoven afterward is from 1825, ten years later. From that year on, the friendship was as good as it had been in former days. Beethoven became fond of Stephan's son Gerhard. Gerhard would later write down his memories of his many meetings with Beethoven in a book: *Aus dem Schwarzspanierhause (From The House of The Black-Robed Spaniards*; a house where Beethoven had lived).

Stephan von Breuning became increasingly involved in the planning of Karl's future and it was he who arranged for his admission into the army. He even agreed to become Karl's guardian, but died in June 1827, shortly after Karl had left Vienna to join the army.

FRANZ LOBKOWITZ

The ancestors of Prince Lobkowitz had shown a great interest in music and his father had been a patron of the famous opera composer Gluck. Franz Lobkowitz was a great music lover and an enthusiastic violinist himself. A physical disability – he walked with a crutch – made a military or diplomatic carrier impossible. Instead, he devoted most of his time to enhancing musicians' careers. Prince Lobkowitz was one of the biggest benefactors of music of all time, but he was also a spendthrift; his boundless generosity and his extravagant lifestyle would ultimately cause his financial ruin.

Franz Lobkowitz (1772–1816)

The first documented contact between Lobkowitz and Beethoven dates from March 1795, when Beethoven played at his palace in Vienna. Lobkowitz was also one of the subscribers to the Piano Trios Opus 1. The collaboration between Beethoven and Lobkowitz proved to be an excellent one and reached its zenith in 1804 when Lobkowitz allowed Beethoven to use his private orchestra to practice several versions of his Third Symphony before its first public performance.

As one of Beethoven's leading patrons, Lobkowitz received several dedications of Beethoven's masterpieces, including Symphonies 5 and 6, the String Quartets Opus 18 and Opus 74 and the Triple Concerto.

During a rehearsal for the opera *Leonore*, Beethoven was fuming with rage because the third bassoon (the contrabassoon) was missing. Franz Lobkowitz pointed out that the other two were present and that would have to suffice for the time being. The perfectionist Beethoven did not share his opinion. On his way home, Beethoven passed the Prince's palace, went to the entrance and shouted, *"Lobkowitzischer Esel!"* (*"Lobkowitzian ass!"*). Shortly afterward he wrote to his patron, "If his Serene Highness plays with the instruments like this, I do not give a shit for it."[66]

But Prince Lobkowitz had a laxer and less demanding character compared to Prince Lichnowsky. He seemed not to take offense to the things Beethoven said or wrote in his rage and although they did quarrel on a regular basis, there are no reports of major clashes.

Prince Lobkowitz was one of three aristocrats who contributed to Beethoven's annuity from 1809 onwards. However, in 1811 Beethoven's payments were suspended. His financial situation was getting worse and worse and inflation was increasing. Because the Prince could still afford to finance his daughter's wedding, which lasted a staggering three weeks and cost many times more than Beethoven's annuity, Beethoven did not hesitate to sue the Prince. Beethoven won the case, but it took until 1815 before the annuity was resumed.

In 1816, Beethoven dedicated the song cycle *To the Distant Beloved* to Prince Lobkowitz, who in 1813 had moved out of Vienna. However, the printed edition of that song cycle did not reach Lobkowitz, because, in December 1816, he died, completely impoverished. His family continued the annuity until the end of Beethoven's life.

NAPOLEON BONAPARTE

Beethoven and Napoleon never met, nor did they write letters to each other. Nonetheless, Napoleon played an important role in the composer's life. Beethoven's attitude towards his peer (Napoleon was born sixteen months earlier) was ambivalent and subject to change.

After his assumption to power in 1799, Napoleon took interest in the music scene of France and supported musicians. Beethoven, therefore, considered moving to Paris to profit from the favorable cultural climate. When his Second Symphony was performed in Paris and he consequently became more famous in France, Beethoven decided to start a marketing campaign. The climax of this campaign would be the composition of a symphony that would surpass all existing symphonies. This Third Symphony would be dedicated to Napoleon and be called *Bonaparte*.

Napoleon's appeal to Beethoven was that he was not highborn, but self-made.

What he achieved, he achieved through his own efforts, not because of noble birth. When such a man rose above the crowd, he would be a natural leader, according to Beethoven's heroic image. In his admiration, Beethoven deemed Napoleon a liberator, a champion of freedom from oppression. And this Third Symphony would not only be dedicated to Napoleon but also be in some way modeled on his character and career and on the larger image of a hero.

Beethoven also saw some opportunism and a need for power in Napoleon's behavior and expressed himself negatively about the Concordat, the agreement between Napoleon and Pope Pius VII, signed in 1801. But Beethoven was not free from opportunism himself. Prince Lobkowitz had gleaned that Beethoven was working on a symphony that would be a big step in the development of the genre, so he offered Beethoven his orchestra and room in his palace to stay and to rehearse. He also offered a considerable amount of money to receive the dedication and the right of performance for half a year, a common practice in those days. This offer was very welcome and Beethoven changed his plans accordingly by dedicating the symphony to Lobkowitz, still calling it *Bonaparte*.

But one day, Ries told Beethoven the news that Napoleon had crowned himself emperor. Realizing that Napoleon was no liberator but was seeking his own power and glory, Beethoven shouted, "So, he too is nothing more than an ordinary man! Now, he will also trample all human rights underfoot and only pander to his own ambition. He will place himself above everyone else and become a tyrant!"[67] Beethoven snatched the title page of the symphony, ripped it in two, and threw it to the floor.

Cover page of the Third Symphony with the hole

A copy had already been made of the symphony. On the title page was written: *Sinfonie grande / intitulata Bonaparte / del Sigr / Louis van Beethoven.* This title page has survived; the words *Intitulate Bonaparte* have been erased so violently that there is a hole in the paper.

Beethoven remained ambivalent towards Napoleon. After Napoleon had won the Battle of Jena in October 1806, Beethoven said, "It is a pity that I do not understand the art of war as well as I do the art of music – I would certainly defeat him!" But, in 1808, Beethoven seriously considered accepting an invitation from the King of Westphalia, to become *Kapellmeister* at his court in Kassel. That King was Jerome Bonaparte, Napoleon's youngest brother.

The Third Symphony, already privately performed several times at Lobkowitz's palace, received its first public performance in April 1805. The audience was perplexed. This was not an entertaining symphony like the ones of Haydn and Mozart. The quality and quantity (fifty minutes) were unprecedented. Halfway through, someone shouted that he desired the thing to stop; he even offered money to attain that goal.

The Third Symphony was published in the fall of 1806. As planned, it was dedicated to Prince Lobkowitz, but on the title page was added: *Sinfonia Eroica, composta per festeggiare il sovvenire di un grand Uomo* (*Heroic symphony, composed to celebrate the memory of a great man*).

Who could Beethoven have had in mind, when he wrote about *the memory of a great man* and *a hero*? If a real person is meant, Napoleon deserves no consideration because he would die in 1821. In fact, only one person is eligible: Louis Ferdinand.

LOUIS FERDINAND

The Prussian Prince Louis Ferdinand was the nephew of the famous King, Frederick the Great. He was well-liked by men as a war hero and beloved by women because of his extremely handsome appearance. He was dear to Beethoven as a brilliant pianist. They first met in 1796 when Beethoven visited Berlin, and they got along with each other very well.

In September 1804, Louis Ferdinand was on his way to attend the fall maneuvers of the Austrian army, so he made sure he had some time to visit Vienna to call on Beethoven. During his stay, an aristocratic hostess offered him a small private concert and a dinner with Viennese nobility. The main musician of the concert was, of course, Beethoven. However, when dinner was served, it appeared to Beethoven that there was no place at the table assigned to him. He fiercely took his hat and left, uttering some coarse language.

A few days later, Louis Ferdinand offered a lunch for a part of the same noble company, including the same aristocratic hostess. From the table arrangement, it appeared that she was asked to sit next to Louis Ferdinand. Beethoven was delighted to find that the other seat next to Louis Ferdinand was reserved for him. Beethoven's favor in return was significant: he dedicated his Third Piano Concerto to Louis Ferdinand.

Louis Ferdinand, himself a talented composer, was greatly impressed by Beethoven's compositions. After the aforementioned maneuvers, he visited Lobkowitz in Bohemia and was overjoyed to find that Lobkowitz's private orchestra would play Beethoven's unpublished and not yet publicly performed Third Symphony. He was so impressed, that he requested the orchestra to play it a second time, and even a third time.

Lobkowitz greatly admired Louis Ferdinand and, in 1806, he wrote him several letters urging him to take control of the "German chaos." In the view of Lobkowitz, only Louis Ferdinand was able to defeat Napoleon and to restore order in Germany. Indeed, later that year, Louis Ferdinand became one of the principal advocates in resuming the war against Napoleon. In September, Prussia and its coalition partners (Russia, Saxony, Sweden, and Great Britain) prepared for war against the First French Empire. But before the fighting started, Louis Ferdinand visited Lobkowitz again in Bohemia, where many important noblemen and a few beautiful women were present. Louis Ferdinand left the Lobkowitz castle on 26 September. He was killed two weeks later at the Battle of Saalfeld on the 10th of October, 1806.

Louis Ferdinand (1772–1806)

On 29 October, the publication of the Third Symphony was announced as the *Sinfonia Eroica, composta per festeggiare il sovvenire di un grand Uomo*. It takes little imagination to understand that it took Lobkowitz little effort to persuade Beethoven to associate "his" Symphony at the last moment – anonymously – with the great man Louis Ferdinand, their hero.

FRIEDRICH HIMMEL

Himmel was the royal *Kapellmeister* in Berlin when Beethoven visited the royal court in 1796. During his stay, Beethoven frequently had contact with Himmel and praised his piano playing (although he thought Louis Ferdinand was the better player). Being aware of Beethoven's reputation, one day Himmel asked Beethoven to improvise. Beethoven complied with the request, after which it was Himmel's turn. After a while, Beethoven (who thought Himmel was just warming up) asked, "Now, then, when will you start in earnest?" Himmel, who believed he had already performed brilliantly, was angry and an argument followed. They reconciled the same day.

After Beethoven left, he stayed in contact with Himmel through letters. Beethoven used Himmel as an information source about Berlin and always inquired about the latest news. This annoyed Himmel, and one day he deluded Beethoven. He did what hardly anybody dared to do, he played with Beethoven's childish naivety. He wrote that the breaking news was that a lamp for blind people had been invented. A credulous Beethoven fell for it and told everyone about it. But how is that possible, people wanted to know. Beethoven wrote back to Himmel that it was awkward that he had not explained how the lamp worked. The next letter Himmel wrote to Beethoven was the last one in their correspondence. The content is unknown. We know of its existence because Beethoven was so foolish as to show it to others, among them Ferdinand Ries.

Friedrich Himmel (1765–1814)

RUDOLF VON HABSBURG

People make allowances for geniuses that they wouldn't make for the average Joe.[68]
ASHLEY STANFORD

The Archduke did put up with everything because he had an unswerving faith in Beethoven's loftiness.[69]
JAN CAEYERS

Archduke Rudolf was the youngest brother of Emperor Franz. For many years, he was both a dear friend and the primary patron of Beethoven. He was one of the three aristocrats who contributed to Beethoven's annuity from 1809 on. This ardent admirer of Beethoven's music not only received piano lessons from Beethoven but – and this was exceptional – composition lessons as well. He wrote chamber music and a set of forty variations on a theme of Beethoven's.

Rudolf von Habsburg (1788–1831)

Beethoven dedicated his Fourth and Fifth Piano Concertos, the Piano Sonatas Opus 81a (*The Farewell, Absence* and *The Return*), Opus 106 (*Hammerklavier*) and Opus 111 (his last piano sonata) and chamber music to Archduke Rudolf. For the enthronement as archbishop and Cardinal in 1820, Beethoven wrote the *Missa*

Solemnis, although the composition was not ready in time.

There are no reports of major clashes between Beethoven and Archduke Rudolf. Only at the beginning of their contact was there a minor issue, which was resolved easily through the kindness of the Archduke. When Beethoven visited Archduke Rudolf he embarrassed his court. The courtiers tried to force him to observe the ceremonial court rules. For Beethoven this was unbearable. He always promised to do better next time, but he never did. One day as they tried again to *court teach* him (as he called it), he turned to the Archduke, annoyed, and said forthrightly, he surely respected him to a high degree, but he disliked the strict observation of the court rules. The Archduke laughed good-humoredly about the case and ordered his court not to bother Beethoven anymore. He explained to his servants, "That's just Beethoven!"

JOHANN VON GOETHE

Goethe was one of the most important and influential German poets and playwrights of all time. Beethoven adored Goethe and his works and set several of his texts to music, culminating in the incidental music to *Egmont* (1810). Beethoven wrote to Goethe in April 1811 to announce his *Egmont* piece and Goethe replied in June to thank Beethoven; he planned to have the music performed in Weimar. He added the desire to meet with Beethoven and hear him play the piano.

In July 1812, Beethoven and Goethe met repeatedly at the Bohemian spa in Teplitz. It is not known what they talked about, but the impression Beethoven made on Goethe is phrased in a letter Goethe wrote to his wife:

> *I have never seen an artist more concentrated, more energetic and more intimate. I can very well understand how singular he stands in his relations with the world.*[70]

With a little more distance, Goethe wrote in September to his musical adviser:

> *I made Beethoven's acquaintance in Teplitz. His talent amazed me. However, unfortunately, he is an utterly untamed personality, who is not altogether in the wrong if he finds the world detestable, but he thereby does not make it more enjoyable either for himself or others. He is very much to be excused, on the other hand, and very much to be pitied, as his hearing is leaving him, which, perhaps, injures the musical part of his nature less than his social. He, by nature laconic, becomes doubly so because of this lack.*[71]

There is a famous story about Beethoven and Goethe walking through Teplitz, and meeting the Empress and her train. Goethe stepped aside and took off his hat. Beethoven pushed his hat firmly on the back of his head and strode through the crowd. However, there is only one source of this story and that source is considered untrustworthy. Fact is that Beethoven wrote shortly afterward that Goethe delighted far too much in the *court atmosphere*, far more than is becoming of a poet.

After 1812, Beethoven and Goethe did not meet again. Beethoven's admiration for Goethe's works did not diminish. Several times, Beethoven started to compose music associated with Goethe's play *Faust*. But he never got far. Only twenty-four lines are set to music and that composition dated back to 1809: *Mephisto's flea song*.

Johann von Goethe (1749–1832)

In February 1823, Beethoven wrote to Goethe, requesting his support in persuading the court of Weimar to subscribe to the *Missa Solemnis*. However, Goethe did not reply and the court did not subscribe.

It is not known whether, apart from the Egmont music, Goethe liked Beethoven's music or gave it special attention. In 1830, the young Felix Mendelssohn played pieces of several composers to Goethe on the piano. Goethe did not want to hear anything from Beethoven, but Mendelssohn insisted on playing the beginning of the Fifth Symphony. Goethe was impressed by that music; "It's tremendous, quite mad; one could fear the whole house might collapse – imagine the lot of them playing it together!"[72]

CARL CZERNY

Czerny received his first piano lessons from his father. At the age of ten, he was able to play many piano works of Mozart and Clementi from memory. In 1800, he made his debut with Mozart's Piano Concerto in C minor (KV 491).

The first time he heard about Beethoven was when his father told him about his short encounter with the piano virtuoso Gelinek. Gelinek had an upcoming piano duel with a young foreigner. Gelinek was sure about his victory. The next day, the two men met again. Father Czerny asked how the duel went. Gelinek replied:

O, yesterday I will never forget. That young man is possessed by the devil. Never have I heard anyone play the piano like that. And he improvised on a theme I had given him in a manner I have not heard even Mozart equal. Then he played some of his own compositions that are miraculous and mighty in the highest degree. Playing the piano, he produces the most difficult things and effects that none of us would ever have dreamed of. [73]

The curious Czerny senior desired to know who the opponent was.
"He's a small, ugly, swarthy, fractious person [...] and his name is Beethoven." [74]

In 1801, Czerny was introduced to Beethoven. Father Czerny desired Beethoven to become Carl's piano teacher. A shabby-looking servant showed them in. The room was messy, papers and garments lay on the floor. The walls were bare and there was hardly any furniture. Next to several suitcases, there was a ramshackle chair in front of the piano. Beethoven's appearance reminded Czerny of Robinson Crusoe. He also noticed that Beethoven had cotton in his ears that had been drenched in a yellow liquid.

Undisturbed by the seven other people in the room, Beethoven requested that Czerny play the piano. Czerny first played from Mozart's Piano Concerto in C major (KV 503) and Beethoven's Piano Sonata in C minor (Opus 13). Then, he accompanied his father in Beethoven's song *Adelaide*. Beethoven reacted enthusiastically and accepted Czerny as his pupil. Although the lessons lasted less than two years, it laid the foundation of Czerny's reputation as the authority in the field of playing Beethoven's piano music. Already as a teenager, Czerny was called upon by Prince Lichnowsky who desired him to play piano works by Beethoven. The Prince simply cited an opus number and Czerny would play the requested work from memory.

Czerny and Beethoven stayed in close contact for the rest of their lives. Czerny arranged many of Beethoven's orchestral works for piano; for example, all nine symphonies for piano duet. Between 1816 and 1818, he taught piano lessons to nephew Karl. After Beethoven's death, he wrote several publications about Beethoven, both about the man and about his music.

Czerny became one of the most sought-after piano teachers in Vienna; Franz Liszt was one of his pupils. His lasting fame is not based on most of his many piano compositions – his piano sonatas are hardly played – but only on the etudes he wrote. His *Schule der Geläufigkeit* (*School of Velocity*) became one of the most popular (or notorious) didactical piano works of all time.

Czerny rarely played in public. One of the exceptions was the Vienna premiere of Beethoven's Fifth Piano Concerto in 1812. More often, he performed in private concerts. One example was an evening in February 1816, when several parts of Beethoven's chamber music were performed. Beethoven arrived late, but not too late to hear how Czerny added a number of his own flourishes to the Piano Quintet (Opus 16). Afterward, Beethoven's *raptus* came down on the dumbfounded Czerny, in spite of the witnesses. This did not add to the good mood of the evening. The next day Beethoven wrote an apologetic note: Czerny had played beautifully, but Beethoven preferred to hear his music as he had composed it.

Carl Czerny (1791–1857)

GIOACHINO ROSSINI

Rossini was the most successful Italian opera composer of the first quarter of the nineteenth century. In the years after 1815, after Napoleon was defeated, the audience in Vienna looked for something airy and accessible. They found what they were looking for in the operas of Rossini, which soon dominated the music scene in Vienna and the rest of Europe.

In March 1822, Rossini went to Vienna for three months and in April, he paid Beethoven a short visit at his apartment. Rossini, who lived in a splendid villa, was escorted into an attic that was "terribly untidy and dirty." A hole in the ceiling allowed rainwater to pour in.

The conversation was hindered by language problems and by Beethoven's deafness. Beethoven congratulated Rossini on *The Barber of Seville*. He continued by advising Rossini only to write *opera buffe* (comic operas) because that genre suited the Italian language and temperament better. To succeed in the *opera serie* (serious operas) was not the destiny of the Italians, so Beethoven told him. Then Rossini's companion, who also was the translator of the conversation, drew Beethoven's attention to the fact that Rossini had composed some *opera serie* (like *Otello* in 1816). Beethoven replied that he had taken a look at them, but that the *opera seria* did not go with the Italian character. Italians did not have enough musical knowledge to treat the real drama, so Beethoven added. However, in the realm of the *opera buffa*, the Italians are the real masters, Beethoven concluded.

That evening Rossini was guest at a gala dinner with many people of nobility. He suggested that they should take better care of Beethoven. The response was cool and Rossini was told that Beethoven was the architect of his own misery.

Gioachino Rossini (1792–1868)

CARL PETERS

[...] a series of negotiations to sell the Missa Solemnis in which his conduct was extremely questionable.[75]
ANNE-LOUISE COLDICOTT

Carl Peters (based in Leipzig) was one of the best-known music publishers of the nineteenth century. Sheet music with his logo (EDITION PETERS) continues to sell well into the twenty-first century.

Peters was one of the publishers to whom Beethoven offered his *Missa Solemnis*. It took Beethoven several years to write this masterpiece and during those years he signed three contracts and received down payments from two publishers. These publishers sometimes asked about the progress of the work. In November 1822, Beethoven wrote to Peters that he had finished one mass long ago, but that he had not yet finished another. He (Beethoven) was not sure which one he would send to Peters. (To make things clear: that second mass existed mainly in Beethoven's fantasy. Only a few sketches of another mass have been found.)

In the winter of 1823, Beethoven even wrote about three masses. (To clarify: that third mass too only existed in Beethoven's fantasy.) The letter included some smaller compositions, some even over twenty-five years old. Peters was not amused, was disappointed about the quality of the compositions (he even sent them back!) and the delay of the mass. In his letter to Beethoven, he added that his criticism applied to Beethoven the businessman, not Beethoven the artist. That last remark is interesting because, at that time, Beethoven's behavior with regard to the selling of the *Missa Solemnis* seems to have been highly influenced by his brother Johann, who was his business adviser.

In a letter during the summer of 1823, Beethoven accused Peters of not knowing what he wanted and asked him to refrain from sending further letters on the basis of his conduct as a publisher being inappropriate. After all, he (Beethoven) had not asked him for the down payment, he had accepted it to stop the gossip. "Let me tell you that more sums [from other publishers] are waiting for me. Other publishers are more willing to be patient, out of respect for my art and out of indulgence for my poor health. I misjudged you with respect to morality, or better: with respect to commerce and music. Be sure I will not take more money from you. I know what I have to do and do not have to prove my honesty to you."[76]

Beethoven paid back the down payment ... two years later. Peters did not publish the *Missa Solemnis* or any other work of Beethoven's, as long as Beethoven lived.

FERDINAND WOLANEK

In March 1825, Beethoven received a letter from the copyist Ferdinand Wolanek.

> *To Mister Ludwig van Beethoven!*
> *I can only finish inserting the Finale into the score by Easter, and as by that time you will not want it anymore, I send you all the parts together with the already commenced Finale. I am grateful to you for the honor shown to me by giving me work. So far as the otherwise disagreeable behavior toward me is concerned, I can regard it smilingly as merely an assumed outburst of temper. There are many dissonances in the ideal world of tones. Why, then, should it not be so in the real world? All that comforts me is the firm conviction that, had those celebrated artists, Haydn, and Mozart been employed by you as copyists, they would have shared the same fate as mine. I, therefore, request you not to rank me among those common copying fellows who, even when treated like slaves, think themselves lucky to be able to earn a living. For the rest, be assured that I have not the slightest cause to blush on account of my behavior to you.*
> *With high esteem,*
> *Yours truly, Ferdinand Wolanek*[77]

Beethoven was very busy, but he took the time to write a reply. First, he made a cross on the paper. Then he wrote:

> *Stupid fool, conceited ass of a fellow.*
> *To such a rascal, who really robs one of one's money, am I to pay compliments instead of pulling his ass's ears?*

Beethoven continued his reply on the reverse side.

> *Scribbler!*
> *Stupid fool!*
> *Correct your own faults caused through ignorance, arrogance, self-conceit, and stupidity. This is far better than to try to instruct me; for this would be just like the sow trying to teach Minerva.*
> *[left margin] It was resolved yesterday, and even earlier, not to engage you any more to copy for me.*
> *[right margin] Honor Mozart and Haydn by not mentioning their names.*[78]

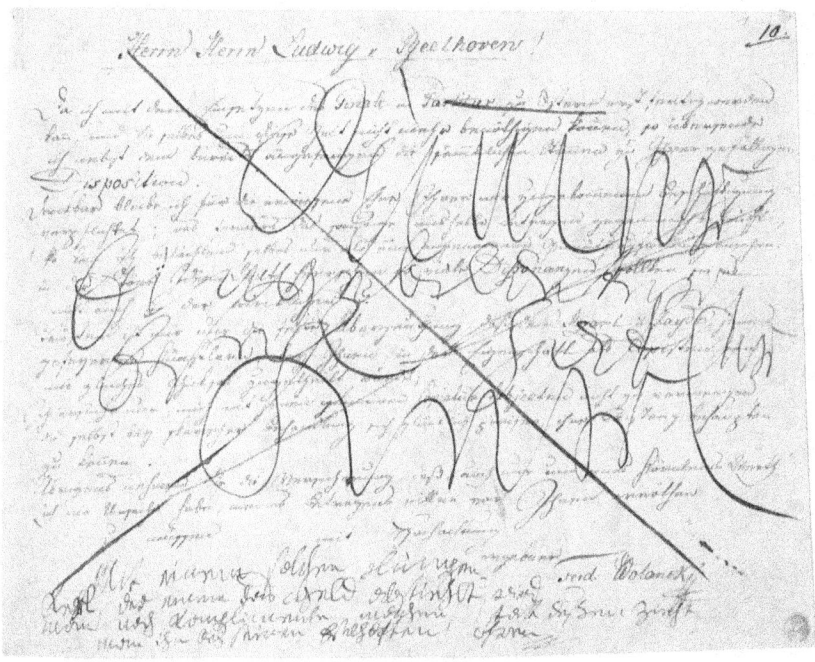

Wolanek's letter to Beethoven

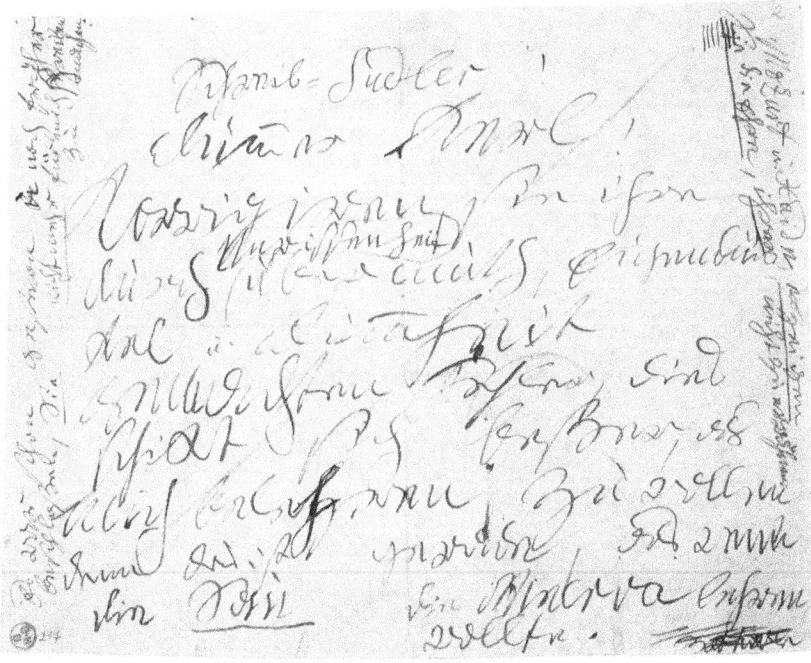

Beethoven's letter to Wolanek

CHAPTER

3

"Love demands everything"

WOMEN IN BEETHOVEN'S LIFE

Many aspergers lead solitary lives and do not marry and have children.[79]
HANS ASPERGER

He did not marry and appears never to have had an intimate relationship
with a woman.[80]
ANNE-LOUISE COLDICOTT

In Beethoven's dealings with men, there were two aspects: friendship and business. In his dealings with women, a third element was added: love. Reports about Beethoven's love life during his teenage years are limited and vague. There is no mention of a girlfriend.

Reports are also scarce about Beethoven in his twenties. Franz Wegeler reports that Beethoven was "always involved in love affairs,"[81] but fails to give any details and there is no other source to confirm this statement. Wegeler does not mention Magdalena Willmann, a soprano Beethoven proposed to in 1795 or 1796, but who rebuffed him, apparently "because he was so ugly, and half-crazy."[82]

Ferdinand Ries is more specific about Beethoven's love life during his thirties. He does not mention the names of women Beethoven was in love with, we know from other sources. But he does write the following:

Beethoven did look readily at women, especially beautiful, young faces. If we walked past a rather attractive girl, he would turn around, take a closer look at her with his glasses, and laughed or grinned when he realized that I had noticed it. He was often in love, but mostly for a short time. One time, I teased him about a beautiful lady and he acknowledged that this one had captivated his attention the strongest and the longest; that was: seven months.

One evening, I visited him in Baden, to receive a lesson. A beautiful young lady was sitting next to him on the sofa. Because I assumed I had come at a bad time, I wanted to leave, but Beethoven held me back and said, "Do play something in the meanwhile!"

He and the lady stayed behind me, seated. I had played for quite a while when Beethoven all of a sudden shouted, "Ries, do play something amorously!" A little later, "Something melancholic!" Even later, "Something passionate!"

From what I could hear I deduced that he probably had offended the lady and now wanted to make amends with a joke. Eventually, he jumped up and shouted, "But those are only my pieces!" What I actually had done was connect parts of his own works with small transitions. That seemed to please him. The lady left soon and to my astonishment, Beethoven did not know who she was. I was told that she arrived just before I did, to meet Beethoven. We soon followed her to find out where she lived in order to determine her class. We did see her in the distance (the moonlight was bright), but suddenly she disappeared. For one-and-a-half hours, we walked through the beautiful adjacent valley, talking about several subjects. When I left, Beethoven said, "I have to know who she is and you have to help me." Long afterward I met her in Vienna and discovered that she was the beloved of a foreign prince. I told Beethoven, but neither from him nor from anyone else have I heard anything about her.[83]

In the following text, ten women who played an important role in Beethoven's life will be introduced. Just as in the chapter about men, the women are presented in chronological order, according to the time of the initial point of the essential (sometimes brief) contact. As with the men, the women will be presented separately. Compared to the men, there is much less interconnectedness between the women. At the end of the chapter, I will elaborate on one woman who, although in waves, played a very important role in Beethoven's life for more than twenty years. It is justifiable to state that she was the most important person in Beethoven's life.

ELEONORE VON BREUNING

Eleonore von Breuning was one of four children of Helena von Breuning. As described in Chapter One, the teenage Beethoven frequented the house of the Breuning family. He gave piano lessons to Eleonore and was in love with her for some time. It is unclear to what degree the love was mutual. However, in 1792 they had a disagreement, although it is unknown what the quarrel was about. In the summer of that year, Beethoven wrote Eleonore a letter to thank her for the handmade scarf she had sent him. In that letter, he wrote that he was sorry for his bad behavior towards her and assured her he would never forget her and her mother. He stressed that he would not be able to bear the loss of their friendship. As a counter-gift, he sent her two small compositions. And he wished her all the best for their coming summer sojourn.

In November 1793, having lived for a year in Vienna, Beethoven wrote his second (and last) surviving letter to Eleonore. Here is the beginning:

> *Honored Eleonore, my dearest friend!*
> *I shall soon have been in this capital for a whole year, yet only now do you receive a letter from me, but you were certainly constantly in my thoughts. Frequently, indeed, did I converse with you and your dear family, but, for the most part, not with the peace of mind I should have liked. Then it was that the fatal quarrel hovered before me, and my former behavior appeared to me really detestable. But the past cannot be undone, and what would I not give if I could blot out of my life my former conduct so dishonoring to me, so contrary to my character. Many circumstances, indeed, kept us at a distance from each other, and, as I presume, it was especially the insinuations resulting from conversations on either side which prevented all reconciliation. Each of us believed that we were convinced of the truth of what we said, and yet it was mere anger, and we were both deceived. Your good and noble character*

guaranteed that I have long since been forgiven. But true repentance consists, so it is said, in acknowledging one's faults, and this is what I intended to do. And now let us draw a curtain over the whole story, and only learn the lesson from it that when friends fall out it is always better not to have a go-between, but for a friend to turn directly to their friend.[84]

It is unknown who the go-between was. In the remainder of the letter, Beethoven did give some explanation about a composition he included with the letter. He also asked Eleonore to ask her friend Babette Koch why she did not answer his two letters.

Babette Koch was the daughter of the owner of *Zum Zehrgarten*, a very popular restaurant in the center of Bonn, frequented by many representatives of the cultural establishment. Babette was a beautiful and well-educated young woman, who had many admirers. She was born in 1771 and died in 1807. Thirty years later, Franz Wegeler, at that time still married to Eleonore (since 1802) and normally moderate in his opinions, writes that Babette "of all the members of the female sex whom I have met in my rather active and long life, came closest to the ideal of the perfect woman."[85] Babette Koch must have been very engaging.

Eleonore von Breuning (1771–1841)

GIULIETTA GUICCIARDI

In 1800, the noble Guicciardi family moved from Trieste (in today's Italy) to Vienna, where the beautiful countess, Giulietta, rapidly became very popular at the dancing balls. During the fall of 1801, she received piano lessons from Beethoven, and in his November letter to Wegeler, Beethoven wrote:

> *My life is somewhat more pleasant now because I mix in society. You would find it hard to believe what an empty, sad life I have had for the last two years. My poor hearing haunted me everywhere like a ghost; and I avoided all of human society. I seemed to be a misanthrope and yet I am far from being one. This change has been brought about by a dear charming girl who loves me and whom I love. After two years I am again enjoying a few blissful moments; and for the first time, I feel that marriage might bring me happiness. Unfortunately, she is not of my class. And at the moment I certainly could not marry; I must still bustle about a good deal.*[86]

Giulietta Guicciardi (1782–1856)

In January 1802, Beethoven received a gift from Giulietta's mother. It is unknown what the gift was, but it can be deduced that it was money, for example, a purse with coins. The gift made Beethoven both angry and sad. It became clear to him that his piano lessons to Giulietta were seen as something that had to be paid for, not as a kind turn. It also stressed the fact that the mother saw Beethoven only as a piano teacher, not as a suitor. The hurt Beethoven dedicated his Piano Sonata in C-sharp minor *quasi una fantasia* (Opus 27/2) to Giulietta as a kind of farewell gift. This piano sonata was later referred to as the *Moonlight Sonata*.

In November 1803, Giulietta married someone else. The couple moved to Naples and had many children. In 1822, the family moved back to Vienna, after which Giulietta and Beethoven appear not to have had any significant contact.

DOROTHEA ERTMANN

Around 1803, Dorothea Ertmann and her husband moved to Vienna. The Baroness was an outstanding pianist. In those days, Beethoven's piano music was much spoken of and sometimes in a negative way, because it was regarded as incomprehensible and boring. When a new piano sonata by Beethoven was published, the curious Ertmann went to the music shop and played there by sight-reading. A self-conscious man in his early thirties stood in the corner and listened attentively. After Ertmann ceased playing, the man approached her, took her hand and thanked her for the excellent interpretation of *his* sonata. It was Beethoven himself!

This was the beginning of a long friendship. Beethoven gave her several piano lessons and Ertmann became one of the greatest Beethoven exponents of that period. Her favorite piece was the Piano Sonata Opus 27/2 (*Moonlight*). She played it often and with pleasure, for example in 1831, when Felix Mendelssohn visited her in Milan.

Dorothea Ertmann (1781–1849)

When she lost a child, she was surprised that Beethoven did not visit her. He did not show up for weeks. But one day Beethoven did appear. He nodded, took a seat behind the piano and started to improvise. However, Ertmann was under the impression that she did not hear a piano; instead, she heard "a choir of angels welcoming her child to the World of Light."[87] After an hour Beethoven ceased playing, pressed her hand and left without a word.

During the last decade of his life, Beethoven wrote completely different piano music compared to the masterworks he wrote in his thirties when he composed the piano sonatas later referred to as the *Moonlight*, the *Waldstein* and the *Appassionata*. One of the earliest creations of that last decade was the Piano Sonata Opus 101, which was incomprehensible and boring to the lay music lover and hard to play for the amateur pianist. As a statement, Beethoven did not dedicate it for money to an aristocrat or to a beautiful woman like Giulietta Guicciardi. He dedicated it to a pianist who completely understood his music: Dorothea Ertmann.

Although Ertmann and Beethoven had a friendship that lasted many years, there is no report of any quarrel. How Ertmann managed to accomplish that, she explained later:

He was very touchy, very irascible, very irritable and because of that often unfair and distrustful toward his best friends. But who could be angry with a man who was so unhappy due to his increasing deafness. One has to consider his physical and mental suffering and forgive him everything. In this fashion, we had an untroubled friendship for many years.[88]

ANNA ERDÖDY

Countess Anna Erdödy was an invalid; swollen feet kept her bedridden most of the time. She could not walk, only limp. Despite her handicap, she was reported to have a happy disposition.

She had lived in Vienna from 1803, and, being an excellent pianist, organized musical soirees at her house. Beethoven was one of the contributors. Such a warm, not romantic, friendship developed between the two – he even called her his *Beichtvater* (father confessor) – that Beethoven moved into a room in her large house in the fall of 1808.

But in the first week of March 1809, Beethoven left the room in a fury and moved into another room nearby. The precise reason for his rage is unknown, but it is certain that a servant was involved. It could simply be that Beethoven became aware (or thought) that Erdödy paid a servant to stay in Beethoven's service, which hurt his pride. A few days later, Beethoven wrote a letter to Erdödy:

My dear countess, I have acted wrongly, it is true – forgive me. If I offended you, it was certainly not due to deliberate wickedness on my part. Only since yesterday evening have I understood how things are; and I am very sorry that I behaved as I did. Read the note calmly, and then judge for yourself whether I have deserved it and whether you have not paid me back six fold for all I have done. If I insulted you unintentionally, please do write just one word to say that you are fond of me again. If you do not do this, I shall suffer infinite pain. I cannot do anything if this situation continues. I expect your forgiveness.[89]

Reconciliation followed and Beethoven and Erdödy stayed friends. In 1809, Beethoven dedicated the Piano Trios Opus 70 to the Countess, out of gratitude for her involvement in the realization of the annuity Beethoven received from that year on. In 1819, Beethoven dedicated the Vienna edition of the Cello Sonatas Opus 102 to the Countess, who had close contact with a cellist.

Anna Erdödy (1778–1837)

THERESE MALFATTI

Therese Malfatti, the daughter of a wealthy Viennese merchant, received piano lessons from Beethoven in the winter and spring of 1810. Beethoven was introduced to the Malfattis by his friend Gleichenstein and he soon became their family friend.

In his letter of 2 May 1810 to Wegeler, Beethoven asked him to send a copy of his baptismal certificate to Vienna. This meant that he intended to marry Therese. He pressed Wegeler to do this "soon." To make things clear, Beethoven was thirty-nine and Therese was eighteen years old.

Therese Malfatti (1792–1851)

At the beginning of May 1810, the Malfattis moved to their summer residence near Krems, some thirty miles west of Vienna. Later that month, Beethoven sent a letter to Therese. Here is the beginning:

> *With this letter, beloved Therese, you are receiving what I promised you. And indeed, if the most powerful obstacles had not prevented me, you would be receiving still more, if only to show you that I always do more for my friends than I promise. I hope and have every reason to believe that you are nicely occupied and pleasingly entertained; but I hope not too much, so that you may also think of me. No doubt I should be counting too much on you or*

*valuing my worth too highly if I were to apply to you the saying, "People are
united not only when they are together; even the distant one, the absent one
too is present with us."[90] Who would ascribe anything of the kind to the lively
Therese, who takes life so easily?*

*In connection with your pursuits be sure not to forget the pianoforte or,
in general, music as a whole. You have such a splendid gift for music, why
don't you cultivate it seriously? You who have so much feeling for all that is
beautiful and good, why will you not direct it to discerning in such a glorious
art that is fine and perfect, a quality which in its turn ever radiates beauty
upon us?*

*I am leading a very lonely and quiet life. Although here and there certain
lights would like to awaken me, yet since you all left Vienna, I feel within
me a void which cannot be filled and which even my art, which is usually so
faithful to me, has not yet been able to make me forget.[91]*

Beethoven went on to say that he had ordered her a piano, that she is lucky having
the opportunity to stroll in the countryside (something he loves to do himself), that
she should read Goethe and Shakespeare (he can send her the books in question),
that he loves to visit her, but only for half an hour (he does not want to bother her
longer) and he finishes his letter as follows:

*Farewell honored Therese. I wish you all that is good and beautiful in life.
Keep me, and willingly, in remembrance. Forget my wild behavior [das Tolle].
Be convinced that no one more than myself can desire to know that your life is
joyous and prosperous, even though you take no interest in Your most devoted
servant and friend, Beethoven.
NB It would really be very nice on your part to send me a few lines in what
way I can be of service here.[92]*

To the astonishment of Beethoven, the letter was not well received at all. Therese's
parents were displeased with the advances of this famous but eccentric fellow.
Gleichenstein was sent as a messenger to tell Beethoven that he was still welcome
as a musician, but not as a suitor. In June 1810, Beethoven wrote a letter to
Gleichenstein. Here is the beginning:

*Your news has again plunged me from the heights of the most sublime ecstasy
down into the deepest depths. Why did you add the remark that you would let
me know when there would be music again? Am I then nothing more than a
music-maker for yourself or the others? This is how I should explain it.[93]*

In the remainder of the letter Beethoven is full of self-pity: "For you, poor Beethoven, no happiness can come from outside, you must create everything for yourself in your own heart; and only in the world of ideals can you find friends."[94]

When the baptismal certificate arrived, Beethoven's "wild behavior" towards Therese, whatever it referred to, was over. Stephan von Breuning wrote to Wegeler, "I believe his marriage project has fallen through."[95]

When Therese died, she owned an autograph of a Beethoven bagatelle (a short unpretentious instrumental composition). In 1865, a Beethoven scholar discovered the autograph but was only allowed by the then owner to copy it. The bagatelle was published in 1867. The autograph has never shown up again, but allegedly the date of 27 April (without an indication of a year) was written on top of it, as were the words, "as a memento" of Ludwig van Beethoven. This bagatelle could very well be the *"promised"* thing Beethoven refers to at the beginning of his letter of May 1810 to Therese. This is only a hypothesis; other hypotheses exist. But if this hypothesis is correct, the Beethoven scholar must have misread the dedication. For this bagatelle has become world famous under the title, *Für Elise*.

BETTINA BRENTANO

Bettina Brentano came from a culturally prominent family. In the first decade of the nineteenth century, her brother Clemens (together with Achim von Arnim) published a collection of folk poems, titled *Des Knaben Wunderhorn* (*The Boy's Magic Horn*), one of the most successful and influential publications during the German Romantic period.

Bettina Brentano (1785–1859)

Bettina, who had multiple talents, was in frequent contact with many important representatives of German culture. She was rather flirtatious and her hobby was pursuing well-known men. Her biggest conquest was the leading German poet Goethe (more than thirty years her senior); this to the displeasure of his wife who forced a break between them in September 1811.

Between 8 May and 3 June 1810, she visited Vienna. Together with her sister-in-law Antonie, she met with Beethoven, who was captivated by her flirtatious behavior. He walked with her hand-in-hand and took her to orchestral rehearsals where she sat in the front row.

Beethoven wrote his song *Neue Liebe, Neues Leben* (*New Love, New Life*, words by Goethe) for her and wrote *Für Bettine von Brentano* on top of the autograph. But he failed to answer the letters she wrote him during the next months. Only after the urging of Antonie did he reply in February 1811. At the conclusion of the letter, Beethoven wrote, "And now goodbye, dear, dear B., I kiss you on the forehead, and thus press on it as with my seal all my thoughts for you. Write soon, soon and often to your friend Beethoven."[96]

In March 1811, Bettina married Achim von Arnim. In July 1812, she was in Teplitz where Goethe did not want to see her and Beethoven could hardly hear her.

After her husband passed away (1831), Bettina applied herself to the terrible plight of the poor, the sick, women, and Jews. She was among the first women who favored the abolition of the death penalty.

ANTONIE VON BIRKENSTOCK

The influential scholar and statesman Johann von Birkenstock had one daughter and he wanted to take good care of her. So, when she was eighteen years old, he looked for a protective husband for her and found the rich merchant Franz Brentano, fifteen years her senior and a half-brother of Bettina and Clemens. Even on the wedding day, the newlyweds hardly knew each other.

They moved to Frankfurt, Franz's hometown, where Antonie was unable to adjust. Her husband was busy most of the time; she respected him but did not love him. From 1806 on, her health declined. Clemens described her as a glass of water that had been left standing for a long time.

In 1809, she heard that her father lay dying and she was eager to move her family (Franz and their four children) to Vienna in order to take care of her father during his last weeks (he died in October 1809). While Franz commuted between Vienna and Frankfurt, Antonie was able to prolong her stay in Vienna until 1812, taking care of her father's immense legacy; he had been a fervent art collector.

Antonie von Birkenstock (1780–1869)

In May 1810, she visited Beethoven together with her sister-in-law Bettina. After this visit, she came to know Beethoven closely and developed a great liking for him. She called their relationship a case of *Wahlverwandtschaft* ("elective affinity"). Some days she was so tormented by headaches that she was bedridden the whole day. On such days, Beethoven would pass by. He went to the pianoforte in the room next to her bedroom and started to improvise. That music brought her more relief than any doctor could have accomplished. Beethoven left the way he came: in silence.

During the summer of 1812, Beethoven spent quite a bit of time with Antonie and her family, as they both visited spas in Bohemia, before the family moved back to Frankfurt that following fall. Antonie and Beethoven never saw each other again but stayed in close contact through letters. Beethoven frequently expressed his affection for the Brentanos, for instance in 1816, "I recall to my mind with pleasure the hours I spent in the company of you both, which are the most unforgettable of my life."[97]

Franz lent Beethoven large sums of money; it is not certain whether Beethoven paid back all the money. But he did acknowledge the Brentanos by dedicating his Piano Sonata Opus 109 to their daughter Maximiliane and the *Diabelli Variations* (his most important variations) to Antonie.

FANNY GIANNATASIO DEL RIO

From February 1816 till January 1818, nephew Karl stayed at the boarding school of Cajetan Giannatasio del Rio. Beethoven got along with the family of Spanish roots and became a regular visitor. Cajetan had two daughters: Fanny and Nanni. Fanny was deeply impressed by Beethoven (twenty years her senior), both the artist and the man. She fell more or less in love with him, which eluded him completely. She kept a lengthy diary in which she, for example, wrote about the artist Beethoven who composes music that will be admired in centuries to come (there she was foresighted). Regarding the man Beethoven, she liked his superb character and his deep understanding of the good and the noble. She regretted that Beethoven seemed to prefer her younger sister. One time, she and Beethoven had a conversation of about half an hour, but the moment Nanni entered the room, Beethoven shifted his attention and seemed to forget Fanny completely. An example of how Fanny wrote is this diary entry 26 February 1816:

> The day before yesterday Beethoven visited us again for several hours. This evening left me with an extremely pleasant impression, which urged the longing for more evenings like this one. He allowed us to see in him the goodness of heart which is his special characteristic. Whether he spoke of his friend, or of his excellent mother, or gave his opinion on those men who think they can match up with him, he proved to us that his heart is as well cultivated as his head. On the whole, I think that most of what he speaks is worth to be written down; it is so just and sound. When he would attach himself to us, it would make me very happy![98]

It took a year before the usual quarrels showed up. The raptus letter Beethoven wrote is lost; the reaction of Fanny is not. On 1 March 1817, she wrote in her diary:

> It saddens me a lot that Beethoven is angry with us lately. However, the art in which he expressed himself turned my sadness into bitterness. It is true that father was unkind to him. But people like us, who express their respect and love all the time, should not be rejected by him with stinging mockery. He certainly wrote this letter in one of his misanthropic moods and I do forgive him gladly.[99]

This rejecting mood continued for two weeks. Then Beethoven reappeared as if nothing had happened. The question whether he was still angry resulted in the answer that he did not think himself important enough to still be so.

Fanny Giannatasio del Rio (1790–1876)

However, Fanny's forgiving mood was put to the test in August of the same year. In her diary, she again wrote about a letter to her father, in which Beethoven expressed "such an extreme offensive opinion" about her that she was "rather hurt, even indignant. [...] Never in my life did I have such an injurious experience. It hurt me even more because it came from a man who I respect in the highest degree."[100]

In a later entry, she expounded on what had happened. "Once I had a nasty conflict with Beethoven because he believed I disagreed with the way he treated his nephew."[101]

NANETTE STREICHER

The piano manufacturer Stein could consider Mozart and Beethoven as his fans. Mozart also praised the piano playing of his daughter when she was only eight years old. Beethoven visited the renowned manufacturer in Augsburg during his first journey to Vienna (1787). It is likely he also met Nanette.

When her father died, Nanette took over the firm. She married Johann Streicher and they moved to Vienna. For many years, Beethoven showed a liking for the pianos made by her company. But really intense contact between Beethoven and Nanette developed during the years 1816 to 1818 and had nothing to do with music. Beethoven extensively consulted Nanette regarding apartments, staff, laundry, garments, utensils, and foodstuff. It was Beethoven's intention to bring nephew Karl into the house, which took until January 1818.

Beethoven wrote many letters to Nanette. A good example is the letter of June 1818, from his summer residence in Mödling, in which he complains about his staff (an older woman, Frau D. and a younger one, called Peppi). Here is the beginning:

Nanette Streicher (1769–1833)

Dear Frau von Streicher!
It was not possible to answer your last letter sooner. I had already some days ago written to you before the servants were sent away, but I always hesitated about my decision until I perceived that especially Frau D. kept Karl back from confessing everything. She said to him that "he ought to spare his mother," and Peppi joined in in the same strain; naturally they did not wish to be found out. Both disgracefully played into each other's hands, and allowed themselves to be used by Frau van Beethoven; both received coffee and sugar from her, Peppi money, the old woman probably also; but there is not the slightest doubt that she went herself to the house of Karl's mother. She also told Karl that if I sent her away, she would at once go to his mother. This occurred on an occasion when I was reproaching her with her behavior, for I had often cause to be dissatisfied. Peppi who often listened when I was talking to Karl, seemed disposed to confess the truth, but the old woman told her she was a fool, and gave her a good blowing up – and so she again was stubbornly silent and sought to lead me on a wrong track. The story of this horrible deception may have lasted for about six weeks; both of them would have had a worse time of it with a less magnanimous man. Peppi borrowed from me 9 or 10 fl.

for stuff for shirts, and I afterwards made her a present of the money, and instead of 60 fl. she received 70 fl.; she might at least have denied herself those wretched bribes. As for the old woman who behaved worse, hate may have had something to do with it, as she always thought herself thrust into the background (although she received more than she deserves), for through her scornful face one day when Karl embraced me, I suspected treachery, and how disgraceful in such an old woman, and how backbiting she could be. Imagine, two days before, when I betook myself here, Karl went without my knowledge one afternoon to his mother, and both the old woman and Peppi were aware of it. But now hear the triumph of a hoary-headed traitress; when I drove hither with Karl and her, I spoke to Karl in the carriage about the matter, although I did not know everything, and indeed I expressed fear lest we might not be quite safe in Mödling, she called out I need only rely on her. Oh, how disgraceful! Only twice has anything of the sort happened to me with people of an otherwise venerable age.[102]

One day, Beethoven offended Nanette seriously. But his anger was not directed at her. She happened to be present when he erupted. Beethoven wrote her one of his apologetic letters the next day:

I ask you a thousand times to forgive me about yesterday. We had a meeting on the question of my nephew [...] and on such occasions, I am really always in danger of losing my head. And that's what happened yesterday. I only hope that you may not have felt offended.[103]

JOSEPHINE VON BRUNSVIK

Josephine von Brunsvik was born in Pressburg (now Bratislava in Slovakia). This Countess enjoyed a carefree youth in a magnificent castle in Martonvásár, near Budapest. Together with her brother Franz and sisters Therese and Charlotte she received a classical education from tutors. They all learned to play an instrument: Franz, the violoncello and the three sisters, the piano. All had musical talent, but Josephine most of all. The only blemish was the premature death of their father in 1792. During the last years of the century, the Brunsvik family became particularly impressed by the compositions of a young man who had made his reputation in noble circles as an excellent pianist. The name of this man: Ludwig van Beethoven.

In May 1799, their mother, Anna, took Therese and Josephine to Vienna. Part of the purpose of the visit was to have the sisters take piano lessons with Beethoven.

They were told that he disliked teaching and were advised to visit him at home. It was 5 May 1799 when Anna, accompanied by two of her daughters, took the winding stairs to Beethoven's apartment. When Beethoven saw Josephine, he fell in love at first sight. He liked the way the sisters played the piano and promised to come to their hotel to teach them on a daily basis. And so he did. For the next sixteen days, he appeared every day at noon and gave piano lessons for one or two hours, staying until 4 or 5 p.m. He refused any payment.

Beethoven composed a song for the two sisters: *Ich denke dein* (*I think of you*, lyrics by Goethe). He wrote three lines in their diary:

> *Ich bin bei dir*
> *Du seist auch noch so ferne*
> *Du bist mir nah!*

> *I am with you,*
> *Even if you are so far away.*
> *You are near me!*

Later Beethoven wrote six variations on *Ich denke dein* for piano four hands and the printed version was dedicated to Therese and Josephine.

That same day, Anna and her daughters visited a famous art gallery (the Wax Museum and Curiosities Cabinet of Joseph Müller). Joseph Müller (born in 1752) saw Josephine and fell in love at first sight. However, Müller was not Joseph's real surname.

Many years earlier Count Joseph von Deym had to leave the country after an escalated duel. On his return, years later, he adopted the name Joseph Müller. In May 1799, Joseph Müller turned to his friend, the Emperor, explained his situation, was reprieved and allowed to use his noble title again.

One morning, Joseph Müller entered the hotel at nine and desired to speak to Anna von Brunsvik in private. After a few minutes, Josephine was invited into the room and introduced to Count Joseph von Deym. She was asked if she wanted to marry him. Josephine understood that her mother disliked being contradicted and that the question was a rhetorical one. She answered affirmative and a few minutes later she threw her arms around Therese's neck and wept uncontrollably.

One month later, the wedding took place in Martonvásár. The couple settled in Vienna and the free piano lessons with Beethoven were continued, although only twice a week. Beethoven was very friendly to Joseph and composed small pieces for his mechanical clock as Haydn and Mozart had done before. And, of course, Beethoven contributed to the musical soirees at the Deym's.

Despite the difference in age (more than a quarter of a century) Joseph and

Josephine got along with each other very well. Besides, Vienna with all its balls was an attractive city for a young and engaging countess. Josephine quickly became a party animal. The only thing that puzzled her was the presence of several young women in a wing of Deym's large house (eighty-four rooms). Joseph explained to her that these women were his three adopted daughters. This number was surpassed by the children Josephine gave birth to: two sons and two daughters.

Josephine von Brunsvik (1779–1821)

With the same zeal she had used to make the wedding happen in 1799, Anna tried to undo the marriage of Joseph and Josephine in 1800. The reason was that Joseph was not as rich as she had understood. But Anna stood alone; her daughter Josephine loved her husband and she did not wish to divorce the father of her first child. And so the marriage continued, although Joseph von Deym in his turn was somewhat disappointed with the small dowry.

The contact with Beethoven was still positive. During the summer of 1800, he visited Martonvásár when he was in Budapest for a few weeks to give concerts. In December, during a private concert, Schuppanzigh played a violin sonata by Beethoven and Josephine played the piano part.

All these concerts and balls were very nice, but they cost a lot of money, and the couple was not excessively wealthy. So, in June 1803, they moved to a smaller house in a city where life was cheaper: Prague. They took their oldest child with them and the two youngest were Aunt Therese and Grandmother Anna.

Count Deym died suddenly of pneumonia in January of 1804. In his will, it was stipulated that his (pregnant) wife inherit his possessions and become guardian of the children. In those days, that was not automatic. Josephine moved to Vienna and received the moral support of the Emperor – "Don't weep: your children are my children" – however, no practical support ensued.

Back in Vienna, Josephine continued the good life, and renewed her contact with Beethoven, although she had worries and suffered a nervous breakdown. Beethoven visited her frequently, with "piano lessons" as a pretext for his visits. The love he had felt in May 1799, which had been suppressed when she married someone else, was rekindled now that Josephine was an available widow. Beethoven was well aware of obstacles on the road towards marriage. If Josephine married him, she would lose her noble title and would have to give up her guardianship over her four noble children. But this awareness did not influence his hopes. So, in the spring of 1805, he wrote a song *An die Hoffnung (To Hope)* and wrote a dedication on the title page of the autograph. This autograph still stood on the piano when Lichnowsky visited Beethoven. Lichnowsky drew his own conclusions but did not mention anything at that time. Later he asked Zmeskall whether he knew if Beethoven visited Josephine frequently.

The next time Lichnowsky visited Beethoven, he asked him whether that dedication had any meaning and whether Beethoven entertained certain feelings regarding Josephine. And no, of course, he had not mentioned that dedication to anyone else, discretion being his middle name. He had only asked Zmeskall a few innocent questions.

Josephine disliked the idea of an amorous Beethoven visiting her frequently, becoming gossip. Her sister Charlotte had already called Beethoven's visits "dangerous." Thus, Josephine asked Beethoven for clarification. First, Beethoven answered her orally, but he felt the need to revert to the subject by letter. And, while writing the letter, he took the opportunity to express his feelings for her.

> As I said, the issue with Lichnowsky is not so bad, my beloved Josephine, as they made you think – quite by chance Lichnowsky saw the song An die Hoffnung at my home although I did not notice it and he did not utter a word about it, but he gathered from this that I must have some affection for you, and then when Zmeskall went to his home for the affair in which you and Aunt Guicciardi were involved, he asked him if he knew whether I went to see you fairly often, Zmeskall said neither yes or no, after all, there was nothing he could say, for I withdraw from his attention as much as possible – Lichnowsky said that he thought he had noticed by chance (the song) that I must have some affection for you, but he did not say anything about it as Zmeskall solemnly assured me – and Zmeskall was to have a word with Aunt Guicciardi to suggest that she should speak to you so that you might encourage me more to finish my opera, as he believed that this might do a lot

of good, for he knew for certain what a great regard I cherished for you – this is all that happened – Zmeskall magnified it and Aunt Guicciardi likewise; meanwhile – you can rest assured, seeing that no one other than these two persons are involved – Lichnowsky himself said that as for him, he would know very well how to act with delicacy so as not to mention a single word, if he assumed with certainty the existence of a closer relationship – on the contrary, there was nothing which he desired more than the formation of such a relationship between you and me, if it were possible, which could not but be advantageous to me for what I had told him about your character. – basta così – It is true that I have not been as diligent as I ought to have been – but an inner grief – robbed me for a long time of the energy I usually have, for some time after the feeling of love for you, my adored Josephine, began to stir within me, this grief increased even more – as soon as we are together again with no one to disturb us, then you shall hear all about my real sorrows and the struggle with myself between death and life in which I was engaged for some time – For a long period a certain event made me despair of ever achieving any happiness during life on this earth – but now things are no longer so bad, I have won your heart, oh! I know it with certainty, I have greatly appreciated it, my activity will increase again and – here, I promise you solemnly that here, in a short time, I will be standing more worthy of me and you – oh! give it some value to found – to increase – my happiness through your love, oh! beloved Josephine, it is not the drive to the opposite sex that attracts me to you, no, only you, the whole of your Being with all its singularities – has my respect – all my feelings – all of my sensibility is chained to you – when I came to you – I was firmly determined not to let even a spark of love germinate in me, you have overcome me – did you want it? – or did you not? – some day you could solve this question Josephine. – Oh! Heaven, how I wish to tell you everything – how I think of you – what I feel for you – but how weak, how poor are words, at least my words – A Long – long – time – may our love last – it is so noble – so founded on mutual respect and friendship – even the great similarity in so many things, in thoughts and feelings – oh! let me trust that your heart – will beat for me for a long time – mine can only – stop beating for you – when – it no longer beats at all – beloved Josephine. My best wishes for you – I also hope – that through me you may be a little happy – otherwise I would be – selfish.[104]

More love letters followed. Here is the beginning of one of them:

There should be no proof – of how I was pleased to come to your house today – but – only an overwhelming amount of work – and besides tonight I got home only at half past two – yesterday you were so sad dear Josephine. – I cannot do anything for you – and you do so much for me – you make me so happy – do not abandon yourself to your propensity to sadness too much, how it hurts me to see you so – and all the more so, when I do not know how or where I can help – here your – your – Andante.[105]

This *Andante* was initially written as part of a piano sonata (Opus 53), as mentioned in the section about Ferdinand Ries. Beethoven removed it from the sonata and gave it its own existence, named: *Andante favori.*

In his letter, Beethoven emphasized that this *Andante* is Josephine's *Andante.* The publication in 1805 was without dedication. Josephine was Beethoven's big love and whoever mocked this *Andante*, touched Beethoven deeply. Herewith we have the reason for Beethoven's vehement reaction to the innocent practical joke Lichnowsky played. Normally, if Beethoven said something in anger, he could revise it later. But the vow to never play the piano again in the presence of Ries was kept forever.

Josephine did love Beethoven in return, but marrying him would mean losing her children and she did not want to make that sacrifice. Also, her mother Anna would oppose a marriage with a commoner, although Josephine had learned not to take her mother's opinion completely seriously. Thus, she wrote to Beethoven:

You have long had my heart, dear Beethoven [...] receive, through this confession, through this confidence, the greatest proof of my love – of my esteem! [...] Do not tear my heart apart – Do not try to rush me further – I love you inexpressibly – as one pious spirit loves another – Are you disposed to this covenant? – I am not receptive to other forms of love for the present.[106]

This was a love confession, but still a bitter pill to swallow for Beethoven because the request was based on mutual suppression of feelings. This made him angry and his distress was heightened in the spring of 1806 when he heard about Anton von Wolkenstein. At a ball in Budapest, Anton saw Josephine and fell in love at first sight. The thing that made Beethoven mad was that Josephine had not completely rejected the advances of this Tiroler nobleman. An agitated Beethoven wrote the song *Empfindungen bei Lydiens Untreue* (*Emotions at Lydien's Unfaithfulness*; later published as *Als die Geliebte sich trennen wollte – When the beloved wanted to part*). But Josephine wrote to Beethoven that she suffered more, much more. And if he, Beethoven, loved her, she would appreciate a little empathy from his side. And, above all, he should not doubt her actions.

In July 1807, Josephine lived in a summer residence in Baden, together with her four children and her mother. Beethoven happened to be there, too. Contact between Josephine and Beethoven was impeded by the presence of Anna. Beethoven was deeply shaken when he took a walk and Anna passed by. Her strongly rejecting glance gave him a foreboding that he would see Josephine less and less in the future.

In September, Beethoven wrote another letter to Josephine, the beginning of which is presented here

> *Dear, beloved, only Josephine! – Again just a few lines of yours – make me feel great joy – how often, beloved Josephine, I have struggled with myself not to violate the ban I am imposing upon myself – but in vain, a thousand voices whisper to me that you are my only friend, my only beloved – I am no longer able to obey what I am imposing upon myself, oh! dear Josephine let us walk again without worries on that path where we were often so happy – Tomorrow or the day after I will see you, may heaven bestow upon me an undisturbed hour, when I can be with you to have the long awaited talk, when my heart and my soul can meet you again.*[107]

However, the walk and the talk did not take place. Beethoven repeatedly knocked at her door and was informed by servants that the Countess was not at home. A few short letters followed, but did not change the situation; Beethoven gave up.

In the summer of 1808, Josephine's sons were at an age – the eldest had just turned seven – that they had to attend school; or at least receive lessons. Josephine wanted the best of the best for her children and traveled together with her boys and Therese to the pedagogical institution with the highest reputation in the world: the one of Pestalozzi in Yverdon (at the south of Lake Neuchâtel, in Switzerland). Pestalozzi had a young staff member, the handsome Baron Christoph von Stackelberg from Estonia. Stackelberg saw Josephine and fell in love at first sight. He became the teacher of both sons and traveled with them to Hungary. To avoid the rambling French armies north of the Alps, they traveled via Italy. Josephine had already become very ill in Geneva and was ailing for the rest of the journey, which took about half a year. One time when Josephine was recovering, but still very weak, Stackelberg grabbed his chance and impregnated her.

When they arrived in Hungary, Stackelberg stated that he could only continue the education of the two boys as her husband. Anna was not impressed with this poor, protestant, lower aristocrat. But Stackelberg had one big trump card: he was the father of the girl Josephine gave birth to in December 1809. And thus, Anna reluctantly gave her approval for the marriage that took place in February 1810. Anna herself was absent. Nine months later Josephine's sixth child was born. Josephine remained very ill for a long time.

From the outset, the marriage was bad. The family had moved to Vienna, but already in May of 1810, Stackelberg wanted to buy an estate in Moravia. The whole enterprise was one big failure. So, at the end of the year, a lot of money was lost, including a big part of Josephine's inheritance. Stackelberg was skilled at losing money and as a theoretical pedagogue, but not as a practical pedagogue and spouse. He was primarily involved with himself, read esoteric books in his room and mostly left that room only to scold the rest of the family, in a near-psychotic manner.

After her recovery in 1811, Josephine refused to share the bedroom with Stackelberg. The couple had big differences of opinion regarding the upbringing of the children. Josephine was an advocate of kindness and compassion, but Stackelberg preferred to handcuff the children regarding smaller offenses and confine them to bed (tied with a rope) over bigger offenses.

In the spring of 1812, Josephine wrote in her diary that Stackelberg was not behaving as a husband: he continued reading, rather than helping with all the accumulating problems. She also wrote that they were no longer married (this she meant not in a legal way), that Stackelberg was not sincere, not reliable, and that he had an evil character. On top of that, he talked religious nonsense.

In April, the couple had a violent quarrel. Stackelberg left the house, only to return a few weeks later. He packed his suitcases and left the family. One day in June, Josephine wrote in her diary that the current day had been a difficult day for her, that the hand of fate was resting ominously on her, that she saw besides her own deep sorrows also the suffering of her children and that almost all courage had deserted her.

And soon afterward she wrote that Stackelberg wants to leave her on her own, but that she will never let the children be taken from her. She added that because of Stackelberg she had ruined herself physically, in that she had incurred so much distress and illness through him.

While Stackelberg lay in tears in a small, rented room praying to God for relief and ease, Josephine traveled incognito to Prague. She stayed in the house of a sister of Deym, near the inn *Zum Schwarzen Ross*. Here, a man, who had an appointment with a diplomat about financial matters, had taken lodgings. However, that evening (Friday 3 July 1812) the appointed man did not show up. Weeks later, this man wrote a letter of excuse to the diplomat, stating that a circumstance that he could not foresee had prevented him from spending the evening with the diplomat.

This circumstance was that this man and Josephine, both unaccompanied, met completely unexpectedly. What followed is not documented, but it must have been ecstatic. The name of this man: Ludwig van Beethoven.

The next morning, Beethoven left for the spa in Teplitz, one day's journey northwest of Prague. He arrived late in the night of Sunday 5 July. After the first full night in an inn, Beethoven started to write a letter in three installments, which he finished the next morning:

6th July, in the morning.

My angel, my all, my very self. – only a few words today, and in pencil (with yours) – I shall not be certain of my rooms here until tomorrow – what an unnecessary waste of time – why this deep grief, where necessity speaks – can our love exist but by sacrifices, by not demanding everything. Can you change it, that you are not completely mine, that I am not completely yours? Oh God, look upon beautiful Nature and calm your mind about what must be – love demands everything and rightly so, that is how it is for me with you, and for you with me – only you forget too easily, that I must live for myself and for you as well, if we were wholly united, you would not feel this as painfully, just as little as I would – my journey was terrible. I did not arrive here until 4 o'clock yesterday morning. As there were few horses, the mail coach chose another route, but what a dreadful one this was! At the last stage but one I was warned not to travel at night; attempts were made to frighten me about a forest, but that only made me more eager. – I was wrong. The coach broke down on the awful road, a road without a proper surface, a country one. If the two coachmen had not been with me, I would have remained stranded on the way. Esterhazi traveled the usual road here and had the same fate with eight horses that I had with four. – Yet I did get some pleasure out of it, as I always do when I successfully overcome difficulties. – now quickly to the interior from the exterior. We will probably see each other soon, only, today I cannot convey to you my observations, which I made during these few days about my life – If our hearts were always close together, I would have no such thoughts. My heart is full with so much to tell you. – Oh – There are times when words are simply no use – be cheerful – remain my faithful only darling, my all, as I am yours. The rest is up to the gods, what must be for us and what is in store for us. – your faithful Ludwig –

Monday evening, 6th July.

You are suffering, you my dearest creature – only now do I realize that letters have to be posted very early, on Mondays – Thursdays – the only days when the mail is delivered to K. – you are suffering – Oh, wherever I am, you are with me, I talk to myself and to you; arrange [it] that I can live with you, what a life!!!! as it is!!!! without you – Pursued by the goodness of mankind here and there, the goodness that I wish to deserve as little as I deserve it. – Man's humility toward man – this pains me – and when I consider myself in relation to the universe, what am I and what is He who is called the greatest? – And yet, – therein lies the divine element in man. I weep when I think that you will probably not receive first news of me until Saturday. However as much as you love me – I love you even more deeply, but – but never hide yourself from me

– Goodnight – as I am taking the baths I must go to bed. ~~Oh go with me, go~~ ~~with me~~ – Oh God – so near! so far! Is our love not truly sent from Heaven? – And is it not even as firm as the firmament of Heaven?

Good morning, on 7th July.
While still in bed my thoughts turn toward you my Immortal Beloved, now and then happy, then sad again, waiting whether fate might answer us – I can only live either wholly with you or not at all, yes I have even decided to wander about far away, until I can fly into your arms, and feel at home with you, and send my soul embraced by you into the realm of the Spirits – yes unfortunate it must be – you will compose yourself all the more since you know my faithfulness to you, never can another own my heart, never – never – O God why do I have to separate from someone whom I love so much, and yet my life in V[ienna] as it is now is a miserable life – Your love makes me at once most happy and most unhappy – at my age I would now need some conformity [,] regularity of my life – can this exist in our relationship? – Angel, I have just heard that the mail coach goes every day – and thus I must finish so that you may receive the letter immediately. – be patient – only through quiet contemplation of our existence can we achieve our purpose to live together – Be calm; – love me – today – yesterday – What yearning with tears for you – you – my life – my all – farewell – oh continue to love me – never misjudge the most faithful heart of your Beloved L[udwig]
Forever thine
forever mine
forever us.[108]

The letter, known as the "Letter to the Immortal Beloved," was never sent. Josephine started to calculate, went back to Vienna and restored her marriage with Stackelberg, although for a short time, but long enough to make him believe that he was the father of her seventh child …or could pretend he was to the outside world. Josephine's behavior is understandable because if it did come to light that she had an illegitimate child, she would probably lose custody of her children, including the Deym children.

On 8 April 1813, Minona was born. She was named after a beautiful, music-minded person from *The Sorrows of Young Werther* by Goethe, whose name is also interesting when read backward. The child was more or less offered to her godmother Therese.

Shortly after the birth, Stackelberg left his family and traveled to Estonia. In May 1814, he popped up in Vienna and asked Josephine and the children to join him in Russia, to estates he had just inherited. Josephine refused. Stackelberg went to the police and depicted his family life in a way that was half true and half lie. The truth was that his family was in a bad condition and that Josephine neglected the children. He failed to mention his part of the situation. Untrue was that one of the Deym boys had violated one of the Stackelberg girls.

One has to keep in mind that in Vienna at that time, not only was it a class society, it was also a police state, although the heyday of the spy system was still to come. The legal position of women (noble or not) was weak (Beethoven would use these laws to his advantage in his legal battle with his sister-in-law Johanna.)

So, after Stackelberg had told his story, the police (without seriously listening to the other side) came into action and removed the three Stackelberg children from their mother. The intervention of the emperor himself was necessary to prevent the removal of the four Deym children. Stackelberg took his three children (including Minona) to a Deacon in Bohemia.

That Stackelberg did not tell Josephine where he left the children might have been done on purpose. That he did not provide the Deacon with the necessary financial resources can be attributed to his forgetfulness. In the meantime, Josephine tried to fix the education of the four Deym children. In September 1814, she appointed a private teacher, Adrian. Adrian saw Josephine and fell in love at first sight. Josephine was permanently weakened and was not able to resist his advances. So, in September 1815 her eighth child was born, somewhere in a shanty in the Wienerwald (Vienna Woods), far away from the Viennese nobility. Josephine turned Adrian out, including the child, who died in September 1817 because of measles. Josephine paid for the funeral costs.

In April 1815, Stackelberg, who had just received another inheritance, showed up in Vienna again. He probably did not see through Josephine's pregnancy, asked her again to join him (which she refused again), told some slander to the police and left.

In January 1816, Josephine received a letter from a Bohemian Deacon (unknown to her) who told her about three children he took care of. He was out of money and the father had not shown up. Josephine immediately sent some money. In his next letter, the clergyman wrote about the emotional state of the children and how they longed for their mother. Josephine and Therese started to collect money for the homeward journey of the three children, which took some time. The collected money was sent and the Deacon prepared everything for the departure of the three children. But at the final moment, a brother of Stackelberg's appeared. In the name of the father, he took the children with him to Estonia. The connections Stackelberg had with the Viennese police proved their value, even when he was far away. Josephine did not get her money back. The whole story was a big blow to the weak Josephine, but the education of the four Deym children called for all her attention.

As to the years 1813–1815, it is unclear if there was any contact between Beethoven and Josephine. But on 11 February 1816, the Schuppanzigh's goodbye-concert was held at Josephine's place, with Josephine as hostess. Only pieces by Beethoven were played. It was a private concert that was spoiled by Beethoven because he scolded Carl Czerny in front of other people.

Beethoven and Josephine could also have met in Baden, where they both stayed during the summer months. During the fall, after her children did not return, Josephine became depressed. Her mother, Anna, who had become more of a background figure, informed her by letter that there was only one person to blame for her misery: Josephine herself.

"DETACHMENT AND RESIGNATION"

Long intermezzo

Beethoven has documented this important moment of detachment and resignation in the song cycle An die ferne Geliebte *(op. 98) which he had finished in April 1816.*[109]
JAN CAEYERS

An die ferne Geliebte *is what its verses say it is: private anguish universalized and transcended in its singing.*[110]
JAN SWAFFORD

Beethoven's career as a composer can be divided into three periods. The first period lasted until 1802, at which time Beethoven talked about *a* "new path" that he want-ed to follow. Beethoven traveled about ten years on this new path, which resulted in the compositions he is most famous for, the symphonies, numbers three up to and including number eight, the Piano Concertos 4 and 5, the Violin Concerto, his only opera (*Leonore/Fidelio*) and six piano sonatas of which Opus 53 (*Waldstein*) and Opus 57 (*Appassionata*) are the most important. But from the year 1812, his out-put decreased considerably. He did complete two symphonies (Symphonies 7 and 8) that were first performed in 1813 and 1814, respectively. But in the years after 1812, no more new symphonies were composed, no more solo concertos, only some minor orchestral music of which one became very popular at that time: *Wellingtons Sieg oder die Schlacht bei Vittoria* (the "Battle Symphony"). And during the years 1812–1815, Beethoven wrote only one piano sonata (Opus 90). Also, during these years, *Leonore/Fidelio* (in its third version) became popular at last.

The year 1816 is the turning point in this story. Beethoven had met a young physician, Alois Jeitteles, who wrote poems in his leisure time. Beethoven read some of these poems and six thereof (that were never separately published as poems) acted like condensation nuclei for thoughts and feelings that had hovered in Beethoven's soul since 1812. Within a few weeks, the poems were set to music. The six songs are connected with transition notes, so, in fact, they form one whole piece of music. In October, they were published titled *An die ferne Geliebte* ("To the Distant Beloved").

In the first song, the protagonist sits on a hill and laments the distance between him and his beloved. Only music is deemed as an appropriate means to make contact:

Denn vor Liebesklang entweichet
Jeder Raum und jede Zeit,
Und ein liebend Herz erreichet,
Was ein liebend Herz geweiht!

Because all space and all time
Dodge due to love tones;
And what is dedicated to a loving heart,
Will reach a loving heart!

In the second song, the protagonist is still sitting on the hill and articulates his longing to be somewhere else:

Ach, mich zög's nicht von hier,
Könnt ich, Traute, bei dir
Ewiglich sein!

Oh, I would not want to leave from here,
If, dear, I could forever be with you!

In the third song, the protagonist realizes that clouds and brooks travel to his beloved and he requests them to greet her:

Flüstr' ihr zu mein Liebesflehen,
Lass sie, Bächlein, klein und schmal,
Treu in deinen Wogen sehen
Meine Tränen ohne Zahl!

Whisper to her my love appeal;
Little and small brook,
Please let her faithfully see in your waves
My innumerable tears!

In the fourth song, the protagonist proceeds with his talks to clouds and brooks and ends with a request in case his beloved looks into the brook:

Hin zu dir von jenen Hügeln
Emsig dieses Bächlein eilt,
Wird ihr Bild sich in dir spiegeln,
Fliess zurück dann unverweilt!

Please, brook, hurry zealously
From the hills to her;
If it happens that her image is reflected in you,
Please flow back immediately.

In the fifth song, the spring and especially the month of May are amply praised as the season and month of love:

Wenn alles, was liebet,
der Frühling vereint,
Nur unserer Liebe
kein Frühling erscheint,
Und Tränen sind al ihr Gewinnen.

The spring unites everything
And everyone that loves each other.
Only to our love spring does not emerge.
And tears are all that is gained.

In the sixth song, the protagonist offers all the six songs to his beloved and expresses his hope that she will sing them too. The song starts calmly (*Andante con moto, cantabile*) and seems to stand still halfway. But then an enormous rush (*Allegro molto e con brio*) follows that culminates in the renewed realization that only with music can contact be made.

Dann vor diesen Liedern weichet,
Was geschieden uns so weit,
Und ein liebend Herz erreichet,
Was ein liebend Herz geweiht.

What has severed us so profoundly,
Will give way to these songs;
And what is dedicated to a loving heart,
Will reach a loving heart!

In order to ensure for Josephine that she was his Distant Beloved, Beethoven repeats those last four lines several times (with increasing elation) and refers in the music to the first few bars to "her" *Andante* from more than ten years before.

When he had met Josephine for the first time (1799), Beethoven had written in her diary the following words by Goethe:

Ich bin bei dir
Du seist auch noch so ferne
Du bist mir nah!

I am with you,
Even if you are so far away.
You are near me!

In 1812, he had written, "Oh God – so near! so far!" and, "I have even decided to wander about far away, until I can fly into your arms." When it became clear that he could not fly into her arms, it took Beethoven more than three years to process that fact. But with the song cycle *An die ferne Geliebte*, his hitting rock-bottom was overcome. It is striking that during the same month, Beethoven wrote *An die ferne Geliebte*, he also started to write Piano Sonata Opus 101 (dedicated to Baroness Ertmann, an outstanding pianist), which is considered as the first masterpiece of his third period. During this period, he would write rather wayward music, not suited for the general public, with one exception, the Ninth Symphony, in which he expressed his desire that all men would become brothers. That was a message to all mankind, just like *An die ferne Geliebte*.

This is more than a message to the beloved; it is a message to the world. By
setting to music these poems and by publishing them, Beethoven indeed made
a public statement that included both the confirmation of the existence as
well as the distancing himself of his 'immortal beloved'. But this nostalgic

hymn to his lost love is above all a paean to art, the only surviving means of communication to the beloved.[111]
JAN CAEYERS

Two loving hearts drawn apart are united in music, the poet's song and his heart echoing in the song and heart of the beloved. In the most direct yet profound way, in that moment Beethoven is united with his own lost beloved in the only way he can be, and no less with all beloveds and all lost loves – which is to say, with all humanity.[112]
JAN SWAFFORD

*   *   *

In March 1817, Stackelberg reappeared again in Vienna. Again, he asked Josephine to come with him and again she refused. Once more he tried to cajole some money from her; here he was more successful. After some months, he left.

In 1819, Stackelberg reappeared in Vienna, this time with his children, including Minona. Josephine was too ill to take an interest in anything or anyone. But Therese wrote in her diary:

It was remarkable how the child had developed. Without being beautiful, she was strong and commanded her older sisters so much that we used to call her the governess. It was also evident that she had the most genius among the sisters.[113]

Stackelberg did not try to take Josephine with him; nor did he try to cajole money. It must have been clear to him that regarding Josephine the end was near. However, it took more than a year before her suffering was completely over.

On 31 March 1821, Countess Josephine von Brunsvik died. Her funeral at the Währing Cemetery in Vienna was only modestly attended. There were only two persons present, her sister Therese and her eldest daughter. Mother Anna did not think a gravestone was necessary. Thus, Josephine disappeared into anonymity, where she would remain over 130 years. Not until 1957 were Beethoven's love letters to her published.

"INDESCRIBABLY SORROWFUL"

Short intermezzo

Here is music rising from Beethoven's own sorrow to become universal, what the Romantics called Weltschmerz, *"world-pain."*[114]
JAN SWAFFORD

No source reports Beethoven's reaction regarding Josephine's death. But it is very tempting to take a look at the first main composition Beethoven wrote in the months that followed.

In those years, Beethoven was writing three piano sonatas (his last three) commissioned by a publisher. The first (Opus 109) had been completed during the fall of the year before. During the first half of 1821, Beethoven was ill for several weeks and feeling poorly for several months. Somewhere in the spring or summer, Beethoven began composing the second sonata (Opus 110). It is no surprise that a Beethoven piano sonata is full of contrasts, but this one is extreme. This sonata starts with a *Moderato cantabile molto espressivo* (at a moderate speed, in a singing style, very expressive) and is lyrical in nature.

The second movement (*Allegro Molto*) is bizarre. It is an adaptation of two German folk songs (*"My cat has had kittens" and "I'm a slob, you're a slob"*). The third and final movement (*Adagio ma non troppo*) starts with very slow music, which Stafford calls *"indescribably sorrowful."*[115] After eight long bars, Beethoven starts an *Arioso dolente* ("plaintive song") which refers to Bach's *Es ist vollbracht* ("It is accomplished") from the *St John Passion*.

The sonata ends with two fugues, which are parted by the return of the plaintive song. This piece of music ends with a Beethovian life corroborative, triumphal fortissimo, like the song cycle "the Distant Beloved." Of course, it is highly speculative, but it looks like composing this piano sonata was Beethoven's way of coming to terms with Josephine's death and set the stage for what would become his final years, wherein he would compose his Ninth Symphony, including the chorus *Ode to Joy*. Also remarkable, the Piano Sonata Opus 110 is the only one of the five late piano sonatas that has no dedication, just like the *Andante favori*. It is only natural that Opus 110 has been called, "clearly a requiem for Josephine."[116]

*   *   *

What happened to Minona? After Stackelberg passed away (1841), she went to live with her Aunt Charlotte in Transylvania. The arranging of the elaborate library was made around long trips by horse. Around 1851, Minona moved to her other aunt in Vienna. Therese tried to make her a pianist but to no avail. Minona never married, nor did she have children. She died in 1897.

Almost exactly six years after Josephine's funeral at the Währing Cemetery, a man who had died on 26 March was buried near her grave. In previous years this man had been seen several times at that cemetery, although nobody understood his business there. Different from the 1821 funeral, this 1827 funeral was well attended; although the number of persons present would not have exceeded twenty thousand. The name of this man: Ludwig van Beethoven.

CHAPTER

4

"Beyond music he did not understand anything about the sociable life"

BEETHOVEN AND THE ASPERGER FEATURES

Beethoven's character and personality were a mass of contradictions.[117]
ANNE-LOUISE COLDICOTT

We will see that Beethoven was in some ways a hard man.[118]
JAN SWAFFORD

Besides we receive the first testimonies of Beethoven's complicated psyche and his tendency to be introverted – other contemporaries labelled this already with 'misanthropy'.[119]
JAN CAEYERS

In many cases the social problems are so profound that they overshadow everything else. In some cases, however, the problems are compensated by a high level of original thought and experience. This can often lead to exceptional achievements in later life.[120]
HANS ASPERGER

Aspergers – with their lack of flexibility and, often, stunning egocentricity – have major problems coping with 'normal' life. At the same time, many are 'free thinkers' and may be scientifically and aesthetically highly skilled people.[121]
CHRISTOPHER GILLBERG

The diagnostic criteria were shockingly familiar – my mind whispered, "This is him." Everything made sense. Everything fell into place.[122]
ASHLEY STANFORD

"ONE WOULD CONSIDER HIM A MISANTHROPE."

Social impairment (extreme egocentricity)

It has been my aim to show that the fundamental disorder of aspergers is the limitation of their social relationships. [...] The nature of these children is revealed most clearly in their behavior toward other people.[123]
HANS ASPERGER

This symptom is often perceived as 'extreme egocentricity'. This, in turn, is usually a catchphrase for the reduced capacity to go beyond the limits of 'the self' and to take the cognitive and emotional perspectives of other people.[124]
CHRISTOPHER GILLBERG

We speak our mother tongue intuitively. The native speaker does not think about what is correct: "he walk" or "he walks." And she knows without ever attending the course "mother tongue." Whoever learns a foreign language has to learn the grammar intellectually. It will take some time before the rules have been internalized.

The same is true regarding our social behavior. "Much of what governs our social interactions is intuitive, and something which is expected to be known almost without explicit training."[125] Which social behavior is appropriate depends on the social setting.

The core problem for aspergers is that their social behavior does not have the same self-evidence as the speaking of the mother tongue. Their behavior stands out in their social environment, just as when someone says "he walk." The underlying problem has hardly anything to do with bad intentions. It has everything to do with a lack of skills.

It is important to realize that the incomprehension is mutual. According to aspergers, other people behave strangely. For example, aspergers like to tell the truth. Other people may not. Their lies vary between white lies that act as social grease and blatant lies that can harm people. Some people withhold an inconvenient true statement out of habit, where aspergers would not.

"Certain things you just do not say in certain settings"[126] is a difficult instruction for aspergers. What are "certain things" and what are "certain settings?" The situation can arise when an asperger is referred to as "someone with a manual." For the asperger, the situation is the other way around. He is the one without a manual: he is speaking the truth, he is pure and authentic. The others are the ones with a manual, they lie when it suits them; but because all the others use more or less the same manual, the illusion can take root that there is no manual involved at all.

There is not just one language. Language is a cultural product. As there are many cultures, so there are many languages. Social behavior is also a cultural product. Whether certain behavior is regarded as appropriate depends on the culture in question. "Peculiar social behavior" is always peculiar social behavior within the context of a certain culture. To assess whether a certain social behavior is peculiar, one has to regard the cultural context of that behavior. The peculiarity can best be assessed by people from within that culture.

*   *   *

Already as a child he was introverted and grave. He never enjoyed the usual child's plays.

Beyond music he did not understand anything about the sociable life. Therefore he was moody in the company of other people, could not participate in their conversations and would withdraw from them. One would consider him a misanthrope.[127]
BERNHARD MÄURER (CELLIST FROM BONN)

The two remarks quoted above date from 1777 (when Beethoven was six years old) and from 1780 (when Beethoven was nine years old) and are the oldest indications that Beethoven was seen by his contemporaries as socially different. Later, other characterizations would follow: "Grand Mogul" (Joseph Haydn), "an utterly untamed personality" (Johann von Goethe), "disagreeable behavior" (Ferdinand Wolanek), "his misanthropic moods" (Fanny Giannatasio del Rio) and "very touchy, very irascible, very irritable" (Dorothea Ertmann). Archduke Rudolf was most laconic: "That's just Beethoven!"

Beethoven appeared to show socially inappropriate behavior. To his patron Franz Lobkowitz he wrote, "If his Serene Highness plays with the instruments like this, I do not give a shit for it." He also called him a "Lobkowitzian ass!" After a small private concert, it turned out that no place at the dinner table had been assigned to Beethoven. He left in a fury. Prince Louis Ferdinand was present during the incident, had ample social skills and offered a lunch where the aristocratic hostess was seated next to him and Beethoven at the other side. To the pianist Friedrich Himmel, zealously improvising, Beethoven said, "Now then, when will you start in earnest?" He also became irritated when Archduke Rudolf's personnel tried to "court teach" him.

Beethoven scolded pianist Carl Czerny in front of other people when he added a number of his own flourishes to a composition by Beethoven. The highly successful composer Rossini got some unsolicited advice about what kind of operas he should compose (and as to what kind of opera he did not have any talent at). Music publisher Peters was kept dangling by Beethoven (and his brother Johann Nikolaus) till Peters gave up on Beethoven. The intensity of copyist Ferdinand Wolanek's annoyance in his letter to Beethoven was easily surpassed by the intensity of the annoyance in Beethoven's reply.

Beethoven quarreled with most of his friends. In his twenties, Beethoven argued with his lifelong friend Franz Wegeler. After Beethoven's hyperbolic letter, the friendship was restored. Differences of opinion with Stephan von Breuning (another lifelong friend) in 1804 about who was responsible for the canceling of the rental contract of Beethoven's apartment escalated in minutes. Beethoven terminated the friendship; months later, Beethoven changed his mind. When Breuning contradicted Beethoven with regard to the treatment of his nephew Karl, Beethoven froze the friendship for ten years.

When, in 1806, his patron and friend Prince Lichnowsky requested him to play the piano for a French general, Beethoven refused. Lichnowsky's urging resulted in Beethoven's untimely departure from Bohemia and the end of their contact. Lichnowsky's bust was smashed by Beethoven. To clarify things, Beethoven wrote, "There have been and will always be thousands of princes. There is only one Beethoven."

In 1808, Ferdinand Ries was ignored by Beethoven for several weeks when the latter mistakenly thought that Ries preyed upon a position that was offered to him (Beethoven) behind his back. It took Ries a lot of effort to convince Beethoven that he had misinterpreted the situation.

Nikolaus Zmeskall adored Beethoven, but could only endure contact with him by ignoring his contempt. And violinist Ignaz Schuppanzigh had to put up with Beethoven's repeated references regarding his corpulence, including the song *Praise to the fat man.*

Beethoven also quarreled with women. In his twenties, he had a row with Eleonore von Breuning. In 1809, Beethoven abruptly left Anna Erdödy's large house (where he was living) and sought new lodgings. There seems to have been a dispute over a servant. The dispute was settled quickly, but Beethoven did not return.

Fanny Giannatasio del Rio had an "injurious experience" with Beethoven when he thought she disapproved of the way he dealt with his nephew. Beethoven's rage also came down on Nanette Streicher, although her only "mistake" was that she was present when there was a meeting about his nephew Karl. Otherwise, Nanette Streicher seemed to have been immune with respect to his negative aspects.

Beethoven only had two male friends with whom he never quarreled: Lorenz von Breuning (who died at the age of twenty-one) and Karl Amenda (who had spent a year and a half in Beethoven's proximity, before the friendship was continued by correspondence). The contact between Beethoven and Antonie von Birkenstock seemed to be free of misunderstandings (their time together in Vienna was a little over two years.) Dorothea Ertmann forgave Beethoven's "unfair and distrustful" behavior in advance, a strategy also used by Fanny Giannatasio del Rio, although in her case it was not always successful.

It is striking that during a tantrum (and the subsequent span of anger that could last for weeks) Beethoven did not want or was not able to speak with the other person directly, but looked for a go-between. That was the case in the row with Eleonore (with an unknown intercessor). In his letter to her, he states that it is better "for a friend to turn directly to their friend." But, in 1804, he ignored Stephan von Breuning and his letters altogether and instead wrote letters to Ries and requested him to talk to Breuning. During the period of misunderstanding with Ries himself, he even ignored him and his letters without looking for a go-between. Beethoven never learned to avoid his raptus tantrums completely, as his letter to Wolanek of 1825 shows.

Beethoven was socially at his best when he was quiet and played the piano. Then he could give great relief to the ill (Antonie von Birkenstock) and great comfort to the sad (Dorothea Ertmann).

Beethoven was attracted to women; he liked looking at them and sought their friendship (Eleonore von Breuning, Anna Erdödy, Dorothea Ertmann, Antonie von Birkenstock, and Nanette Streicher) and sometimes their love (Magdalena Willmann, Giulietta Guicciardi, Therese Malfatti, and Josephine von Brunsvik). When considering proposing, the estimation of his chances was rather low. He had both difficulties in gauging whether the woman in question felt the same way and whether the parents would welcome him as a suitor (Magdalena Willmann, Giulietta Guicciardi, and Therese Malfatti). It was easy for Beethoven to make a social mistake and to be confused by the reactions he received (Marie Bigot). In his letter to Eleonore von Breuning, starting with "Honored Eleonore, my dearest friend!" he apologized for not writing to her for a year. Yet later in the same letter, he asked his "dearest friend" to ask Babette Koch why she had not reacted to the two letters he had sent her. It seemed to elude Beethoven that this would cause some confusion on the side of Eleonore.

Several women visited his apartment to make acquaintance with the genius Beethoven (from the unknown "beloved of a foreign Prince" to Bettina Brentano). This never led to any long-term contact.

In Beethoven's life, there was one long-term love, Josephine von Brunsvik. Before he got to know her, he had been fascinated by women and had made one proposal. But almost immediately after their acquaintance, Josephine married someone else. The two times Beethoven proposed afterward were at times when Josephine was married. When Beethoven thought about marrying Giulietta Guicciardi, Josephine was married to Joseph Deym. When Beethoven thought about marrying Therese Malfatti, Josephine had (just) married Christoph von Stackelberg. Between her two marriages, the noble widow Josephine received many love letters from the commoner Beethoven. After he had met her by sheer coincidence in Prague in 1812, Beethoven wrote a most impressive love letter (which he did not send). After it had become clear to him that a marriage with Josephine was out of the question forever, Beethoven turned to "detachment and resignation," of which the song cycle *To the Distant Beloved* is the most striking result. Even towards Josephine, Beethoven behaved somewhat clumsily, but that was not the reason they did not marry. That was caused by external factors according to the Shakespearean motto, "The course of true love never did run smooth."

The biggest social problems in Beethoven's life showed up in his dealings with family members. The contact with his brothers Casper Carl and Nikolaus Johann was sometimes rough and he caused his sister-in-law Johanna much pain. Beethoven was a bad substitute father and his poor understanding of his nephew Karl's emotional needs pushed the boy towards a suicide attempt. In the months that followed this episode, Karl summarized Beethoven's egocentricity eloquently: "You must remember that other people are also human beings."

"I CANNOT GIVE YOU A LESSON TODAY; I STILL HAVE WORK TO DO."

Narrow interest

We see here something that we have come across in almost all aspergers, a special interest which enables them to achieve quite extraordinary levels of performance in a certain area.[128]
HANS ASPERGER ABOUT ONE OF HIS PUPILS

Even when interests change, the style in which they are adhered to rarely does. Again, it has to be said that it is not the interest in itself, but rather the character of the person's relationship to the interest, that is the problem. The asperger so engrosses himself in the interest that it becomes tedious, indeed often painfully so, for other people. So much time, energy and thought are spent on it, that there is little or no time left for anything else.[129]
CHRISTOPHER GILLBERG

Although the narrow interest can cause problems in one's social life, it can also – initially – be viewed as very attractive. This is what Ashley Stanford states about her asperger spouse: "One of the many reasons I fell in love with my husband was that I marveled at his ability to lose himself in his work. Never in my life had I met someone who could focus so intensely on one particular topic of study."[130] However, she also writes about the disadvantages of the narrow interest: "Unfortunately, as it is with all human nature, there were plenty of drawbacks to this trait that required work-arounds in order for us to function as a couple and as a family."[131]

Provide an asperger with the opportunity to indulge his area of narrow interest, and he will most assuredly do so. As one asperger woman writes: "We are obsessers. For each of us, the desire to spend time and thought with a favored passion is extremely gratifying. Our obsessions are our enchanters."[132]

*　　　*　　　*

For me there is no greater satisfaction than to pursue and present my art.[133]
LUDWIG VAN BEETHOVEN

Beethoven's narrow interest was obviously his music. Making and composing music was not restricted to his working hours. He was preoccupied with his art, anyplace, anywhere. Some contemporaries testify to this:

If one speaks with him for a long time and waits for an answer, he will suddenly utter a lot of sounds, take his staff paper and start to write.[134]

He only lives for his art and no worldly passion distorts his practice; he is incredibly diligent and prolific.[135]

The moment he is seated at the piano, he is evidently unconscious that there is any thing [sic] in existence but himself and his instrument.[136]

He stared at his staff paper, drummed, wrote and had forgotten his neighbor completely. Eventually I left quietly but he would be so preoccupied with his thoughts that he did not even notice.[137]

The events of the outside world hardly touch him; he is completely engrossed in his art.[138]

As early as his childhood years, Beethoven could be so absorbed in his thoughts that he sometimes forgot all about the world around him. One morning, Ludwig was sitting at the open window, supporting his head with his hands and staring at a point in the far distance. The landlord's daughter saw Ludwig and asked him what he was looking at. There was no answer. Later that day, she asked again. Ludwig apologized and said that he had been engrossed in such a beautiful thought, that he could not permit himself to be interrupted.

In the last decades of his life, Beethoven would always carry a notebook with him in which he would jot down ideas as they occurred to him. Even in the middle of the night he would regularly get up and write in his notebook because otherwise, he would forget his ideas.

Should a musical idea occur to him at the time he had to leave for an appointment with a pupil – Archduke Rudolf of all people – then the jotting down of this idea would take preference. Evidence of this is provided in the excuse letter that followed: "The bad habit (which I have had from early childhood on) to immediately jot down my ideas as they occur to me, has once again harmed me."[139]

During the summer months, Beethoven would vacation in the countryside, as many Viennese did; however, these were not holidays in the usual sense because there, his creativity would be at its richest. He loved to hike and he would always take his notebook while doing so.

Provide Beethoven with the opportunity to indulge his music, and he will most assuredly do so. In his later years, for example, Beethoven visited a restaurant to have lunch. He called for the waiter, but the waiter did not appear immediately. Beethoven called again. In the meantime, he took out his notebook and started to write. The waiter came, but the deaf Beethoven did not hear him. The waiter knew Beethoven and tried again later. For a long time, Beethoven was writing in his notebook, was completely absorbed in his thoughts and was not approachable. Finally, he called for the waiter again and wanted to pay. He had ordered nothing, let alone eaten anything.

After years of silence, Beethoven wrote a letter to his friend Franz Wegeler in Bonn. He felt that he had to explain his silence. First, he stated that writing letters had never been his strong point. Then he explained how he occupied his time: "I only live for my music, and I have scarcely begun one thing when I start on another. The way I am now working, I am often engaged in three or four compositions at once."[140]

Beethoven was quite aware of the fact that composing was the only thing he could do well, especially during his final decade, when he was too deaf to play music. In a letter to Ferdinand Ries he wrote, "Beethoven can write music, thank God, for he cannot do anything else on earth."[141] And to an acquaintance, he said, "Everything I do other than music is badly done and stupid."[142]

Friedrich Treitschke reported how Beethoven visited him one evening. Treitschke had been asked to rewrite the text of the opera *Leonore*. One particular aria text had just been finished and was offered to Beethoven. Treitschke had already written several versions of that text, but all had been rejected by Beethoven. That evening's version had a completely different effect on Beethoven. He read the text, walked around, mumbled, growled, took a seat behind the piano and started to improvise. Dinner was served but was ignored by Beethoven. Hours passed. The meal remained untouched by Beethoven. At the end of the evening, Beethoven hugged Treitschke and ran home. The next day the aria was composed.

Enthusiasm for his music made Beethoven easily forget physical discomfort. Ferdinand Ries recalled the time after a lesson when they were speaking about themes and fugues. Ries was sitting at the piano and Beethoven was seated next to him in a position that made it awkward for Beethoven to comfortably play the piano using both hands. Ries played a theme and Beethoven started to replay the theme with his left hand. His right hand soon accompanied his left, and he played like that for half an hour, without interruption. "I still cannot understand how he was able to endure this extremely uncomfortable position. His enthusiasm made him numb to perceptual impressions."[143]

The clearest example of Beethoven being so completely engrossed in his music that he was oblivious to the world around him took place when Beethoven composed the third part of the Piano Sonata that was later referred to as the *Appassionata*. This scene, too, was witnessed by Ferdinand Ries, and it took place during the summer when Beethoven lived in the countryside. As mentioned previously, during his vacationing time he was highly active as a composer, especially while he was hiking. Ries appeared for a lesson, but Beethoven preferred to go for a walk first.

> *The entire way he hummed, or sometimes even howled, to himself – up and down, up and down, without singing any definite notes. When I asked what this was, he replied: "A theme for the final Allegro of the sonata has occurred to me" (in F major, Op. 57). When we entered the room he rushed to the piano without taking off his hat. I took a seat in the corner and he soon forgot all about me. He stormed on for at least an hour with the new finale of the sonata, which is so beautiful. Finally he got up, was surprised to see me still there, and said: "I cannot give you a lesson today; I still have work to do."*[144]

THE PLEASURE OF BEETHOVEN (AND THE DISPLEASURE OF HIS DOWNSTAIRS NEIGHBORS)

Rigid routines and obsessive rituals

In everything he did, it was said, he had his particular rituals. He was especially concerned with his clothes, did not tolerate a grain of dirt on them, washed his hands very frequently and observed his body and its functions very closely. His pedantries tyrannized the household and he was in general very difficult to cope with.[145]
HANS ASPERGER ABOUT ONE OF HIS PUPILS

An almost obsessive desire to introduce routines and rituals of different kinds are the rule in Asperger syndrome.[146]
CHRISTOPHER GILLBERG

Aspergers have – more than most other people – an inclination to perform certain (daily) activities again and again in the same way, for years. That inclination comes from within and is not enforced by any person or circumstance. These activities may not only be related to their narrow interest, but also to daily activities like (un) dressing, washing, having breakfast or dinner, watching television, going to school, or work. Some aspergers are of the opinion that before certain activities can be performed, other activities have to be performed first, or they impose activities on others. In both cases, others have to wait. For example, an asperger child wants to put his toy cars in a certain order before going to school, even if the school bus is about to leave. Regarding this, he can be very persistent. His parents, however, can be on the verge of despair. Their explanation that the toy cars can also be put in order after school is not appreciated by the child.

An asperger's wife explained that before dinner, someone has to cook and afterward someone has to do the dishes. At first, they did this in turns, but then she always had to eat the same food when it was his turn. Now she cooks all meals and that way, she ensures there is some variation. She even enjoys the creative side. He always does the dishes and has his fixed order, first the glassware, then the cutlery, followed by the dinner-service, and finally he does the pots and pans. This division of tasks is satisfying for both.[147]

Of course, cooking can be a narrow interest and, in that case, the other extreme shows up: the asperger prepares the most innovative dinners and exaggerates regarding time investment and attention.

Asperger rituals are individualized. A second trait is that these rituals are not performed to avert some fear, like the interminable hand washing that can occur with obsessive-compulsive disorder. Aspergers like their rituals and do not want to get rid of them.

The purpose these asperger rituals serve is that they can provide satisfaction in performing something that is so familiar. These rituals always have the same result and always cause the same emotion. This is the opposite of what normally happens in the social world, which is characterized by change and unpredictability.

This can be the reason why the above-mentioned child wants to put his cars in order *before* he goes to school and not afterward. He can experience the social life at school as chaotic and likes to create his daily portion of order before he enters this confusing part of the world. Without the rituals, aspergers can feel like they have insufficient control over the world and in a way, fall apart. Or like one asperger writes, "Routines are often the very glue that holds us together."[148]

*   *   *

Aspergers are capable of so much, but flexibility is not on the list. Aspergers tend to thrive on predictability, a stable environment, and a visible, set schedule.[149]
ASHLEY STANFORD

Beethoven organized his working days with a lot of discipline.[150]
JAN CAEYERS

His daily routine varied little.[151]
ANNE-LOUISE COLDICOTT

When Beethoven had no appointments, his days in Vienna were more or less the same. Contemporaries have described what a typical Beethoven day looked like.[152] First, he would make coffee – he made coffee in the predecessor of the coffee machine – whereby he would count sixty beans, no more, no less. Next, he went to his desk to compose. There he would work until two o'clock in the afternoon or a little later – his customary dinner time. Often, he would go for a short walk, but because he continued to compose in his mind, the term *spazieren arbeiten*[153] ("walk-working") is more suited. In the late afternoon he went for a longer walk – preferably one time around the city – regardless of the weather (even during a bleak winter day), followed by the visit to a tavern where he read the newspapers. Beethoven spent his evenings reading books. He would only work in the evening when necessary. At ten he would go to bed.

*   *   *

A small number actually develop severely compulsive washing rituals[154]
CHRISTOPHER GILLBERG

Paradoxically he had an almost obsessional attitude towards washing.[155]
ANNE-LOUISE COLDICOTT

Around 1806, Beethoven became acquainted with a singer, who came to his apartment a few days after they met. A somewhat older servant did not know what to tell him because Beethoven was busy washing. The singer knew this because he heard the water flow, which the "noble eccentric" poured over himself in excess, accompanied by a roaring groaning, which, in this case, appeared to be an "expression of pleasure." This "pleasure" makes clear that the washing ritual of Beethoven has nothing to do with the repetitive washing that people with obsessive-compulsive disorder display.

The singer witnessed Beethoven's washing ritual. This ritual is paradoxical because it appears to be in contrast with his much-reported disorderliness regarding his dress and household.

Contemporaries who knew Beethoven in his fifties have described this washing ritual in great detail.[156] One even wrote that washing and bathing were "indispensable needs"[157] to Beethoven. If, while he was working, he did not go out, he would stand at the washbasin and splash a jug of water over his heated head. At the same time, he would howl or, for a change, growl out the whole gamut of the scale, ascending and descending. Then he would pace the room, his eyes rolling or fixed in a stare, jot down a few notes and again return to his water pouring and howling. His servants had a laughing fit. Then Beethoven had a fit of rage. That caused his servants to have another bout of laughing.

The ones who could not laugh at all were the downstairs neighbors when, once again, water leaked from the ceiling. This washing ritual actually took place in extreme concentration. Beethoven would make only a hasty gesture of drying his thick and unruly hair, paying not the slightest attention to the large amount of water he spilled. The water soaked through the floor and leaked through the ceiling of the apartment below, whose tenant complained to the house manager, then to the owner, and, finally, the rent contract with Beethoven was terminated.

"LUDWIG VAN BEETHOVEN, BRAIN OWNER."

Speech and language peculiarities

*They, and especially the intellectually gifted among them, undoubtedly have
a special creative attitude toward language. They are able to express their own
original experience in a linguistically original form. This is seen in the choice
of unusual words which one would suppose to be totally outside the sphere
of these children. It is also seen in newly formed or partially restructured
expressions which can often be particularly accurate and perspicacious, but
also, of course, often quite abstruse.*[158]
HANS ASPERGER

The "special creative attitude toward language" of aspergers emerges for example
if they like to say something, but lack the words. Then they will use a neologism.
Hans Asperger quotes a child who said:

Mündlich kann ich das nicht, aber köpflich.[159]

I can't do this orally, only headily.

The child means that he understands the thing in his head, but cannot express
his thoughts verbally. This expression is meant seriously but can be perceived by
others as funny.

Aspergers can be rather formal and pedantic. They can experience stress when
someone says "Holland" instead of "the Netherlands" or uses the word "star" when
"planet" should be the right word. According to some aspergers, language should
be used properly, regardless of how informal the context might be. When someone
says "Let's go out to lunch," an asperger might say, "It appears to be the hour in
which our bodies require nourishment."[160] And a six-year-old asperger child told
his child psychiatrist, "Well, well, considerable time has elapsed since this room
had the pleasure of the presence of a maid. Ashes to ashes and dust to dust if you
please, well, well. You might say that this place is not up for sale but up for dusting.
You might equally say that dust is rather similar to dusk, it will soon be dusk and
then the dust will be visible no more."[161] Not your average child language.

Prosody is about the stress and intonation patterns of an utterance. Aspergers can
speak in a slightly muted, muffled, or mumbling way. Some have muddled speech. A lot
have a flat prosody, a monotonous voice. Many speak too loud, too low, too fast, or too slow.

But aspergers may also have difficulties with the understanding of things other
people say because they are not aware of the importance of the prosody. They do

not understand that the next sentence can have seven meanings, depending on the accentuation: I didn't say she stole my money.[162]

Because aspergers tend to take language literally, they can have a hard time with expressions. Especially for aspergers, there is *An Asperger Dictionary of Everyday Expressions*. When it rains cats and dogs, does it literally rain cats and dogs? According to this dictionary, it does not. It explains that *to rain cats and dogs* means to "rain heavily." "There are numerous explanations of the phrase, but in no instance is it implied that either cats or dogs are actually falling from the sky."[163]

Finally, aspergers can misunderstand the speaker's intention. They tend to interpret everything that is said as matter-of-fact information or as a matter-of-fact question. "'Could you open the door for me?' somebody might say, and the child with Asperger syndrome may respond 'Yes', but do nothing. She understood the question to mean: 'Do you have the ability to open the door for me?', not the 'hidden' prompt to actually do so."[164]

A cognitively impaired asperger might have difficulties understanding the meaning of what other people say. But a gifted asperger might like to play games with their intentions. So, in asperger country, next to wordplay, intention-play is a popular pastime.

*   *   *

There are times when words are simply no use.[165]
LUDWIG VAN BEETHOVEN

This is a sentence from the letter to the Immortal Beloved. Years before, Beethoven had already complained about language, especially in the realm of love. To Josephine he wrote, "But how weak, how poor are words, at least my words."[166]

Others too observed that language was not Beethoven's chief selling point. A contemporary wrote in a letter: "Beethoven received me with open arms. I have already been at his place several times. He is a very odd man. Big thoughts hover in his soul, but he is only able to express them with musical notes. Words are not at his service."[167]

Nevertheless, there were moments, given that he felt comfortable and especially when he was talking about music that Beethoven was like a verbal waterfall. Three examples:

At such moments when he talked, completely engrossed in the subject, the abundance of ideas that poured from his mouth seems truly miraculous.[168]

Beethoven talked gladly and a lot [...] Now he talked ceaselessly [...] and because he continued talking incessantly[169]

He talked almost without interruption.[170]

* * *

*But writing, as you know, was never my strong point. Even my best friends
have not received any letter from me in years.*[171]
LUDWIG VAN BEETHOVEN

In the Dutch publication of Beethoven's letters, Jos van der Zanden writes in the
preface: "Beethoven disliked writing letters. He regarded it as difficult and time-
consuming. It took concentration and attention that he preferred to put into writing
music. As with other ways of communication, he had some trouble complying
with common manners and observing conventions. Most of the time he was not
civil or tactful in his statements and his interest in his circle was poor. If ever he
did decide to write a letter, then usually the message was crucial, with hardly any
embellishment."[172]

* * *

*Another characteristic of asperger children is the absence of a sense of humor.
[...] When making puns, however, aspergers sometimes shine, and may even be
highly creative. This can range from simple wordplay and sound associations
to precisely formulated, truly witty remarks.*[173]
HANS ASPERGER

*Most aspergers have a type of humor that differs from that of people in general.
Some appear to be totally devoid of humor. [...] Others love to play with words
and statements made by famous people or to draw attention to the many
absurdities of life.*[174]
CHRISTOPHER GILLBERG

Both in his letters and during conversations, Beethoven used a lot of wit and often
made puns.

Carl Czerny: *Beethoven, who was always merry and mischievous in company
[...]*[175]

Carl Czerny: *He was able to make a pun everywhere.*[176]

Bettina Brentano: *[...] because of his strange sense of humor*[177]

Fanny Giannatasio del Rio: *[...] his funny puns [...] and so he was full of jokes and puns [...] Sometimes he was very funny and teasing [...] And so he was often cheerful with many puns and jests [...]*[178]

A contemporary: *Peculiar are all his expressions; always mixed with satirical humor.*[179]

Gerhard von Breuning: *This preference for making jokes, even of a strange nature, at every possible occasion, one encounters very often with Beethoven.*[180]

It is hardly known which puns Beethoven made orally. An example (toward Fanny Giannatasio del Rio) is the play with the two meanings of the verb *to believe*, as in the religious sense and as in *to assume*. The pun is immediately followed with a next wordplay, about two words in the title of a song

[...] *als ich ihm sagte, ich hätte geglaubt, er wäre schon in Baden, antwortete er mir lachend, er höre immer mehr auf zu glauben und ich glaube immer. Wegen einem Lied, das er mir geschenkt und wieder ausgeliehen, sagte er, nun müsse er es mir wohl bald wiederbringen, schon meiner Liebe zur Wahrheit wegen! Es war "Das Geheimnis, Liebe und Wahrheit" von Wessenberg.*[181]

...; *when I told him, I believed him to be in Baden, he replied laughing: he believed less and less and I always believe. As to (the score of) a song, which he had given to me and had borrowed back, he said that he had to give it to me again soon, because of my love for the truth. The song was "The secret, Love and Truth" by* [the poet] *Wessenberg.*

Beethoven disliked writing letters, but the letters, especially, give an impression of his puns. A first example is the wordplay with the German verb *stechen* which means *to sting* (of an insect) as well as *to engrave* (prior to the pressing of a composition). In a letter to a publisher Beethoven complained about all the misprints in a string quartet, published by another publisher:

... *das heiß ich stechen, in Wahrheit meine Haut ist ganz voller Stiche und Ritze – von dieser schönen Auflage meiner Quartetten*[182]

... *that I do call to engrave/to sting, really, my skin is full of stings and scratches – because of this beautiful print of my quartets*

A second example is the pun with the two meanings of the German noun *Gehalt*. *Gehalt* means *salary* (when it is neuter) or *content* (when it is masculine). In a time of inflation (1822), Beethoven wrote in a letter to a publisher:

Wäre mein Gehalt nicht gänzlich ohne Gehalt, ich schrieb nichts als große Symphonien, Kirchenmusik, höchstens noch Quartetten.[183]

Would my salary not completely be without content, I would write nothing but big symphonies, church music and quartets at the most.

In 1823, Beethoven made the same pun in a letter to Goethe:

- mein Gehalt ist ohne Gehalt[184]

- my salary is without content

Beethoven favored the binovular twins *Not* and *Note*.
Not (plural: *Nöte*) means distress or misery.
Note (plural: *Noten*) means musical note; the plural can also mean sheet music or simply music. Here are two examples of Beethoven's wordplay with these twins.

Das Leben ist zu kurz, um Buchstaben oder Noten zu malen; und schönere Noten brächten mich schwerlich aus den Nöten.[185]

Life is too short to draw letters or musical notes; and more beautiful music would hardly relieve my distresses.

Following Beethoven's convalescence after an illness, a physician asked Beethoven for "a few insignificant notes;" he had mainly wanted something handwritten from Beethoven. In his reply letter, Beethoven added a canon:

Doktor sperrt das Tor dem Tod, Note hilft auch aus der Not.[186]

Doctor bar the door for the death, musical notes save also from distress

During the summer of 1815, Beethoven took up his lodging in the small town of Baden. From there he wanted to visit Countess Erdödy, who lived in Jedlersee, on the other side of river Danube. Jedlersee could be reached by road or by boat (quicker, but less comfortable). The Countess offered Beethoven her coach to pick him up, but he refused, punning with the noun *Wagen* (coach) and the verb *wagen* (to dare/to venture).

Ich setze übrigens getrost den Weg wie vorhin über die Donau, mit Muth gewinnt man allenthalben, wenn er gerecht ist. [...] Schicken Sie also keinen Wagen; lieber [es] wagen, als einen Wagen.[187]

I prefer to cross the Danube [by boat] *like last time. With courage one wins all about, when it is sincere. ...Please, do not send a coach; better to dare/to venture than a coach.*

In September 1815, Countess Erdödy moved to her family estate in Croatia. In a letter to the Countess, Beethoven inquired how she was doing after her relocation. To anticipate her likely question of how he was doing, he wrote:

Von mir nichts - das heißt vom Nichts nichts.[188]

From me nothing [new]; *that means from Nothing nothing.*

In a letter to Ignaz von Gleichenstein, Beethoven relates that he had spent an evening with an acquaintance who had had the upper hand in their conversation. In German, the noun *Unterhaltung* means conversation and the adverb *unten* means below. Beethoven had to cheat a little because the fifth letter of *Unten* is different from the fifth letter of *Unterhaltung*.

Er verschaffte mir eine sehr gute Untenhaltung, wenigstens konnte ich niemals oben sein, aber ziemlich tief Unten.[189]

He provided me with a very good conversation, at least I could never be above, though rather deeply below.

To nephew Karl, Beethoven wrote:

Denn teurer Sohn, du bist auch wieder sehr teuer![190]

For dear son, you are also again very expensive.

*   *   *

Beethoven favored taking names literally or making a wordplay with them in another way. The name of the (according to Beethoven) incompetent conductor *Gebauer* was pronounced by him as *Geh-Bauer*[191] (*Go, peasant*). When the musician Anton Halm (Stalk) made a mess of something, Beethoven wrote:

Nicht jeder Halm gibt Ähren![192] (Ähren sounds like *Ehren* (honor))

Not every stalk produces ear [of corn]*!*

At another occasion, Beethoven simply added the word Stroh in front of the name Halm, resulting in *Strohhalm (Straw)*

What did Beethoven think of the composer Bach? The German noun *Bach* means brook.

Nicht Bach, sondern Meer sollte er heißen, wegen seines unendlichen, unerschöpflichen Reichtums an Tonkombinationen und Harmonien.[193]

Not Bach/brook but Sea should be his name, because of the rightness of tone combinations and harmonies.

When the German composer Friedrich Kuhlau visited Beethoven, he received a canon:

Kühl, nicht lau.[194]

Cool, not tepid

Ernst Hoffmann did not visit Beethoven, but nevertheless had the pleasure of discovering his name in the canon *Auf einen, welcher Hoffmann geheißen (On a person named Hoffmann).*

Hoffmann, sei ja kein Hofmann.[195]

Hoffmann, do not ever be a courtier.

In his only letter to Hoffmann, Beethoven mentioned mister *Starke*. But because *Stärke* means "power" or "force," Beethoven couldn't resist referring to this gentleman as the "weak Mister Starke." Just as with Kuhlau/Kühl, Beethoven had to cheat with the umlaut mark.

After hearing one of Carl von Weber's (Weaver) overtures, Beethoven said:

Hm! S'ist eben gewebt.[196]

Hm! It's woven properly.

The maiden name of *Nanette Streicher* was *Stein*. *Streich* means "prank" and *Stein* means "stone." And if you are in a jolly mood writing a letter, why not try to use a pun also with *eher* ("sooner"), *ehe* ("before") and *Ehe* ("marriage").

Ich konnte wegen dem schlechten Wetter nicht eher als Donnerstag hereinkommen, und sie waren schon fort von hier. Welcher Streich von der Frau Streicher!!!! [...]
Wegen der Haushälterin, die Sie kennen und wenigstens als brav geprüft haben, könnte man ja das Kochen versuchen, ehe sie zu mir käme. Dieses lässt sich nun nicht eher bewerkstelligen, bis Sie wieder in die Stadt kommen; wann? Übrigens lassen Sie sich nicht durch Ihren Mann zu gewissen Ehestreichen verführen[197]

Due to the bad weather, I could not come sooner than Thursday and you had already gone. What a prank of Madam Streicher!!!!! [...]
Because of the housekeeper, the one you know and at least had tested as proper, one could try cooking, before she would come to me. This will no sooner be achieved, than till you return to the city; when? For the rest: do not let your husband tempt you into certain matrimonial pranks.

In another letter to Nanette, Beethoven wrote to her about the publisher Steiner.

Was die Frau von Stein anbelangt, so bitte ich selbe, dass die den Herrn von Steiner nicht versteinern lassen, damit er mir noch dienen könne, oder die Frau von Stein möchte nicht zu sehr von Stein sein in Ansehung des Herrn von Steiner usw. [...] Beste Frau von Streicher, spielen Sie Ihrem Männchen keine Streiche – sondern heißen Sie lieber gegen jedermann Frau von Stein!!![198]

Concerning Madam von Stein, so do I request that you do not petrify Mister von Steiner, so that he can still be of service to me, or Madam von Stein could be not too much [made of] stone glancing at mister Steiner etc. [...] Dear Madam von Streicher, do not prank with your little man – better to call yourself Madam von Stein toward every man!!!

Hauptmann means "captain" and *Nebenmann* means "neighbor." In a letter to Anna Milder-Hauptmann Beethoven wrote:

Wie es auch sei, alles um sie her darf sich nur Nebenmann nennen, ich allein nur führe mit recht den ehrerbietigen Namen Hauptmann und nur ganz im Stillen[199]

However, everyone around you is only allowed to call himself Nebenmann/
neighbor. Only I address myself with the honorable name Hauptmann/captain
and I do so in utter silence.

Sometimes you cannot pun with a name, but in that case, maybe you can play a
word game with someone's title. Count Moritz Lichnowsky (younger brother of
Prince Karl Lichnowsky) had given Beethoven some unsolicited advice, which
turned out unfavorable. It is time for the final canon.

Lieber Herr Graf,
Sie sind ein Schaf.[200]

Dear Mister Count,
You are a sheep

*   *   *

When, in November of 1815, the municipal authorities of Vienna informed him that
he had been appointed citizen of honor, Beethoven's prompt reply was:

Ich habe nicht gewusst, dass es auch
Schandbürger in Wien gibt.[201]

I did not know there are also citizens of
shame in Vienna.

On a New Year's greeting card, Nikolaus Johann stressed his material acquisitions
by writing under his name: *Gutsbesitzer* (*real estate owner*). After reading this,
Beethoven did not hesitate at all and sent the card back, signed on the back with:

Ludwig van Beethoven Hirnbesitzer[202]

Ludwig van Beethoven, Brain owner

Of course, Beethoven realized that an appointment was concerned respectively
an expression of pride. But this appointment was on bad terms with Beethoven's
aversion regarding everything that promoted humility between people. And this
pride annoyed him because he perceived his brother Nikolaus Johann as greedy.
In both cases, he played an intention game, mocking in an unconventional fashion
what the other person had said or written.

So how did Beethoven sign his reply to a letter of a *"Stellvertreter* [deputy]" of the chairman of a society? With: "Beethoven, *Selbstvertreter* [self-advocate]!"[203]

Finally, it is striking that Beethoven had such a profound inclination to play with words, that he did it even when he was very emotional. In the letter to the Immortal Beloved, he punned with *fest* (firm) and *Veste* (firmament).

... ach Gott – so nah! so weit! ist es nicht ein wahres Himmelsgebäude unsre Liebe – aber auch so fest, wie die Veste des Himmels.[204]

Oh, God – so near! so far! is our love not truly sent from Heaven? And is it not even as firm as the firmament of Heaven?

"AT THE BEGINNING OF A FORTE HE JUMPED INTO THE AIR."

Non-verbal communication problems

His eye gaze is strikingly odd. It was generally directed into the void, but was occasionally interrupted by a momentary malignant glimmer. When somebody was talking to him, he did not enter into the sort of eye contact which would normally be fundamental to conversation. He darted short 'peripheral' looks and glanced at both people and objects only fleetingly. It was 'as if he isn't there'.[205]
HANS ASPERGER ABOUT ONE OF HIS PUPILS

Non-verbal communication problems are paramount in Asperger syndrome. Facial mimicry may be extremely poor, gestures stereotyped, and the gaze stern, fixated, staring or wide-open. Some are said to have 'poker faces'. [...] There is often a naive, clumsy or merely restricted 'body language'.[206]
CHRISTOPHER GILLBERG

* * *

His build was fierce, his figure medium-sized, his gait decisive, just like his vivacious movements; his garments were more middle-class than distinguished; and yet there was something in his whole appearance that did not fit in any classification.[207]
GERHARD VON BREUNING *about Beethoven*

Beethoven's appearance impressed his contemporaries. One account, among many others, is from Gerhard von Breuning, who knew Beethoven during the last years of Beethoven's life. He described Beethoven's appearance us unusually striking, due to the nonchalance of his clothing. When Beethoven was outside, he was mostly absorbed in thought; he muttered and gesticulated with his arms. When he walked with others, he talked excitedly and loudly. When Beethoven passed by, lots of people turned around, urchins scoffed at him and called him names. Nephew Karl disliked being seen with his uncle, because of his foolish appearance, which made Beethoven feel offended and hurt.

* * *

Although I heard about it several times, I was very surprised when I saw Beethoven conducting for the first time. Beethoven had trained himself to convey the desired expression of the music by making odd body movements. As soon as a sforzando[208] *appeared, he parted his arms – which had been crossed over his chest – with vehemence. At a* piano *he stooped; the quieter, the deeper. As soon as a* crescendo *appeared, he raised his body slowly. At the beginning of a* forte *he jumped into the air. To strengthen the* forte, *he also screamed, without knowing it.*[209]

LOUIS SPOHR (composer, violinist, and director)

His contemporaries described Beethoven's body language and especially his gestures as peculiar. This was most striking when he was conducting. One visitor to Vienna wrote that Beethoven "stood as on an isolated island and conducted the stream of his dark, demonic harmonies into the human world with the most odd body movements."[210]

In combination with his increasing deafness, failure was imminent. It happened during a final rehearsal of the opera Fidelio, in November of 1822. Wilhelmine Schröder (age seventeen), the most important interpreter of *Leonore* (the main character of the opera) of the nineteenth century, made her debut. Beethoven had stipulated that he should conduct the final rehearsal and the performance. Wilhelmine had never seen him before. She was frightened of the deaf man with his swinging arms, his unkempt hair, his upset appearance, and his scary shining eyes. If *piano* was intended, he disappeared behind the desk; if *forte* was intended, he jumped and uttered weird sounds. All the musicians (instrumentalists and singers) became confused and afterward the *Kapellmeister* had to tell Beethoven the painful news that it would be impossible to let him direct the performance.

During his final year, Beethoven's appearance became even more eccentric. While staying at his brother Nikolaus Johann's estate in Gneixendorf, Beethoven became known as a very strange figure in the neighborhood. He strolled through the fields, shouted, waved his hands, and alternated walking very slowly and very quickly. He could stop abruptly and would then write something in his notebook. One peasant told of how Beethoven had approached him, yelling, gesticulating like a madman.

In his final decade, Beethoven looked like a beggar or a vagrant. Since he made notes all the time, another impression of this strangely behaving man was that he was a spy. One time, Beethoven was arrested and forced to go to the town hall in one of the towns around Vienna. He was only released after a music-loving member of the council confirmed he was Beethoven, which other people found hard to believe.

*   *   *

Beethoven's facial expression had three extreme settings. The first was his non-expression, his poker face: "At large it was difficult, even impossible, to decipher approval or displeasure from his facial expression. He remained the same, seemingly cold and closed in his judgments about colleagues. Only his spirit was ceaselessly active inside; physically he looked like soulless marble."[211]

In pleasant company, Beethoven could express another extreme: "In friendly conversations his face became kind and mild, especially if he liked the conversation. Every mood of his soul was expressed clearly and immediately in his features."[212]

The third extreme appeared when he played piano. "The muscles of the face swell, and its veins start out; the wild eye rolls doubly wild; the mouth quivers, and Beethoven looks like a wizard, overpowered by the demons, whom he himself has called up."[213]

*   *   *

Beethoven's eyes impressed his contemporaries and were mentioned many times. Here are some examples:

During the morning, Ludwig van Beethoven was in his bedroom (which faced the inner courtyard), sat at the window, held his head in both his hands and gazed at a spot [in the air].[214]

[…] with small, sparkling eyes […][215]

[…] with bright eyes […][216]

[…], burning eyes, which are small though, but deep-seated, round and full of immense life[217]

His eyes were blue-gray and extremely vivid[218]

[…] profound, melancholic eyes, […][219]

[…] his eye is full of rude energy"[220]

[…] Beethoven with his usual cloudy look […][221]

[…] his eyes testify to abysmal depths of feeling […][222]

[…] *with beautiful, expressive eyes* […][223]

[…] *restless, shining, indeed with a fixed look, almost cutting eyes;* […] *in the expression of his face, his eyes especially are full of spirit and life; a mix of instantaneous alternation of heartily good nature and of shyness* […][224]

[…] *with unearthly enthusiastic eyes* […][225]

[…] *he looked at me with a piercing, almost demonic expression* […][226]

Franz Liszt: He looked at us for a while […] *the dark burning look of the great master was pervasively imposed on me.*[227]

[…] *his very grave eyes*[228]

[…] *there was in those small piercing eyes an expression which no painter could render. It was a feeling of sublimity and melancholy combined.*"[229]

[…] *not big, but deep, sparks emitting eyes* […][230]

[…] *his piercing eyes* […][231]

His big, deep-seated, piercing eyes seemed to lighten up and made sure they entered the soul of the person in front of him […][232]

[…] *dark, piercing eyes* […][233]

Shortly afterwards a man of stocky stature of average height with friendly gestures and a benign look in his eyes emerged and invited me in his room."[234]

Someone had expressed some negative comments regarding Beethoven's symphonies. "The play of his eyes and face answered me: 'What do you, Dumbo, and other smartasses who castigate my works understand of it? You all lack the assiduity, the audacious eagle flight to comprehend me.'"[235]

[…] *with such a look of good nature and at the same time of suffering* […][236]

[…] *with small, pale blue but at the same time expressive eyes* […] *in his gentle eyes* […][237]

[...] particularly the wonderful, almost creepy flashiness of his eyes exceeded everything in this kind [...] who then fixed me with a shrewd look [...] never will I forget these human eyes, in which dazzling abyss I did look from such a small distance! [...] he once directed his small, lightning eyes toward me; half with disconcertment, half with contempt [...][238]

[...] the expression of cutting, keen eyes, that looked around erratically [...][239]

In his eyes there was something extremely dynamic and bright.[240]

Rossini stated that most portraits of Beethoven resemble the composer. "But what no etcher's needle could express was the indefinable sadness spread over his features - while from under heavy eyebrows his eyes shone out as from caverns, and, though small, seemed to pierce one."[241]

Beethoven's eyes did impress his contemporaries, that's for sure. Some descriptions come close to the wording of Gillberg: "stern, fixated, staring, or wide-open."[242]
Very interesting is the description of the painter August von Kloeber, who made a portrait of Beethoven in 1818: "Beethoven always looked very grave, his extremely vivid eyes swarmed often with a somewhat dark, moody look upwards. I have tried to depict that in the portrait."[243]

Image 1: Portrait of Beethoven by August von Kloeber (1818)

The big difference between this portrait (image 1) and many others is that Beethoven did not pose. Von Kloeber portrayed Beethoven the way he experienced him in daily life. In the picture, Beethoven's look is directed into the void, instead of at his fellow man.

Image 2: Portrait of Beethoven by Ferdinand Schimon (1818 or 1819)

Also, in the portrait of Ferdinand Schimon (image 2) Beethoven is said not to have posed. Here he looks into the void as well.

Image 3: Portrait of Beethoven by Ferdinand Waldmüller (1823)

Another interesting portrait is that of Ferdinand Waldmüller (image 3), commissioned by a publisher. Beethoven did pose but was not in the mood because of time pressure. The Waldmüller painting is made of a man who, at that very moment, does not require any company at all.

Image 4: Portrait of Beethoven by Joseph Stieler (1819-1820)

The most famous Beethoven portrait is by Joseph Stieler (image 4). In this idealized painting, Beethoven looks into the void, but does so posing and doesn't seem under any time pressure.

Image 5: Portrait of Beethoven by Blasius Höfel (1814)

As a comparison, a portrait of a posing Beethoven is provided (image 5), where he looks straight at the spectator. Beethoven was very pleased with this painting.

"POSSESSED BY THE DEVIL."

Motor clumsiness

The majority of aspergers have motor incoordination or motor 'fluency'
problems of various kinds.[244]
CHRISTOPHER GILLBERG

Possessing poor motor skills is one of the characteristics that Hans Asperger discussed in his landmark paper. There are two kinds of motor skills: fine and gross. *Fine motor skills* utilize small scale movements and most typically refer to digital (finger) coordination. Tasks such as writing, typing and tying shoelaces are all performed using fine motor skills. Furthermore, fine motor skills typically require attention and concentration. *Gross motor skills*, on the other hand, require large scale movements of the body and typically utilize whole limbs to perform. Walking, swimming, and kicking a ball are all performed using gross motor skills. Often, but not always, these movements are performed more subconsciously and do not require much concentration. Development of gross motor skills precedes development of fine motor skills. For example, if a toddler throws a ball with his right hand (a gross motor skill), then this hand is the dominant one and later on writing (a fine motor skill) will be done with the same hand. Asperger children – and sometimes adults – can have difficulty determining the position of their body in relation to objects. This lack of kinesthetic awareness may cause them to trip, bump into objects, and spill drinks.

Fine motor movements may be clumsy and ill coordinated, particularly in social
settings. Some of those who appear to be the most clumsy can perform astonishingly
well in activities for which they are highly motivated and well trained.[245]
CHRISTOPHER GILLBERG

*   *   *

Oh, yesterday I will never forget! That young man is possessed by the devil.
Never have I heard anyone play the piano like that! And he improvised on a
theme I had given him in a manner I have not heard even Mozart equal. Then
he played some of his own compositions that are miraculous and mighty in the
highest degree. Playing the piano he produces the most difficult things and
effects that none of us would ever have dreamed of.[246]
JOSEPH GELINEK (PIANIST) ABOUT BEETHOVEN

Based on this quote, one would surmise that Beethoven did not have motor control problems. Indeed, how could Beethoven, an accomplished pianist, be considered to possess motor skill problems? The answer is that such perceptions can be deceiving. The above quote is only about Beethoven's motor skills *as a pianist*. Ferdinand Ries wrote the following about Beethoven's motor skills in general:

> Beethoven was most awkward and bungling in his behavior; his clumsy move-
> ments lacked all grace. He rarely picked up anything without dropping or
> breaking it. Thus, he frequently knocked his inkwell into the piano. No piece
> of furniture was safe from him, least of all anything valuable. Everything was
> knocked over, soiled, or destroyed. How he ever managed to shave himself at
> all remains difficult to understand, even considering the frequent cuts on his
> cheeks. He never learned to dance in time with the music.[247]

In his description, Ries mentions problems with both gross motor skills (knocking over furniture and not being able to dance) and fine motor skills (inability to pick up objects and problems with shaving). His first sentence ("Beethoven was most awkward..."), is consistent with the description by Gillberg when he expounds on "motor incoordination" or motor "fluency" problems.[248]

Supplementary to the observations of Ferdinand Ries are those by Gerhard von Breuning: "Just like Beethoven – with his characteristic clumsiness – was hardly able to cut quill pens, so were his awkward fingers less capable to sharpen a pencil, without breaking it. This will have been the reason that he preferred to buy pencils of a thickness that carpenters used to use."[249] (This was one of the reasons why Beethoven liked to have contact with Zmeskall, who was very proficient at cutting quill pens.) Beethoven's handwriting was consequently notoriously careless and hard to read, indicating poor fine motor skills. His remarkable piano-playing skills are consistent with the fact that even "those who appear to be the most clumsy can perform astonishingly well in activities for which they are highly motivated and well trained."[250]

"AS SOON AS ANYONE SHOUTS, IT IS UNBEARABLE FOR ME."

Sensory problems

Perceptual problems are commonplace in Asperger syndrome. In a sense, Asperger syndrome is a disorder of unusual perceptions. [...] Unusual reactions to sound [...] are almost universal.[251]
CHRISTOPHER GILLBERG

There is hyposensitivity too against noise. Yet the same children who are often distinctly hypersensitive to noise in particular situations, in other situations may appear to be hyposensitive. They may appear to be switched off even to loud noises.[252]
HANS ASPERGER

Because an asperger does not know how different his perception is compared to the perception of others, this phenomenon can be a source of misunderstanding. The American professor of animal science Temple Grandin writes that a problem for most people in the autism spectrum is that they do not realize that their sensory processing is different. Grandin is autistic herself and states, "It came as a kind of revelation, as well as a blessed relief, when I learned that my sensory problems weren't the result of my weakness or lack of character."[253]

Three types of problem noises are recognized.[254] First, there are sudden, unexpected noises, like the barking of a dog or the ringing of a telephone. An asperger can perceive such noises as sharper than most other people do. Second, there are high-pitched, continuous noises such as those from small electric motors like from a food processor or a hairdryer. Third, there are confusing, complex or multiple sounds, like those in shopping malls or noisy social gatherings. Temple Grandin states that as a child, birthday parties were like "torture"[255] to her. All these noises can give an asperger a lot of stress, which can impede proper function.

Oversensitivity to certain frequency and volume ranges of sound is called hyperacusis. It is not restricted to Asperger syndrome but is reported by many people with ailments as diverse as fibromyalgia and migraine. Hyperacusis can occur temporarily after a whiplash or the removal of ear wax. Loss of hearing can be accompanied by hyperacusis. Half-deaf people are less sensitive to soft noises but can be more sensitive to loud noises.

It has to be stressed that sound can also be a source of repose and relaxation to an asperger. Several authors describe the stress-reducing effect of listening to self-chosen music.[256]

The different experiences of sound can lead to remarkable phenomena.[257] One asperger child's narrow interest was buses. Waiting at a bus stop, he could not only tell when a bus was about to arrive before others did, but he could also tell the correct number plate of the imminent bus. The boy was able to do so because he knew all the different sounds of all buses in that area and he also knew their number plates. The same boy disliked playing in the garden; he could not stand the noise of butterflies' wings.

*   *   *

He became hypersensitive to unexpected loud noises that turned up and to loud shouting people.[258]
JAN CAEYERS

Sometimes too I can scarcely hear a person who speaks softly; I can hear sounds, but cannot make out the words. Yet, as soon as anyone shouts, it is unbearable for me.[259]
LUDWIG VAN BEETHOVEN

Beethoven wrote the aforementioned words in a letter to his friend Franz Wegeler in 1801. A clear case of hyperacusis is described and can easily be attributed to Beethoven's increasing deafness during that time. To attribute this hyperacusis to Asperger syndrome, we have to look at the time before Beethoven's deafness started.

One contemporary stated that Beethoven, before he became deaf, had extremely good hearing and that all noisy sounds (*Übellaut*) were experienced as painful.[260] This information points in the direction of hyperacusis, as does the statement of Beethoven that in his youth he could not bear the overwhelming force (*Gewalt*) of the organ, that "giant instrument."[261]

Food processors or hairdryers did not exist during the first half of the nineteenth century, but both sudden and complex noises did, and Beethoven was bothered by both. Of course, these noises did not bother him anymore when he was completely deaf, but in the years before, those noises annoyed him all the more.

An accumulation of sudden, unexpected noises (problem noise type one) occurred in May 1809, when the French army bombarded Vienna. Beethoven was very anxious and preferred to stay in the cellar of his brother Casper Carl's house and to cover his ears with pillows.

Shopping malls did not exist either in the first half of the nineteenth century, but noisy social gatherings did. A very good example of this problem noise type three was the bathhouse in the spa Teplitz. Beethoven stayed there during the summers of 1811 and 1812. Besides the therapeutic, the social aspect was important as well. Everyone looked at everyone and the behavior of well-known people was well-observed and could easily become news in Vienna. For most guests, it was honorable and prestigious to be part of this party game.

> *Our imagination falls short to fit Beethoven into this picture.* [...] *Also the reverberating music in the colonnades must have been nerve-racking to him. And the resounding noise of the chatting crowd in the bath rooms must have caused pain in his ears. Normal talk was often too much for him, let alone echoing small talk.*[262]
> JAN CAEYERS

"EAGER TO ACCOMPLISH GREAT DEEDS."

Strengths

Aspergers almost always have major strengths that may, wholly or partly, compensate for the major difficulties. Almost all the core features of the syndrome have 'positive' opposites. Good general IQ, perseverance, stubbornness and perfectionism are just a few of the strengths often shown by individuals with Asperger syndrome.[263]
CHRISTOPHER GILLBERG

There are features that are commonplace in aspergers, but that are not regarded as weaknesses and thus are no part of the diagnostic criteria. These characteristics are hardly mentioned in most asperger literature, but Gillberg devotes one chapter to the strengths. Beethoven was one of the top in his field, so it is likely that he not only had to deal with the disadvantages of Asperger syndrome but also took advantage of its benefits. I like to examine to what degree Beethoven showed perseverance, stubbornness, and perfectionism. (I will not address issues about his general IQ.) I will start with stubbornness.

* * *

The obsession to go his own way in all circumstances and the exclusive use of his own self-invented procedures can prevent the child from assimilating the calculation methods the school wishes to instill.[264]
HANS ASPERGER

Beethoven certainly wanted to learn, but not on command, and his knowledge and erudition he had to acquire later by self-teaching.[265]
JAN CAEYERS

Beethoven's contemporaries referred to stubbornness rather early during his life. In 1791, his piano playing was publicly praised because of the almost inexhaustible richness of his ideas. "His style of treating his instrument is so different from that usually adopted, that it impresses one with the idea, that by a path of his own discovery he has attained that height of excellence whereon he now stands."[266]

Some contemporaries even used the terms *stubborn* and *stubbornness* literally.

It makes me very sad when I see this fine and great man in a gloomy and suffering mood. However, I am convinced that his best and most original works can only be created in such a stubborn and deeply moody frame of mind.[267]

Even among his oldest friends he must be humored like a wayward child.[268]

However, his stubbornness is still terrible.[269]

Soon after his arrival in Vienna, Beethoven took lessons from Haydn. Later he had two other first-rate teachers. All three were unanimous in their opinion about their pupil: "Beethoven was always so stubborn and so bent on having his own way that he had to learn many things through hard experience which he had refused earlier to accept through instruction."[270]

In 1820 – during the first part of his third creative stage in which he composed his most advanced works – Beethoven wrote in his conversation book:

The world is a king and desires flattery in return for favor; but true art is perverse and will not submit to the mold of flattery.[271]

*   *   *

Perfectionism is common, even though it is often limited to certain areas of functioning, and may well be coupled with a glaring lack of orderliness in other domains.[272]
CHRISTOPHER GILLBERG

Contrary to his daily life, where he was very chaotic, Beethoven was very methodical regarding composing.[273]
JAN CAEYERS

To the perfectionist, not only is the big picture important, but something is only perfect if all of the details are perfect. Even if only one detail is not perfect, the whole is affected in the perception of the perfectionist. This leads to VDVW thinking: a Violation of a Detail is a Violation of the Whole.

According to Beethoven, a composition was finished when it was perfect. Haydn and Mozart had been *intuitive* composers, who used musical ideas as such. Beethoven was a *constructive* composer, who used a musical idea as a starting point and he took his time to let the idea ripen.[274] For Beethoven, it would have been impossible to write more than a hundred symphonies like Haydn or even more than forty like Mozart. The process of ripening took too long for that in Beethoven's case.

So, we are left with fewer than ten Beethoven symphonies; however, the quality balances the quantity.

During the beginning of the composition process, Beethoven concentrated only on the big picture. But step by step, the details became more important. During the final phase, the details were the only things that mattered to him. Not only did he write *what* had to be played, but also *how* it had to be played. He did so to a larger degree compared to Haydn and Mozart and this caused friction with publishers who were not used to it. Beethoven wrote many lengthy letters to them regarding the exact length of a slur or the exact position of a sforzando.

The climax regarding the notation of details was his Fifth Piano Concerto. For publishers, it was an anti-climax.

The publication of the Fifth Piano Concerto differed from its predecessors due to the accuracy with which Beethoven wanted to fix all the details of the performance: the articulation marks, the use of the pedal and the many possibilities of sound and expression. Nothing was left to chance.[275]
JAN CAEYERS

Perfectionism is a double-edged sword. It can stimulate exceptional achievements, but can also be the cause of things not being ready in time. In January 1819, Beethoven heard that Archduke Rudolf would become archbishop in March 1820. For Beethoven, this was reason to start to compose a large mass. He had one year to finish it and it had to become something very special. It became something very special. The *Missa Solemnis* is considered one of the most important choral works ever written, but the score was not ready until March 1823, three years after the intended first performance.

Another large composition that was dedicated to Archduke Rudolf was the voluminous Piano Sonata Opus 106 (referred to as the *Hammerklavier*). Playing those forty pages takes more than fifty minutes. When this composition was about to be printed in London (in order to be issued simultaneously with the German version), Ferdinand Ries received a letter from Beethoven with the request to add two notes at the beginning of the *Adagio*.

Ries wondered whether his master had become insane; to add two notes to such a large composition that had been ready for half a year?! But Ries was glued to the spot when he tested the effect of this musical prefix. The two notes changed the color of the whole *Adagio*.

The slow movement now begins with a simple gesture that is the distilled essence of the whole piece.[276]
JAN SWAFFORD

A publisher suggested revising the oratorio *Christus am Ölberg,* because of its inferior text. He was met by Beethoven's VDVW thinking:

> *I know the lyrics are very bad. But even if from a bad text a whole is made, it becomes difficult to change even small details without disrupting the whole thing. Even a single word has to remain like it is, because it can have a great significance. He is a bad composer, who doesn't try and succeed to make the best out of even a bad text. If this is the case, changes will not improve the whole thing.*[277]
> LUDWIG VAN BEETHOVEN

A Scottish publisher had received a commissioned work from Beethoven. He thought it was brilliant but too complicated for the intended target group. So, he requested Beethoven to make some adjustments. The request was dismissed by Beethoven's VDVW thinking:

> *I never had the habit to revise my compositions. I never did such a thing, because I am convinced of the truth that every part alteration will change the character of the whole composition.*[278]
> LUDWIG VAN BEETHOVEN

When, in 1805, Beethoven's only opera *Leonore/Fidelio* had its first performance, it flopped. Part of the trouble was the slow beginning of the opera. At Lichnowsky's palace, there was an exhausting crisis meeting. Everybody present agreed that the opera and especially the first act should be shortened. But the number of notes Beethoven was inclined to cut was zero. Hours passed, but Beethoven remained adamant. Parts of the score were played at the piano. Some parts were sung. But the talks reached total deadlock.

It was past midnight when Princess Maria Christiane Lichnowsky took Beethoven's hand and made an ultimate appeal to shorten his work. The request was again dismissed by Beethoven's VDVW thinking.

"Do not ask for that!" he replied moodily. "Not one note may lack!"

"Beethoven!" the princess shouted with a deep sigh. "Thus your great work will be misjudged and slandered?"

"It has already sufficiently been rewarded by your approval, dear princess!" said Beethoven and his hand slid softly trembling out of hers.

When, a little later, Beethoven was able to overcome his great stubbornness and perfectionism, the door was open for *Leonore/Fidelio* to become one of the biggest successes in the history of opera.[279]

*　　*　　*

Many aspergers are impatient and tend to give up easily. Many others are extremely persistent. Others still combine impatience in some settings – usually those that are perceived as uninteresting or 'impossible' – with extreme tenacity and persistence in other situations – not least, of course, in areas of special narrow interests.[280]
CHRISTOPHER GILLBERG

Just like the great heroes he admired, Beethoven had to suffer to transcend himself and to make exceptional achievements for humanity.[281]
JAN CAEYERS

It has become clear that Beethoven could be stubborn and was a perfectionist to a high degree. In fact, these two features were so pronounced that it was one of Beethoven's main challenges in life to find the right balance regarding these two traits. To show Beethoven's perseverance, it suffices to quote just one letter.

Beethoven had a lot of fortune in his life. When he came to Vienna, Mozart had just died, leaving an opportunity for the next musical genius to enter the salons of the nobility. Twenty years later, Beethoven became very popular in Vienna with both the nobility and the commoners just by composing second-grade music to the victories over Napoleon. There were always people around to help him with the next step in his career or in other ways, but the degree of misfortune he had to face was also significant. In the summer of 1801, Beethoven wrote to Wegeler about a huge problem, "I am deaf." In the fall of the same year, Beethoven stated in a subsequent letter, "My hearing, however, has not in the least improved; I really am not quite sure whether it has not become worse."[282]

However, during the next year, it became clear to Beethoven that his deafness was permanent. In October 1802, he wrote a letter to his two brothers, but he seemed to address all the people he knew as well. As with his letter to the Immortal Beloved, this letter was found after his death amongst his belongings. It looks like both letters were never sent. Because this letter was written in the village Heiligenstadt, it has become known as *The Heiligenstadt Testament*.

For my brothers Carl and [Johann] *Beethoven*
O you men who think or say that I am malevolent, stubborn or misanthropic, how greatly do you wrong me, you do not know the secret causes of my seeming, from childhood my heart and mind were disposed to the gentle feelings of good will, I was even ever eager to accomplish great deeds, but reflect now that for six years I have been a hopeless case, aggravated by senseless physicians,

cheated year after year in the hope of improvement, finally compelled to face the prospect of a lasting malady (whose cure will take years or, perhaps, be impossible), born with an ardent and lively temperament, even susceptible to the diversions of society, I was compelled early to isolate myself, to live in loneliness, when I at times tried to forget all this, O how harshly was I repulsed by the doubly sad experience of my bad hearing, and yet it was impossible for me to say to men speak louder, shout, for I am deaf. Ah, how could I possibly admit such an infirmity in the one sense which should have been more perfect in me than in others, a sense that I once possessed in highest perfection, a perfection such as few surely in my profession enjoy or have enjoyed – Oh I cannot do it, therefore forgive me when you see me draw back when I would gladly mingle with you, my misfortune is doubly painful because it must lead to my being misunderstood, for me there can be no recreations in society of my fellows, refined intercourse, mutual exchange of thought, only just as little as the greatest needs command disposition, although I sometimes ran counter to it yielding to my inclination for society, but what a humiliation when one stood beside me and heard a flute in the distance and I heard nothing, or someone heard the shepherd singing and again I heard nothing, such incidents brought me to the verge of despair, but little more and I would have put an end to my life – only art it was that withheld me, ah it seemed impossible to leave the world until I had produced all that I felt called upon me to produce, and so I endured this wretched existence – truly wretched, an excitable body which a sudden change can throw from the best into the worst state – Patience – it is said that I must now choose for my guide, I have done so, I hope my determination will remain firm to endure until it please the inexorable Parcae to break the thread, perhaps I shall get better, perhaps not, I am prepared. Forced already in my 28th year to become a philosopher, Oh it is not easy, less easy for the artist than for anyone else – Divine One thou lookest into my inmost soul, thou knowest it, thou knowest that love of man and desire to do good live therein. Oh men, when some day you read these words, reflect that you did me wrong and let the unfortunate one comfort himself and find one of his kind who despite all obstacles of nature yet did all that was in his power to be accepted among worthy artists and men. You my brothers Carl and [Johann] as soon as I am dead if Dr. Schmid is still alive ask him in my name to describe my malady and attach this document to the history of my illness so that so far as possible at least the world may become reconciled with me after my death. At the same time, I declare you two to be the heirs to my small fortune (if so it can be called), divide it fairly, bear with and help each other, what injury you have done me you know was long ago forgiven. To you, brother Carl, I give special thanks for the attachment you have displayed toward me of late.

It is my wish that your lives be better and freer from care than I have had, recommend virtue to your children, it alone can give happiness, not money, I speak from experience, it was virtue that upheld me in misery, to it next to my art I owe the fact that I did not end my life with suicide. – Farewell and love each other – I thank all my friends, particularly Prince Lichnowsky and Professor Schmid – I desire that the instruments from Prince L. be preserved by one of you but let no quarrel result from this, so soon as they can serve you better purpose sell them, how glad will I be if I can still be helpful to you in my grave - with joy I hasten toward death – if it comes before I shall have had an opportunity to show all my artistic capacities it will still come too early for me despite my hard fate and I shall probably wish it had come later - but even then I am satisfied, will it not free me from my state of endless suffering? Come when thou will I shall meet thee bravely. – Farewell and do not wholly forget me when I am dead, I deserve this of you in having often in life thought of you how to make you happy, be so -
Heiligenstadt 6 October 1802, Ludwig van Beethoven

For my brothers, Carl and [Johann]
to be read and executed after my death.

Heiligenstadt 10 October, 1802, thus do I take my farewell of thee – and indeed sadly – yes, that beloved hope – which I brought with me when I came here to be cured at least in a degree – I must wholly abandon, as the leaves of autumn fall and are withered so hope has been blighted, almost as I came – I go away – even the high courage – which often inspired me in the beautiful days of summer – has disappeared – Oh Providence – grant me at least but one day of pure joy – it is so long since real joy echoed in my heart – Oh when – Oh when, Oh Divine One – shall I find it again in the temple of nature and of men – Never? no – Oh that would be too hard.[283]

CHAPTER
5
In clinical practice

CONCLUSION AND CODA

*To my own amazement, I have seen that asperger individuals, as long as they
are intellectually intact, can almost always achieve professional success, usually
in highly specialized academic professions, often in very high positions, with a
preference for abstract content. [...] There are also several musicians of considerable
stature who were observed by me when children.*[284]
HANS ASPERGER

*Milder episodes of hypomania appear to be very common in Asperger syndrome
and may show as increased activity or restlessness, increased talkativeness, more
pronounced difficulties concentrating, decreased need for sleep, overfamiliarity or
unexpected sociability, or as overspending or other types of reckless or irresponsible
behaviors.*[285]
CHRISTOPHER GILLBERG

*I believe that someday we will wake up as a civilization and realize that the asperger
traits that now confuse us are part of the core of human progress. Geniuses throughout history who have been previously identified as highly eccentric are now being
recognized as having Asperger syndrome and are being authoritatively diagnosed
post-mortem. I believe that as we become more sophisticated in our perceptions, we
will realize some of the brilliance behind the asperger brain.*[286]
ASHLEY STANFORD

DIAGNOSIS

Did Beethoven have Asperger syndrome? To answer this question, we have to look at whether Beethoven's features meet the Gillberg criteria.

Social impairment (extreme egocentricity) is the first and most important feature exhibited by people with Asperger syndrome. This particular diagnostic criterion is described as follows:

1. Social impairment (extreme egocentricity)
(at least two of the following):
(a) difficulties interacting with peers
(b) indifference to peer contacts
(c) difficulties interpreting social cues
(d) socially and emotionally inappropriate behavior[287]

Beethoven meets subcriteria 1a and 1d. He had a lot of difficulties dealing with friends, both male and female, and his biography abounds in examples of inappropriate behavior. There are no reports relating to subcriterion 1c. Beethoven does not meet subcriterion 1b: he often had a big need for friends, again both male and female. That these friendships did not always have the desired quality and quantity was not due to a lack of need; it was due to a lack of social skills.

Narrow interest is the second feature exhibited by people with Asperger syndrome. This particular diagnostic criterion is described as follows:

2. Narrow interest
(at least one of the following):
(a) exclusion of other activities
(b) repetitive adherence
(c) more rote than meaning[288]

By virtue of Beethoven meeting subcriterion 2a (his narrow interest in music regularly leading to the exclusion of other (social) activities), Beethoven satisfies the second diagnostic subcriterion of being positively diagnosed with Asperger syndrome.

Fixed routines and obsessive rituals are the third feature exhibited by people with Asperger syndrome. This particular diagnostic criterion is described as follows:

3. Compulsive need for introducing routines and rituals
(at least one of the following):
(a) which affect the individual's every aspect of everyday life
(b) which affect others[289]

By virtue of Beethoven meeting subcriterion 3a, Beethoven satisfies the third diagnostic criterion of being positively diagnosed with Asperger syndrome. There is no clear information – although it is possible – that he imposed routines and rituals on others, for example, his servants and nephew Karl.

Speech and language peculiarities are the fourth feature exhibited by people with Asperger syndrome. This particular diagnostic criterion is described as follows:

4. Speech and language peculiarities
(at least three of the following):
(a) delayed speech development
(b) superficially perfect expressive language
(c) formal pedantic language
(d) odd prosody, peculiar voice characteristics
(e) impairment of comprehension including misinterpretations of literal/implied meanings[290]

The subcriteria from 4a to 4e can be read as one sentence: although speech development can be delayed, the normal level will eventually be reached, but the use of language will be formal or pedantic and/or the person has an odd prosody or peculiar voice characteristics and/or there is an impairment of comprehension including misinterpretations of literal/implied meanings.

As for Beethoven, it has not been documented that he had any delayed speech development. But it is obvious he reached the normal level. There is no indication Beethoven used any formal pedantic language, nor has there been any contemporary mentioning an odd voice. Beethoven does also not meet subcriterion 4e: although his use of language was notable, he did not show any impairment of comprehension. Consequently, Beethoven does not meet this fourth diagnostic criterion of Asperger syndrome, because meeting at least three subcriteria is required.

Non-verbal communication problems are the fifth feature exhibited by people with Asperger syndrome. This particular diagnostic criterion is described as follows:

5. Non-verbal communication problems
(at least one of the following):
(a) limited use of gestures
(b) clumsy/gauche body language
(c) limited facial expression
(d) inappropriate facial expression
(e) peculiar stiff gaze[291]

Beethoven does not meet subcriterion 5a: his gestures were more exaggerated than limited. There are no reports that point in the direction of subcriterion 5d. With respect to subcriteria 5c and 5e, confirmations can be found; but there are also reports of the opposite. Only regarding subcriterion 5b, there are reports that confirm a *clumsy/gauche body language*, while there are no reports of the contrary.

Motor clumsiness is the sixth feature exhibited by people with Asperger syndrome. This particular diagnostic criterion is described as follows:

6. Motor clumsiness:
poor performance in neuro-developmental test[292]

Obviously, Beethoven cannot now be subjected to neuro-developmental testing. However, descriptions provided by Beethoven contemporaries Ries and Breuning provide evidence of both his poor fine and gross motor skills.

Sensory problems are not part of the diagnostic criteria. Beethoven did have hyperacusis (an asperger feature), but most of it can be attributed to his increasing deafness. There are no reports he had any sensitivity problems with his other senses. However, Beethoven's motor clumsiness is, in fact, also a sensory problem, as movement is sensed by receptor cells in joints and muscles. Aspergers can have a problem with this so-called proprioceptive system, leading to inaccurate perception of the position of body parts and lack of coordination.

In Table 1, all diagnostic criteria and subcriteria of Asperger syndrome are provided, including the degree to which Beethoven fits the subcriteria. By virtue of the information provided in Table 1, Beethoven does not meet the criteria of Asperger syndrome. He scores too few subcriteria with regard to criterion four. However:

In clinical practice, a diagnosis of Asperger syndrome is made if the social interaction dysfunction criterion is met along with at least four of the five other criteria.[293]
CHRISTOPHER GILLBERG

By virtue of this information, Beethoven does meet the criteria of Asperger syndrome. If Beethoven had lived in the twenty-first century, he would be positively diagnosed. In other words, Beethoven did have Asperger syndrome. I like to stress here that this diagnosis is speculation. I do hope that the reader will regard this speculation as well-founded.

Table 1: Gillberg's diagnostic criteria of Asperger syndrome and the degree to which Beethoven fits these criteria.

1. **Social impairment (extreme egocentricity)**

   (at least two of the following):

   (a) difficulties interacting with peers   ++

   (b) indifference to peer contacts   ☐

   (c) difficulties interpreting social cues   ☐

   (d) socially and emotionally inappropriate behavior   ++

2. **Narrow interest**

   (at least one of the following):

   (a) exclusion of other activities   ++

   (b) repetitive adherence   ☐

   (c) more rote than meaning   ☐

3. **Compulsive need for introducing routines and rituals**

   (at least one of the following):

   (a) which affect the individual's every aspect of everyday life   ++

   (b) which affect others   ☐

4. **Speech and language peculiarities**

   (at least three of the following):

   (a) delayed speech development   ?

   (b) superficially perfect expressive language   ++

   (c) formal pedantic language   ☐

   (d) odd prosody, peculiar voice characteristics   ☐

   (e) impairment of comprehension including misinterpretations of   ☐

   literal/implied meanings

5. **Non-verbal communication problems**

(at least one of the following):

(a) limited use of gesture ☐

(b) clumsy / gauche body language ++

(c) limited facial expression +

(d) inappropriate facial expression ☐

(e) peculiar stiff gaze +

6. **Motor clumsiness**

poor performance in neuro-developmental test ++

Table legend:

? No data available; there is no report about the first years of his life.

☐ *Beethoven does not show this feature; it is not described in the many reports about Beethoven.*

+ *Beethoven does show this feature, but there are reports of the contrary.*

++ *Beethoven does show this feature in a sufficient degree to support the diagnosis.*

TWO OTHER EXPLANATIONS: BIPOLAR DISORDER AND HIGH SENSITIVITY

The question is: what is gained with this diagnosis? This becomes clear when the asperger explanation is compared with other attempts to explain Beethoven's peculiar behavior. Throughout Beethoven's life − even during his childhood − Beethoven's behavior was viewed as unusual, and the need has been felt up until the present time to find explanations and frameworks for this behavior.

As a kind of competition, I would like to compare my attempt to clarify the person Beethoven with two other concepts, also brought up in connection with Beethoven during the early twenty-first century. My approach will be practical, meaning that I will not verify whether an explanation is true or not − since I lack the capacity and ability to perform as such. I will assume that all explanations made about Beethoven are true, and consequently examine which one can clarify the most. The two other hypotheses are bipolar disorder and high sensitivity. I will not be considering the two explanations I learned from the radio and during birthday parties. The first explains Beethoven's behavior due to the negative influences of his father, experienced in Beethoven's youth. The second explains that Beethoven's deafness was the reason behind his behavior. Although they both may be true, they are less inclusive, as they only focus on the social capacities of Beethoven, not on other evident parts of his personality.

Bipolar disorder

Building further on the book *Manic Depression and Creativity*, written by Jablow Hershman and Julian Lieb, Peter Davies ascertains in his book *The Character of a Genius* that Beethoven had a bipolar disorder. People with this disorder suffer from periods of (hypo)mania, alternately with periods of depression. There is a lot of literature about this phenomenon. The typical symptoms of a depressive state are[294]:

1 feelings of unhappiness that won't go away;
2 the feeling of wanting to burst into tears for no apparent reason;
3 losing interest in things and being unable to enjoy them;
4 feeling restless, agitated and irritable;
5 losing self-confidence;
6 feeling useless, inadequate and hopeless;
7 negative thinking and thoughts of suicide;
8 finding it hard to concentrate or make decisions;
9 losing appetite and weight;
10 difficulty getting to sleep and waking earlier than usual;

11 feeling exhausted;
12 loss of libido;
13 feeling isolated and avoiding contact with others.

It has been extensively elaborated that Beethoven had periods of depression. The
Heiligenstadt Testament demonstrates suicidal thoughts. The other side of bipolar
disorder is mania. It is almost impossible to function in daily life if a mania is
pathological, and hospitalization is therefore usually required. It should thus
be understood that Beethoven did not suffer from a full pathological mania. He
could function in his daily life, there was no need for hospitalization, and he did
not suffer from occurring psychosis. However, one can state that he had a weaker
condition: hypomania. In a period of hypomania, persons display the following
symptoms[295]:
  1 feeling exceptionally confident with inflated self-esteem;
  2 feeling a need for less sleep, and feeling rested after only a few hours sleep;
  3 being more talkative than usual, or feeling a need to keep talking;
  4 feeling full of ideas with racing thoughts;
  5 being easily distracted, and darting from one activity to another;
  6 increased goal-directed activity;
  7 involvement in pleasurable activities that have a high potential for painful
     consequences (e.g. spending sprees that result in debt, or a sexual encounter
     that is later regretted);
  8 feeling very excited and in a euphonic mood for at least several days on end,
     which can switch to irritability, intolerance, and rage;
  9 increased activity and high energy levels;
  10 being unusually friendly, seeking out people, including strangers;
  11 increased productivity and creativity.

It is true that Beethoven had a great sense of self-confidence. At times, he was very
talkative. It is very well possible that he had racing thoughts, including those of
a musical nature. Distraction (symptom 5) was a one-directional move in the case
of Beethoven: from the outside world into music. If he was occupied with music, it
was almost impossible to distract him from continuing with this. Beethoven did not
display the features 6 and 7; the features 8, 9 and 11 he demonstrated frequently
and intensely. Beethoven displayed the quality of feature 10 now and again, for
example when he met the composer Weber for the first time. Beethoven embraced
Weber at least six times, and shouted, "There you are, mate. You are a great guy
(*Teufelskerl*)! Welcome!" (*Grüss dich Gott!*).

High sensitivity

The term *highly sensitive person* was introduced in 1996 by Elaine Aron in her book, *The Highly Sensitive Person: How to Thrive When the World Overwhelms You*. In this book, the word *arousal* takes a central place. Aron makes two statements. First, nobody feels comfortable if he/she experiences a low or a high amount of arousal for a long time. In the first case, one is bored. In the second case, one is overstimulated. These stimuli can be of sensory nature (like light and sound) but also of a social nature (like people staring at you). Second, people differ to a large degree in respect to their arousal optimum.

Aron's book deals further with the 15–20% of the population with a low-arousal optimum. Aron calls those persons *highly sensitive persons*. Similar to Hans Asperger's remarks that his group of socially impaired patients also had other characteristics, Aron formulates a list of features that appear frequently in connection with high sensitivity individuals. She presents those in a paragraph with the title (obviously addressing the highly sensitive reader): *"Your Trait* [high sensitivity] *Really Does Make You Special."*[296] Highly sensitive persons[297] are:

1   better at spotting errors and avoiding making errors;
2   highly conscientious;
3   able to concentrate deeply (but they do best without distractions);
4   especially good at tasks requiring vigilance, accuracy, speed, and the detection of minor differences;
5   able to process material to deeper levels of what psychologists call "semantic memory;"
6   often thinking about their own thinking;
7   able to learn without being aware they have learned;
8   deeply affected by other people's moods and emotions;
9   specialists in fine motor movements;
10   good at holding still;
11   "morning people" (here there are many exceptions);
12   more affected by stimulants like caffeine unless they are very used to them;
13   more "right-brained" (less linear, more creative in a synthesizing way);
14   more sensitive to things in the air (yes, that means more cases of hay fever and skin rashes).

The two statements made by Aron seem very obvious. But the concept of *high sensitivity* suffers from the lack of clear (diagnostic) criteria. This is why it is impossible to make a distinction between who is highly sensitive and who is not. Furthermore, the concept is presented especially as a self-help concept, which allows the reader to identify with what is written (or not). Aron's book doesn't seem to be composed so as to identify high sensitivity in others. One may recognize a few features in other people such as a careful attitude, intense deep concentration and well-balanced fine motor skills, but some other descriptions are too subjective and too vague to diagnose high sensitivity in other persons. These would include the ability to process material to deeper levels of what psychologists call "semantic memory," thinking about one's own thinking, and able to learn without being aware that one has learned. As a result, the concept of high sensitivity is less robust than both the concepts of Asperger syndrome and bipolar disorder. This would be improved once diagnostic criteria are formulated.

In *"Echte Kunst ist eigensinnig!": Das Leben des Ludwig van Beethoven* ["True Art is Perverse!": The Life of Ludwig van Beethoven] Hans-Georg Klemm claims that Beethoven's personality is highly sensitive. His argumentation is twofold. First, he writes that he is "certainly convinced."[298] Second, he claims that many "symptoms" Aron describes in her book are applicable to the composer Beethoven: "his artistic top talent, his extreme mood swings, his profound connection with his natural environment, his high sensitivity, his – before he became deaf – extraordinary hearing (Beethoven himself hints at this in his 'Heiligenstadt Testament'), and possibly his chronic type of illness."[299]

Klemm's arguments are subject to major weaknesses. His first comment – that he is "certainly convinced" – is not a substantive argument, but rather a subjective belief. His second argument is incomprehensible. There is almost no connection between his list of the Beethoven's "symptoms" and the characteristics Aron mentions. In the absence of diagnostic criteria, Klemm should have at least contemplated Aron's fourteen features.

Klemm refers to Beethoven's motor clumsiness as the "typical accidents" that highly sensitive persons show during moments of *"nervliche Anspannung [nervous tension]."*[300] Quite apart from what *nervous tension* exactly means is his introduction of physical clumsiness – Klemm's own creation as part of the concept high sensitivity – in contradiction to Aron's statement, that highly sensitive persons are specialists in fine motor skills.

Klemm also avoids elaborating on the contradiction between Beethoven's characteristics and characteristics of high sensitivity. For example, Beethoven was not "deeply touched by the emotion of others." Here he rather appeared to be insensitive.

As mentioned above, it is not my aim to assess which explanation is true, as it is even possible that more than one explanation is correct. Of more relevance is which explanation is more sound and comprehensive. Table 2 provides Beethoven's characteristics and the degree to which the three concepts are applicable to him.

Is Beethoven's social impairment also explained by bipolar disorder and high sensitivity? It is obvious that infrequent depression and hypomania can lead to social ills. But social ills were a continuum in Beethoven's life, from his childhood up to his death. This would imply that Beethoven was (hypo)manic-depressive almost throughout his life, an unlikely hypothesis. The systematic lack of social insights and his inability to understand the feelings of others cannot be sufficiently explained by bipolar disorder. Here, the explanatory value of bipolar disorder is less evident than that of Asperger syndrome. Regarding Asperger syndrome, I consider the informal behavior Beethoven displayed toward Weber as social impairment.

Beethoven's social impairment is not explained at all by high sensitivity. One of the features of Aron's list even outright contradicts this: to be deeply affected by other people's moods and emotions.

Is Beethoven's narrow interest also explained by bipolar disorder and high sensitivity? The three aforementioned advocates of the bipolar theory call the said behavior (*I cannot give you a lesson today; I still have work to do*) "work hypomania." The word is comprehensible because it seems like the musical ideas are forced upon Beethoven. This force can be so strong and fast (racing thoughts) that Beethoven is getting away from it all and concentrating his attention solely to music. But the accompanying distractibility is a one-way street: always toward music and never away from it. Bipolar disorder does not account for Beethoven's great creativity during a depression. A very clear example is the summer of 1802 when Beethoven stayed in Heiligenstadt in the hope that his hearing might improve. However, this did not happen and in October he wrote about his increased despair in *The Heiligenstadt Testament*. However, this situation did not hinder him enough that very summer to compose three piano sonatas (Opus 31), each of them dazzling, showing no trace of depression. The composition of these three piano sonatas displays, therefore, that Beethoven was not suffering a bipolar disorder. During the first half of 1821, Beethoven was rather ill and affected by Josephine's death. He suffered certainly not from any work hypomania, rather a depression. However, during that time, Beethoven still composed Piano Sonata Opus 110, which is regarded as one of his masterpieces.

Some features of high sensitivity are in line with the way Beethoven dealt with music: conscientious, deeply concentrated and accurate. But his obsessive way of working, which is explained by Asperger syndrome and its work mania is not explained by this theory. Just like the bipolar disorder, high sensitivity gives only partly an explanation, whereas Asperger syndrome gives a full one.

Both bipolar disorder and high sensitivity do not give any account for the discipline he showed during his working days or his sustained, almost obsessive washing ritual. Also, neither account for his language peculiarities. Asperger syndrome only partly accounts for this, because Beethoven does not fit the (sub)criteria entirely.

Both bipolar disorder and high sensitivity also do not account for his striking non-verbal communication style, like his conspicuous way of conducting. They both also do not account for his motor clumsiness; high sensitivity even contradicts this feature, even though Klemm asserts the opposite.

The core feature of high sensitivity is sensory sensitivity. Beethoven's sensory problems are not explained by bipolar disorder, but rather by Asperger syndrome. There are two clear accounts of Beethoven's sensory sensitivity, one by himself and one by a contemporary. I think both high sensitivity and Asperger syndrome account for these descriptions.

Beethoven's mood swings, his depressive and his hypomanic episodes, were volatile and he was considered unpredictable. Bipolar disorder accounts completely for this, but this is not on the list of criteria of Asperger syndrome. Also, high sensitivity does not account for mood swings, again in spite of Klemm's assertion.

Another hypomanic feature is inflated self-esteem. This overlaps with the stubbornness of Asperger syndrome, but because this is only a feature and not a criterion, I will only count this as half in Table 2.

Table 2: Three ways to explain the features of Beethoven's personality

Features of Beethoven's	asperger syndrome	bipolar disorder	high sensitivity
Social impairment	++	+	□
Narrow interest	++	+	+
Compulsive routines and rituals	++	□	□
Speech and language peculiarities	+	□	□
Non-verbal communication problems	++	□	□
Motor clumsiness	++	□	□
Sensory problems	++	□	++
Mood swings	□	++	□
Inflated self-esteem/ stubbornness	+	++	□
Sleep problems/early bird	□	++	+
Very talkative/racing thoughts	+	++	□
Total well explained	15	10	4

Legend:
++   this feature is very well accounted for by aforementioned concept
+   this feature is fairly well accounted for by aforementioned concept
□   this feature is not accounted for by aforementioned concept

People with bipolar disorder are likely to have sleep problems. Davies [301] gives a bibliographical reference for Beethoven's sleep problems, consistent with both depression and hypomania. The early-bird behavior of Beethoven during summer time is also accounted for by high sensitivity.

Sometimes, Beethoven was very talkative: "At such moments when he talked, completely engrossed in the subject, the abundance of ideas that poured from his mouth seems truly miraculous."[302] This certainly seems to refer to a hypomanic characteristic. However, similar to an asperger who cannot stop once he starts talking about his favorite subject, the hypomanic also has difficulties finding his last sentence. Still, the quotation points more in the direction of hypomania because it resembles highly formulated racing thoughts. Here, bipolar disorder gives a better explanation than Asperger syndrome.

The dissatisfying characteristic of Table 2 is the fact that all features carry the same weight. Also, the allocation of distinctively one or two plusses is to some extent subjective and arguable. If someone else were to complete the table, perhaps it would yield different results. Someone could add features or delete unimportant ones, merge features, or split them further. Despite these shortcomings, Asperger syndrome clearly offers the best explanation: it accounts for most features and only two do not apply. The bipolar hypothesis accounts for two features that do not fit the asperger concept. During a manic episode someone can come across as socially impaired and have a narrow focus, although the nature thereof differs from Asperger syndrome, this does not account at all for these features during a depressive period. The high sensitivity hypothesis hardly accounts for anything: only the sensory problems and partly for two others.

As mentioned above, it was not my aim to assess which explanation is true, but if we assume that they are all true, Asperger syndrome accounts for the most: fifteen of a possible twenty-two points. Bipolar disorder scores fewer than half the points (ten of twenty-two). The explanatory value of high sensitivity is very limited (four of twenty-two). Consequently, Asperger syndrome has won the competition.

WHAT DOES THE ASPERGER BEETHOVEN HAVE TO DO WITH BEETHOVEN, THE GENIUS?

I have mentioned repeatedly that Asperger syndrome occurs at different levels of ability. The range encompasses all levels of ability from the highly original genius, through the weird eccentric who lives in a world of his own and achieves very little, down to the most severe contact-disturbed, automaton-like mentally retarded individual.[303]

HANS ASPERGER

There are often-used terms that defy an exact definition, examples of which are life, love, and science. The term genius also belongs to this category. What exactly a genius is and where it borders with talent seems a question of personal perception, culture, and zeitgeist. There are no formulated criteria for genius, which doesn't suggest that the term genius is unfit for use. There are simply people of whom others find that they do much better in a certain field in the arts or science – because that is what we are mostly talking about – than others.[304] Trying to determine if someone is a genius is to discover whether their work speaks to people in different cultures and later times. The value of the work of a genius has then to transcend the place and time of origin. This means that only many years later can it be established as to whether someone was a genius. An example of a composer who would not be a genius is Giacomo Meyerbeer. This opera composer belongs to the most successful composers of the nineteenth century. However, he did not write any music that survived through the years and, in the twentieth century, his music almost disappeared from the concert halls and opera houses.

An attempt to draw the line between genius and talent almost always turns into a comparison. At a contest of who could build the fastest means of transport over the sea, a talent built the fastest boat of all. The genius built an airplane. This shows that the genius does not just do better than others – just like a talent – but also that he works at a higher level.

However we define a genius, Beethoven is usually seen as one. His music is still being appreciated after two centuries, also outside the culture in which it developed. After this introduction, the question remains of what his genius and Asperger syndrome have to do with each other. Before trying to answer that question, it should be established that granting the label "genius" is a product of the Romantic period.

At school, one will get the impression that the Romantic period was an art movement in the nineteenth century. This is partly true. The Romantic period has penetrated all of Western culture and is so omnipresent that in many obvious cases it is not even clear to most that these are Romantic of nature. One of these cases is the genius cult. The Romantic cultural shift starts slowly in the eighteenth century but gains more the character of a revolution than an evolution during the first quarter of the nineteenth century. The way we view composers essentially has not changed since then. It is very difficult to look at composers from before this period without wearing Romantic glasses. This is partly because interest in the artist, next to interest in their artwork, is itself a product of the Romantic period. One who is interested in a composer from before the nineteenth century is looking at this in a Romantic way at a composer who was not Romantic but rather saw himself as a craftsman.

Until the eighteenth century, a composer was viewed as an artisan. If you would travel by means of a time machine to the second half of the eighteenth century and pay a visit to the mansion of the Esterházy family, Joseph Haydn could not be overlooked. Haydn worked thirty years for this family. He composed many works, including tens of symphonies for the orchestra of these noblemen. Was Haydn viewed as a genius? Not at all, he was seen as a courtier! He had to strictly adhere to the wishes of his employer and he had to wear servant livery.

When an aristocrat visited the family, he'd be guided through the garden in the afternoon, which was followed by a big meal in the early evening. Later in the evening, Haydn and his orchestra would provide relaxation. Haydn would eat with the other household staff members. He had dinner with the gardener and the cook.

In the summer, the Esterházy family moved to their summer palace and all the household staff, including the orchestra, had to join them there. These massive moves started to bore the orchestra and conductor Haydn confronted his employer indirectly. He wrote a symphony in which the musicians, in groups, stop playing during the last part. They blow out their candles, take their music scores, and leave the stage until only two violinists are left.

Half a century later, Robert Schumann wrote a review of a work by Chopin. He did not talk about an excellent artisan. Within half a century, musicians were viewed differently altogether and Schumann wrote the now famous line: *Hut ab, ihr Herren, ein Genie!* [*Take off your hat, you gentlemen, a genius!*]

The term genius was used for musicians and composers in the eighteenth century, but it was used sparingly as such and very differently than in the nineteenth century. Count Waldstein wrote to Beethoven in 1792:

> *Mozart's Genius is still in mourning and weeps for the death of its pupil. It found a refuge with the inexhaustible Haydn but no occupation; through him it wishes to form a union with another. Through uninterrupted diligence you will receive the spirit of Mozart from the hands of Haydn.*[305]

In line with the view in ancient Rome, where a "genius" was viewed as a guiding spirit, a "genius" was thought of as an attribute that can unite with individuals, but at the same time let them go again. From the Romantic period onwards, the belief that the genius of Mozart could also unite with Beethoven has been abandoned. The genius of Mozart and the genius of Beethoven are two different entities. However, in the Romantic period, it was taken one step further: Beethoven was not identified with a genius, Beethoven *was* a genius. The person became one with their genius, and cannot be without it, because the person *is* the genius. This rules out that Beethoven could somehow acquire some of the Mozart genius.[306]

Beethoven seems the personification of the cultural change concerning musicians and composers that took place in the first quarter of the nineteenth century. There are no more indirect confrontations; Beethoven states the truth, no matter whom he faces. When he teaches the archduke, he ignores court etiquette. When he plays music for noblemen but finds that afterward there is no seat reserved for him at the dinner table, he leaves in an angry manner. When a patron orders him to play the piano when he doesn't feel like it, he ends all contact. He emphasizes his uniqueness worthy of a genius: there are many noblemen, but there is only one Beethoven. He was never in the service of a religious or secular employer in Vienna.

The Romantic author Ernst Hoffmann knew right away that Beethoven was a Romantic composer without meeting him. He just listened to his music. Before that it was common to write about Beethoven as in this review of the Third Symphony:

An entirely new symphony by Beethoven is written in a completely different style. This long composition, extremely difficult of performance, is in reality a tremendously expanded, daring and wild fantasy. It lacks nothing in the way of startling and beautiful passages, in which the energetic and talented composer must be recognized; but often it loses itself in lawlessness. The symphony begins with an Allegro in E-flat that is vigorously scored; a Funeral March in C minor follows which is later developed fugally. After it comes an Allegro scherzo and a Finale, both in E-flat. The reviewer belongs to Herr van Beethoven's sincerest admirers, but in this composition he must confess that he finds too much that is glaring and bizarre, which hinders greatly one's grasp of the whole, and a sense of unity is almost completely lost.[307]

Around 1810, Hoffmann wrote in a completely new style about Beethoven:

Should, whenever music is discussed as an independent art, not always be referred to instrumental music which, refusing the help of any other art (of poetry), expresses the unique essence of art that can only be recognized in it? – It is the most romantic of all arts; one would almost want to say, the only truly romantic one, for only the infinite is its model. [...]

Beethoven's instrumental music, too, opens to us the realm of the tremendous and abysmal. Glowing rays of light shoot through the dark night of this realm, and we see gigantic shadows swaying back and forth, encircling us closer and closer, destroying us, but not the pain of infinite longing in which every delight, rising up in joyful voices, sinks and drowns, and only in this pain, consuming love, hope, joy, but not destroying it and aiming at bursting our chests with its unison of all passions, do we live on and are we bewitched clairvoyants! [...]

Beethoven's music moves the levers of fear, of shudder, of the terrifying, of pain and thus awakens that infinite longing that is the essence of romanticism. Therefore, he is a purely romantic composer, and may it not be because of it, that to him, vocal music — that does not allow for the character of infinite longing, but, through words, achieves certain affects, as they are not present in the realm of the infinite — is harder?[308]

The matter-of-fact way of writing as in the Third Symphony review has not been displaced and is still being practiced in newspapers and magazines in the twenty-first century. However, the image of the Romantic genius has not vanished. In the Romantic period, the artist and his work are equally important; from the Romantic period onwards, the interest in composers from the past grows steadily and they are considered to be geniuses in retrospect.

Any specialist in classical music will confirm the musically historical implication of Beethoven, whether they like his music or not. Most will as well confirm that Beethoven was a genius. But what had this genius to do with Asperger syndrome?

My hypothesis is: nothing, in the direct sense. Most aspergers are not geniuses and by far most geniuses were not aspergers. However, if someone is a genius *and* he has Asperger syndrome, then this combination yields enormous advantages. These advantages do not occur at the social level, in fact, it is there that a significant price is being paid. Willfulness and perfectionism are social handicaps that create a lot of interpersonal problems, but in the area of narrow interest, the combination creates huge advantages. When a genius has ideas that far surpass those of his contemporaries, then his willfulness and perfectionism are useful qualities. One quality is exclusively positive and therefore even more important when setbacks in life occur. It is precisely this quality that Beethoven particularly possessed: perseverance.

It is interesting to look at the following sentence about Beethoven and Helene von Breuning:

Helene Breuning was acquainted with these kinds of eruptions, knew how to interpret them and realized that one must be able to live with the dark side of Beethoven's genius to profit from his light side.[309]
JAN CAEYERS

As I see it, Beethoven's eruptions do not directly have anything to do with his genius. These are the tantrums that can accompany Asperger syndrome. I would, therefore, like to reformulate this sentence:

Helene Breuning was acquainted with these kinds of eruptions, knew how to interpret them and realized that one must be able to live with the dark side of Beethoven's Asperger syndrome in order to benefit from his genius, which could shine through that same Asperger syndrome.

Following the aforementioned hypothesis, the genius Beethoven would have accomplished far less without his Asperger syndrome, but the opposite, asperger but no genius, would have been far worse for Beethoven. Hans Asperger stated that because of the unequal distribution of endowment in each asperger child, "it is possible to consider such individuals both as child prodigies and as imbeciles with ample justification."[310]

Such difficult children can develop into distinctive persons. Hans Asperger accounts for this by their means of narrow interest, which gives highly gifted aspergers the lead in their discipline. Herewith he states that the positive and the negative of the syndrome are two sides that cannot be kept apart, that "good and bad in every character are just two sides of the same coin. It is simply not possible to separate them, to opt for the positive and get rid of the negative."[311]

However, I'd like to add that the negative can be channeled and Helene von Breuning did so in exemplary fashion.

For the mentally deficient aspergers, though, the picture is murky according to Hans Asperger: "In the less favorable cases, they roam the streets as 'originals,' grotesque and dilapidated, talking loudly to themselves or unconcernedly to passers-by as asperger individuals would. They are taunted by urchins and react to this with wild but ineffectual outbursts."[312]

Compare this to the descriptions of Gerhard von Breuning about the old Beethoven: "Because of the typical nonchalance concerning his clothing, Beethoven's look was something unusually conspicuous on the street. He was usually grumbling, lost in thought. If he was alone, he gesticulated with his arms. If he was with others, he spoke lively and in a loud voice. Hence most people on the street would turn around and call him names. Nephew Karl hated to be seen with him outside and he once said that he was ashamed to escort him on the streets because of his jester-like looks. Beethoven told us this, and he was deeply hurt and offended."[313]

Moreover, Gerhard von Breuning writes, "His desolation from the outside world expressed itself in truly curious peculiarities. Thus, he would lightheartedly nearly undress himself and carry his clothes on a stick on his shoulders, when he found the summer heat too stifling. He would have especially done that in his favorite forests between Baden and Gaden. My father expressed his deepest concerns repeatedly: this could cause a fuss if he were to meet someone this way."[314]

Gerhard von Breuning finally describes how he and his father escorted Beethoven during a walk through the city. Children tried to knock over a pin with a small ball. "Accidentally that ball hit Beethoven's foot. Presuming that they did this on purpose, he turned to them, quick-tempered, and shouted: 'Who told you to play here? Why do you have to play right here?' He wanted to run over to them to chase them away. My father, familiar with the roughness of street-boys, knew how to calm him down. Besides which the ball hardly hurt him."[315]

Why is the old Beethoven in biographies not exclusively described as the village fool or as a "village oddity?"[316] Because meanwhile, he was working on the Ninth Symphony, the *Missa Solemnis,* his last three piano sonatas and his last string quartets, belonging to respectively the most important orchestra music, choir music, piano music and chamber music ever written.

I am convinced, then, that aspergers have their place in the social community. They fulfill their role well, perhaps better than anyone else could, and we are talking of people who as children had the greatest difficulties and caused untold worries to their care-givers.[317]
HANS ASPERGER

ACKNOWLEDGMENTS

I am immensely grateful to Christopher Gillberg for providing the preface and to Aaltje and Jaap van Zweden for their continuous support throughout the years regarding my *asperger Beethoven project*. I am also grateful to my sister Agnes Heijder and especially my American brother-in-law Todd Winkler for their advice on language matters; they have also assisted me regarding many practical issues.

I like to thank the following people who have helped move this book forward: Tony Attwood, Michael Fitzgerald, Alexander Gavrylyuk, Janine Jansen, John Jebb, Isabelle van Keulen, Dine Koopmans, Lucas van Manen, Leo Samama, Dick Swaab, Candida Thompson, Susan Thompson, Jan Willem de Vriend, Penny van Wolferen and Frank Peter Zimmermann

Finally, I like to thank my wife Lioba for allowing me to spend so much time with my brainchild.

LITERATURE

Aron, Elaine, *The Highly Sensitive Person: How to Thrive When the World Overwhelms You*, London, 1999

Asperger, Hans, *"Autistic psychopathy" in Childhood* (original German edition in 1944) in Frith, Uta (editor) *Autism and Asperger syndrome*, Cambridge, 1991

Attwood, Tony, *The Complete Guide to Asperger's Syndrome*, London, 2007

Breuning, Gerhard von, *Aus dem Schwarzspanierhause. Erinnerungen an Ludwig van Beethoven aus meiner Jugendzeit*, Wien, 1874.

Caeyers, Jan, *Beethoven – een biografie*, Amsterdam, 2010
[German edition: Caeyers, Jan, *Beethoven – Der einsame Revolutionär – Eine Biographie*, München, 2012/2013]

Coldicott, Anne-Louise, "Beethoven as an individual," (pp.101–140) in Cooper, Barry (editor), *The Beethoven Compendium*, London, 1991

Davies, Peter, *The Character of a Genius: Beethoven in Perspective*, Westport, 2002

Fischer, Gottfried, *Familie Beethoven im kurfürstlichen Bonn*, Bonn, 2006 (Neuauflage)

Fitzgerald, Michael, *The Genesis of Artistic Creativity: Asperger's Syndrome and the Arts*, London, 2005

Forbes, Elliot, *Thayer's Life of Beethoven: Revised and Edited*, Princeton, 1967/1991

Gillberg, Christopher, *A Guide to Asperger Syndrome*, Cambridge, 2002

Grandin, Temple, *Emergence: Labeled Autistic*, New York, 1986

Grandin, Temple, *Thinking in Pictures And Other Reports from My Life with Autism*, London, 1995

Hershman, Jablow & Lieb, Julian, *Manic Depression and Creativity*, Amherst, 1998

Hoffman, Ernst, *Fantasiestücke*, Frankfurt am Main, 2006

Klapproth, John, *Beethoven's Only beloved: Josephine!*, Charleston, 2012

Klemm, Hans-Georg, *"Echte Kunst ist eigensinnig!" Das Leben des Ludwig van Beethoven*, Darmstadt, 2011

Kopitz/Cadenbach (editors), *Beethoven aus der Sicht seiner Zeitgenossen*, München, 2009

Roberts, Dan, *Bipolar Disorder: The Essential Guide*, Peterborough, 2011

Schindler, Anton, *Biographie von Ludwig van Beethoven*, Münster, 1860

Stanford, Ashley, *Asperger Syndrome and Long-Term Relationships*, London, 2003

Stuart-Hamilton, Ian, *An Asperger Dictionary of Everyday Expressions*, London, 2004/2007

Swafford, Jan, *Beethoven: Anguish and Triumph*, Boston, 2014

Wegeler, Franz & Ries, Ferdinand, *Biographische Notizen über Ludwig van Beethoven*, Koblenz, 1838/1845

Willey, Liane, *Asperger Syndrome in the Family: Redefining Normal*, London, 2001

Zanden, Jos van der, *Beethoven in zijn brieven*, Haarlem, 1997

NOTES

1   Gillberg p. 32 *Many people with Asperger syndrome lack common sense. Much of what governs our social interactions is intuitive, and something that is expected to be known almost without explicit training. It is difficult to define 'common sense.' Even so, most people, even school-age children have an inkling of what is inferred by the term. People with Asperger syndrome are so severely handicapped in this domain that they may themselves feel that they do not know 'how to live.' They appear lost and forlorn. It is usually only toward the end of the pre-adolescent period that it becomes obvious that individuals with Asperger syndrome are so totally lacking in common sense. [...] It is important to distinguish between having a hobby/interest on the one hand and the kind of obsessive pursuit of narrow interests which is the rule in Asperger syndrome on the other.*

2   Swafford p. 39

3   Kopitz/Cadenbach p. 72 *Das ist nicht genau der Charakter, den ich dem Stück geben wollte, sagte er, aber fahren Sie fort; das bin nicht ganz ich, das ist besser als ich.*

4   Letter to Marie Bigot (4 March 1807) *Meine liebe, verehrte Marie! Das Wetter ist so göttlich schön – und wer weiß, ob's Morgen so ist? – Ich schlage Ihnen daher vor, Sie gegen 12 Uhr heute mittags zu einer Spazierfahrt abzuholen. – Da Bigot vermutlich schon aus ist, so können wir ihn freilich nicht mitnehmen – aber deswegen es ganz zu unterlassen, das fordert Bigot selbst gewiss nicht. – Nur die Vormittage sind jetzt am schönsten – warum den Augenblick nicht ergreifen, da er so schnell verfliegt? – Es wäre der so aufgeklärten und gebildeten Marie ganz entgegen, wenn sie bloßen Skrupeln zu gefallen mir das größte Vergnügen (versagen) wollte. – Oh, was für Ursachen sie auch anführen werden, wenn Sie meinen Vorschlag nicht annehmen, so werde ich es nichts anders als dem wenigen Zutrauen, was Sie in meinen Charakter setzen, zuschreiben – und werde nie glauben, dass sie wahre Freundschaft für mich hegen. Karoline wickeln Sie ein in Windeln von Kopf bis zu Füssen, damit ihr nichts geschehe. – Antworten Sie mir, meine liebe Marie, ob Sie können – ich frage nicht, ob sie wollen – weil das letztere nur von mir zu meinem Nachteile wird erklärt werden – Schreiben Sie also nur in zwei Worten ja oder nein. – Leben Sie wohl und machen Sie, dass mir das eigennützige Vergnügen gewährt wird, mit zweien Personen, an denen ich so viel teilnehme, den frohen Genuss der heitern, schönen Natur teilen zu können. –*
Ihr Freund und Verehrer
L. v. Beethoven

5   Letter to Paul and Marie Bigot (6 March 1807) *Liebe Marie, lieber Bigot! Nicht anders als mit dem innigsten Bedauern muss ich wahrnehmen dass die reinsten unschuldigsten Gefühle oft verkannt können werden – wie Sie mir auch liebevoll begegnet sind, so habe ich nie daran gedacht, es anders auszulegen, als dass Sie mir Ihre Freundschaft schenken – Sie müssen mich sehr eitel und kleinlich glauben, wenn Sie voraussetzen, dass das Zuvorkommen selbst einer so vortrefflichen Person, wie Sie sind, mich glauben machen sollte, dass ich gleich ihre Neigung gewonnen – ohnedem ist es einer meiner ersten Grundsätze, nie in einem andern als freundschaftlichen Verhältnis mit der Gattin eines andern zu stehen,*
The letter in English in full:
Dear Marie, Dear Bigot,
Only with the deepest regret am I forced to perceive that the purest, most innocent, feelings can often be misconstrued. As you have received me so kindly, it never occurred to me to explain it otherwise than that you bestow on me your friendship. You must think me very vain or small-minded, if you suppose that the civility itself of such excellent persons as you are could lead me to believe that – I had at once won your affection. Besides, it is one of my first principles never to stand in other than friendly relationship with the wife of another man. Never by

such a relationship (as you suggest) would I fill my breast with distrust against her who may one day share my fate with me--and so taint for myself the most beautiful, the purest life.
It is perhaps possible that sometimes I have not joked with Bigot in a sufficiently refined way; I have indeed told both of you that occasionally I am very free in speech. I am perfectly natural with all my friends, and hate all restraint. I now also count Bigot among them, and if anything I do displeases him, friendship demands from him and you to tell me so--and I will certainly take care not to offend him again; but how can good Marie put such bad meaning on my actions!

With regard to my invitation to take a drive with you and Caroline, it was natural that, as Bigot, the day before, was opposed to your going out alone with me, I was forced to conclude that you both probably found it unbecoming or objectionable--and when I wrote to you, I only wished to make you understand that I saw no harm in it. And so, when I further declared that I attached great value to your not declining, this was only that I might induce you to enjoy the splendid, beautiful day; I was thinking more of your and Caroline's pleasure than of mine, and I thought, if I declared that mistrust on your part or a refusal would be a real offense to me, by this means almost to compel you to yield to my wish. The matter really deserves careful reflection on your part as to how you can make amends for having spoilt this day so bright for me, owing as much to my frame of mind as to the cheerful weather. When I said that you misunderstand me, your present judgment of me shows that I was quite right--not to speak of what you thought to yourself about it.

When I said that something bad would come of it if I came to you, this was more as a joke. The object was to show you how much everything connected with you attracts me, so that I have no greater wish than to be able always to live with you; and that is the truth. Even supposing there was a hidden meaning in it, the most holy friendship can often have secrets, but on that account to misinterpret the secret of a friend because one cannot at once fathom it--that you ought not to do. Dear Bigot, dear Marie, never, never will you find me ignoble. From childhood onwards I learnt to love virtue--and all that is beautiful and good. You have deeply pained me; but it shall only serve to render our friendship ever firmer. Today I am really not well, and it would be difficult for me to see you. Since yesterday, after the quartet, my sensitiveness and my imagination pictured to me the thought that I had caused you suffering. I went at night to the ball for distraction, but in vain. Everywhere the picture of you all pursued me; it kept saying to me – they are so good and perhaps through you they are suffering; thoroughly depressed, I hastened away. Write to me a few lines.
Your true friend Beethoven embraces you all

6   Caeyers p. 369 & 545

7   Caeyers p. 110 & 145

8   These criteria were first presented during a conference in 1988 and first published in a scientific journal in 1989.

9   Gillberg p. 30

10   Stanford p. 107 *Blatant honesty is a common Aspie trait*

11   Caeyers p. 533 *Beethoven nam nooit een blad voor de mond.*

12   Coldicott p. 104

13   Gillberg p. 134

14   Gillberg p. 134

15   Asperger p. 77

16   Coldicott p. 108

17   *Stammbuch* inscription (29 October 1792) *Lieber Beethowen! Sie reisen itzt nach Wien zur Erfüllung ihrer so lange bestrittenen Wünsche. Mozart's Genius trauert noch und beweinet den Tod seines Zöglinges. Bey dem unerschöpflichem Hayden fand er Zuflucht, aber keine Beschäftigung; durch ihn wünscht er noch einmal mit jemanden vereinigt zu werden. Durch ununterbrochenen Fleiß erhalten Sie: Mozart's Geist aus Haydens Händen.*

18   Gillberg p. 54 *In moments of stress it is not uncommon for people with Asperger syndrome to react with panic, 'hysteria', primitive reactions, fear, rage or childish tantrums. Such reactions may border on, or indeed sometimes develop into, confusion states, during which it is quite impossible to reason with the affected individual or even to establish any form of 'contact'.*

19   Caeyers p. 76 *Beethoven was van goede wil, maar soms werd het hem te machtig en verloor hij zijn zelfbeheersing. Hij kreeg dan uitbarstingen van opgekropte frustratie en verongelijktheid, een gedragspatroon waarmee we later nog meer zullen worden geconfronteerd. Helene Breuning kende dat soort erupties, wist die te duiden en besefte dat men moest kunnen leven met de schaduwzijde van Beethovens genialiteit om te kunnen profiteren van zijn lichtkant. Maar zij kreeg vooral controle over dit fenomeen door er een naam aan te geven: zijn raptus.*

20   Wegeler/Ries p. 24

21   Wegeler/Ries p. 49 *Er hat heute wieder seinen Raptus.*

22   Stanford p. 52 *The Aspie's first impression of new information is extremely important since they tend to stick with their first belief. The Aspie may lack the cognitive flexibility to change the initial impression.*

23   Swafford p. 665

24   Coldicott p. 108

25   Quoted from Swafford p. 658

26   Letter to Giannatasio del Rio (15 February 1816) *Diese Nacht ist diese Königin der Nacht bis 3 uhr auf dem künstlerball gewesen nicht allein mit ihrer Verstandesblöße sondern auch mit ihrer körperlichen – für 20 fl. hat man sich in die Ohren gesagt, dass sie – zu haben – sei o schrecklich!*

27   Gillberg p. 81 *Based on clinical work there can be no doubt that persons with Asperger syndrome find it tiresome and strenuous to reflect about other people's thoughts and feelings. It would not occur to them intuitively to consider other people's perspectives or to go outside their own circumscribed egocentric vantage point.*

28   Coldicott p. 110

29   Swafford p. 696

30   Letter to Karl (22 May 1825) *Bisher nur Mutmaßungen, obschon mir von jemand* *versichert wird, daß wieder geheimer Umgang zwischen Dir und Deiner Mutter! Soll ich noch einmal den abscheulichsten Undank erleben?! Nein! Soll das Band gebrochen werden, so sei es! Du wirst von allen unparteiischen Menschen, die diesen Undank hören, gehaßt werden.*

31   Letter to Karl (31 May 1825) *Nüchternheit ist für die jugend nöthig, u. Du scheinst sie nicht genug beachtet zu haben, da Du Geld hattest, ohne daß ich es wußte u. noch nicht weiß woher? – Schöne Handlungen, in's Theater zu gehen ist nicht rathsam jetzt der zu großen zerstreuung wegen so glaube ich, – die angeschaften 5 fl: des H: Dr: Reißig werde ich unterdessen pünktlich Monathl. abtragen – u. hiemit basta – verwöhnt, wie Du bist, würde es nicht schaden der Einfachheit u. Wahrheit Dich endlich zu befleißen, denn mein Herz hat zu viel bej Deinem listigen Betragen gegen mich gelitten, u. Schwer ist es zu vergessen, u. wollte ich an allem dem wie ein jochochs ohne zu murren ziehen, so kann Dein Betragen, wenn es so gegen andere gerichtet ist, Dir niemals Menschen zubringen, die Dich lieben werden – Gott ist mein Zeuge, ich träume nur, von Dir u. von diesem elenden Bruder u. dieser mir zugeschusterten abscheulichen Familie gäntzlich entfernt zu sejn Gott erhöre meine Wünsche, denn trauen kann ich Dir nie mehr. – Leider Dein Vater oder beßer nicht Dein Vater.*

32   Forbes p. 993

33   Letter to Karl (Summer 1826) *Schon um dessentwillen, daß du mir wenigstens gefolgt bist, ist alles vergeben u. vergeßen, mündlich darüber mit dir heute ganz ruhig. – denke nicht, als daß ein anderer Gedanke in mir als nur dein Wohl herrsche, u. hieraus beurtheile mein Handeln – mache ja keinen Schritt, der <u>dich</u> unglücklich machen u. <u>mir</u> das Leben früher raubte – erst gegen 3 uhr kam ich zum schlafe, denn die ganze Nacht hustete ich – ich umarme dich herzlich, u. bin überzeugt, daß du mich bald nicht mehr <u>verkennen</u> wirst, so beurtheile ich auch dein gestriges Handeln – ich erwarte dich sicher <u>heute</u> um Ein Uhr, mach mir nur keinen Kummer u. keine Angst mehr leb indessen wohl / dein wahrer u. treuer vater. – wir sind allein, ich laße deswegen H.[olz] nicht kommen, um so mehr, da ich wünschte, daß nichts verlauten möge von gestern komme ja. – laß mein <u>armes Herz nicht mehr Bluten.</u>*

34   Letter to Nikolaus Johann (November 1822) *Liebloses Betragen*

35   Letter to Nikolaus Johann (4 August 1825) *Pseudo-Bruder*

36   Forbes p. 1007 Thayer/Forbes translates the German word *Trottel* with *imbecile*. I prefer the translation *dumbass.*

37   Forbes p. 1013

38   Forbes p. 1015

39   Gillberg p. 30

40   Caeyers p. 149 *Beethoven vond het moeilijk om nieuwe vriendschappen te sluiten.*

41   Coldicott p. 106

42   Stanford p. 118 *Over and over again I read in the literature that, despite appearances, Aspies don't intend to inflict hurt on others*

43   Swafford pp. 172-173

44   Letter to Wegeler (around 1795). *Lieber, Bester! in was für einem Abscheulichen Bilde* *hast du mich mir selbst dargestellt! o ich erkenne es, ich verdiene deine Freundschaft nicht, du bist so edel, so gutdenkend, und das ist das erstemal, daß ich mich nicht neben dir stellen darf, weit unter dir bin ich gefallen, ach ich habe meinem Besten, edelsten Freund 8 wochen Lang verdruß gemacht, du glaubst, ich habe an der Güte meines Herzens verlohren, dem Himmel sey dank; nein; – es war keine absichtliche, ausgedachte Boßheit von mir, die mich so gegen dich handeln ließ, es war mein unverzeihlicher Leichtsin, der mich nicht die Sache in dem Lichte sehen ließ, wie sie wirklich war. – o wie schäm ich mich für dir, wie für mir selbst – fast traue ich mich nicht mehr, dich um deine Freundschaft wieder zu bitten – Ach Wegeler nur mein einziger Trost ist, daß du mich fast seit meiner Kindheit kanntest, und doch o laß mich's selbst sagen, ich war doch immer gut, und bestrebte mich immer der Rech[t]schaffenheit und Biederkeit in meinen Handlungen; wie hättest du mich sonst lieben können? – sollte ich den[n] jezt seit der kurzen Zeit aufei[n]mal mich so schrecklich, so sehr zu meinem Nachtheil geändert haben – unmöglich, diese Gefühle des Großen des Guten sollten alle aufeinmal in mir erloschen seyn? nein Wegeler lieber, Bester, o wag es noch einmal, dich wieder ganz in die Arme deines B. zu werfen baue auf die guten Eigenschaften, die du sonst in ihm gefunden hast, ich stehe dir dafür, den neuen tempel der heiligen Freundschaft, den du darauf aufrichten wirst, er wird fest, ewig stehen, kein Zufall, kein Sturm wird ihn in seinen Grundfesten erschüttern können – fest, – Ewig – unsere Freundschaft – verzeihung – vergessenheit wieder aufleben der sterbenden sinkenden Freundschaft – o wegeler verstoße sie nicht diese Hand zur aussöhnung, gib die deinige in die meine – Ach Gott. – ach nichts mehr – ich selbst komm zu dir, und werfe mich in deine Arme, und bitte um den verlohrnen Freund, und du giebst dich mir wieder, dem reuevollen, dich liebenden, dich nie vergessenden Beethowen Jezt eben hab ich deinen Brief erhalten, weil ich erst nach hause gekommen bin –*

45   Letter to Wegeler (29 June 1801) [...] *nur hat der neidische Dämon, meine schlimme Gesundheit, mir einen schlechten Stein ins Brett geworfen nemlich: mein Gehör ist seit 3 Jahren immer schwächer geworden, und das soll sich durch meinen Unterleib, der schon damals wie Du weist elend war, hier aber sich verschlimmert hat indem ich beständig mit einem Durchfall behaftet war, und mit einer dadurch außerordentlichen schwäche, ereignet haben, Frank wollte meinem leib den Ton wieder geben durch stärkende Medizine und mein Gehör durch Mandelöhl, aber prosit , daraus ward nichts, mein gehör ward immer schlechter, und mein Unterleib blieb immer in seiner vorigen Verfassung, das dauerte bis voriges Jahr Herbst, wo ich manchmal in Verzweiflung war, da rieth mir ein Medizinischer asinus das kalte Bad für meinen Zustand, ein gescheiderer das gewöhnliche Lauwarme DonauBad, das that wunder, mein Bauch ward besser mein Gehör blieb oder ward noch schlechter, diesen Winter gieng's mir wircklich elend, da hatte ich wirckliche schreckliche Koliken, und ich sank wieder ganz in meinen Vorigen Zustand zurück; und so bliebs bis ohngefähr 4 Wochen, wo ich zu Wering gieng indem ich dachte, daß dieser Zustand zugleich auch einen Wundarzt erfodere, und ohnedem hatte ich immer vertrauen zu ihm, ihm gelang es nun fast gänzlich diesen heftigen Durchfall zu hemmen, er verordnete mir das laue Donaubad, wo ich jedesmal noch ein fläschgen stärkende sachen hineingießen muste, gab mir gar keine Medizin, bis vor ohngefähr 4 Tagen Pillen für den Magen und einen Thee für's Ohr, und darauf kann ich sagen befind ich mich stärker und besser <ich> nur meine ohren, die sausen und Brausen tag und Nacht fort; ich kann sagen, ich bringe mein Leben elend zu, seit 2 Jahren fast meide ich alle gesellschaften, weils mir nun nicht möglich ist, den Leuten zu sagen, ich bin Taub, hätte ich irgend ein anderes Fach, so giengs noch eher, aber in meinem Fach ist das ein schrecklicher Zustand, dabey meine Feinde, deren Anzahl nicht geringe ist, was würden diese hiezu sagen – um dir einen Begriff von dieser wunderbaren Taubheit zu geben, so sage ich dir, daß ich mich im Theater ganz dicht am Orchester <oder>gar anlehnen muß, um den schauspieler zu verstehen, die hohen Töne von Instrumenten singstimmen, wenn ich etwas weit weg bin höre ich nicht, im sprechen ist es zu Verwundern daß es Leute giebt die es niemals merkten, da ich meistens Zerstreuungen hatte, so hält man es dafür, manchmal auch hör ich den Redenden der leise spricht kaum, ja die Töne wohl, aber die worte nicht, und doch sobald jemand* *schreit, ist es mir unausstehlich, was es nun werden wird, das weiß der liebe Himmel, wering-sagt, daß es gewiß besser werden wird, wenn auch nicht ganz – ich habe schon oft den schöp-fer und mein daseyn verflucht, Plutarch hat mich zu der Resignation geführt, ich will wenn's anders möglich ist, meinem schicksaal trozen, obschon es Augenblicke meines Lebens geben wird, wo ich das unglücklichste Geschöpf gottes seyn werde. Ich bitte dich von diesem meinen Zustand niemanden auch nicht einmal der Lorchen etwas zu sagen, nur als geheymniß ver-traue ich dir's an, lieb wäre mirs, wenn du einmal mit Wering darüber Brief wechseltest, sollte mein Zustand fortdauern, so komme ich künftiges frühjahr zu dir, du miethe[s]t mir irgendwo in einer schönen Gegend ein Hauß auf dem Lande, und dann will ich ein halbes Jahr ein Bauer werden, vieleicht wird's dadurch geändert, resignation : welches elende Zufluchtsmit-tel, und mir bleibt es doch das einzige übrige. – [...]*

46   Letter to Wegeler (16 November 1801) *Du kannst es kaum glauben, wie öde, wie traurig ich mein Leben seit 2 Jahren zugebracht; wie ein Gespenst ist mir mein schwaches Gehör überall erschienen, und ich floh die Menschen, musste Misanthrop scheinen und bin's doch so wenig.*

47   Letter to Wegeler (2 May 1810) *Doch ich wäre glücklich, vielleicht einer der glück-lichsten Menschen, wenn nicht der Dämon in meinen Ohren seinen Aufenthalt aufgeschlagen. Hätte ich nicht irgendwo gelesen, der Mensch dürfe nicht freiwillig scheiden von seinem Leben, so lange er noch eine gute Tat verrichten kann, Längst wär' ich nicht mehr – und zwar durch mich selbst. – O so schön ist das Leben, aber bei mir ist es für immer vergiftet.*

48   Asperger p. 70 *The skills that a child acquires grow out of a tension between two opposite poles; one is spontaneous production, the other imitation of adult knowledge and skills. They have to balance each other if the achievement is to be of value. When original ideas are lacking achievement is an empty shell: what has been learnt is merely a superficial and mechanical copy. Autistic intelligence is characterized by precisely the opposite of this problem. Autistic children are able to produce original ideas. Indeed, they can only be original, and mechan-ical learning is hard for them. They are simply not set to assimilate and learn an adult's knowledge. Just as, in general, somebody's good and bad sides are inextricably linked, so the special abilities and disabilities of autistic people are interwoven.*

49   Swafford p. 147

50   Kopitz/Cadenbach p. 60 *[...] wie überhaupt sein Wesen nichts von äußerer Bildung verrieth, vielmehr unmanierlich in seinem ganzen Gebaren und Benehmen war.*

51   Letter to Lichnowsky (October 1806) *Fürst, was Sie sind, sind Sie durch Zufall und Geburt, was ich bin, bin ich durch mich; Fürsten hat es und wird es noch Tausende geben; Beethoven gibt's nur einen.*

52   Letter to Amenda (25 June 1799) *Lieber Amenda! nimm dieses Quartett als ein kleines Denkmal unserer Freundschaft, [und] so oft du dir es vorspielst, erinnere dich unserer durchlebten Tage und zugleich, wie innig gut dir war und immer seyn wird dein wahrer und warmer Freund Ludwig van Beethoven*

53   Letter to Amenda (1 July 1801) *Mein lieber, mein guter Amenda, mein herzlicher Freund! mit inniger Rührung, mit gemischtem Schmerz und Vergnügen habe ich deinen lezten Brief erhalten und gelesen. – womit soll ich deine Treue deine Anhänglichkeit an mich vergleichen, o das ist recht schön, daß du mir immer so gut geblieben, ja ich weiß dich auch mir vor allen bewährt und herauszuheben, du bist kein Wiener-Freund, nein du bist einer von denen wie sie mein Vaterländischer Boden hervorzubringen pflegt, wie oft wünsche ich dich*

bey mir, denn dein B. lebt sehr unglücklich, im streit mit Natur und schöpfer, schon mehrmals fluchte ich lezterm, daß er seine Geschöpfe dem kleinsten Zufall ausgesezt, so daß oft die
schönste Blüthe dadurch zernichtet und zerknikt wird, wisse, daß ich den für mich edelsten
Theil mein Gehör sehr abgenommen hat, schon damals als du noch bey mir warst, fühlte ich
davon spuren, und ich verschwieg's, nun ist es immer ärger geworden, ob es wird wieder können Geheilt werden, das steht noch zu erwarten, es soll von den Umständen meines Unterleibs
herrühren, was nun den betrift, so bin ich fast ganz hergestellt, ob nun auch das Gehör besser
wird werden, das hoffe ich zwar aber schwerlich, solche Krankheiten sind die unheilbarsten

54   Gillberg p. 30 *The teacher at school may be told that she has a foul breath, is ignorant,
or that she has ill-fitting clothes. Alternatively, she may be 'complimented' on having such a
nice bra. All these things may well be 'true'. The problem is that the child with Asperger
syndrome does not understand social rules, cannot judge the situation, and is unable to
conclude that 'certain things you just do not say in certain settings'*

55   Swafford p. 438

56   *WoO 100*
Schuppanzigh ist ein Lump.
Wer kennt ihn nicht,
den dicken Sauermagen,
den aufgeblasnen Eselskopf?
O Lump Schuppanzigh,
o Esel Schuppanzigh,
wir stimmen alle ein,
du bist der größte Esel,
o Esel, hi hi ha.

57   Gillberg p. 8; the phrase is from the Szatmari criteria

58   Caeyers p. 151 *In het geval van Zmeskall kan men zonder meer spreken over schaam-
teloze minachting en misbruik van vertrouwen.*

59   Letter to Amenda (1 July 1801) [...] *wie traurig ich nun leben muß, alles was mir lieb
und teuer ist meiden, und dann unter so elenden Egoistischen Menschen wie die Zmeskall,
Schuppanzig etc, [...] [Zmeskall] ist und bleibt zu schwach zur Freundschaft, ich betrachte ihn
und S. als bloße Instrumente, worauf ich, wenn's mir gefällt, spiele, aber nie können sie edle
Werkzeuge meiner innern und aüßern* Tätigkeit, *eben so wenig als wahre Teilnehmer von mir
werden, ich taxire sie nur nach dem, was sie mir leisten.*

60   Gillberg p. 54

61   Coldicott p. 106 Coldicott erroneously dates the quarrel "in 1806" rather than 1804.

62   Letter to Wegeler (29 June 1801) *Steffen Breuning ist nun hier und wir sind fast täg-
lich zusammen, es thut mir so wohl die alten Gefühle wieder hervorzurufen, er ist wirklich ein
guter Herrlicher Junge geworden der was weiß, und das Herz wie wir alle mehr oder weniger
auf dem Rechten Flecke hat [...]*

63   Letter to Ries (the week before 24 July 1804) *Breuning habe ich gar nichts mehr zu
sagen. Seine Denkungsart und Handlungsart in Rücksicht meiner beweiset, dass zwischen uns
nie ein freundschaftliches Verhältnis statt hätte finden sollen und auch gewiss nicht ferner
stattfinden wird.*

64   Letter to Ries (24 July 1804) *Mit der Sache von Breuning werden Sie sich wohl gewundert haben; glauben Sie mir, Lieber! dass mein Aufbrausen nur ein Ausbruch von manchen unangenehmen vorhergegangenen Zufällen mit ihm gewesen ist. Ich habe die Gabe, dass ich über eine Menge Sachen meine Empfindlichkeit verbergen und zurückhalten kann; werde ich aber auch einmal gereizt zu einer Zeit, wo ich empfänglicher für den Zorn bin, so platze ich auch stärker aus, als jeder andere. Breuning hat gewiss vortreffliche Eigenschaften, aber er glaubt sich von allen Fehlern frei, und hat meistens die am stärksten, welche er an andern Menschen zu finden glaubt. Er hat einen Geist der Kleinlichkeit, den ich von Kindheit an verachtet habe. Meine Beurteilungskraft hat mir fast vorher den Gang mit Breuning prophezeit, indem unsere Denkungs-, Handlungs- und Empfindungs-Weise zu verschieden ist, doch habe ich geglaubt, dass sich auch diese Schwierigkeiten überwinden ließen; - die Erfahrung hat mich widerlegt. Und nun auch keine Freundschaft mehr! Ich habe nur zwei Freunde in der Welt gefunden, mit denen ich auch nie in ein Missverhältnis gekommen, aber welche Menschen! Der eine ist tot, der andere lebt noch. Obschon wir fast sechs Jahre hindurch keiner von dem anderen etwas wissen, so weiß ich doch, dass in seinem Herzen ich die erste Stelle, so wie er in dem Meiningen einnimmt. Der Grund der Freundschaft heischt die größte Ähnlichkeit der Seelen und Herzen der Menschen. Ich wünsche nichts, als dass Sie meinen Brief läsen, den ich an Breuning geschrieben habe und den seinigen an mich. Nein, nie mehr wird er in meinem Herzen den Platz behaupten, den er hatte. Wer seinem Freunde eine so niedrige Denkungsart beimessen kann, und sich ebenfalls eine solche niedrige Handlungsart wider denselben erlauben, der ist nicht Wert der Freundschaft von mir.*

65   Letter to Stephan von Breuning (November 1804) *Hinter diesem Gemälde, mein guter, lieber Steffen, sei auf ewig verborgen, was eine Zeit lang zwischen uns vorgegangen. Ich weiß es, ich habe Dein Herz zerrissen. Die Bewegung in mir, die Du gewiss bemerken musstest, hatte mich genug dafür gestraft. Bosheit war's nicht, was in mir gegen Dich vorging, nein, ich wäre Deiner Freundschaft nie mehr würdig; Leidenschaft bei Dir und bei mir; aber Misstrauen gegen Dich ward in mir rege; es stellten sich Menschen gegen uns, die Deiner und meiner nie würdig sind. – Mein Portrait war Dir schon lange bestimmt; Du weißt es ja, dass ich es immer Jemanden bestimmt hatte. Wem könnte ich es wohl so mit dem wärmsten Herzen geben, als Dir, treuer, guter, edler Steffen! Verzeih mir, wenn ich Dir wehe tat; ich litt selbst nicht weniger. Als ich Dich so lange nicht mehr um mich sah, empfand ich es erst recht lebhaft, wie teuer Du meinem Herzen bist und ewig sein wirst. Dein
Du wirst wohl auch wieder in meine Arme fliehen, wie sonst.*

66   Quoted from Caeyers (2012) p. 380 *Wenn Eure Durchlaucht nur die Instrumente so besetzen, so scheiß ich drauf.*

67   Wegeler/Ries p. 93 *Ist der auch nichts anders, wie ein gewöhnlich Mensch! Nun wird er auch alle Menschenrechte mit Füssen treten, nur seinem Ehrgeiz frönen; er wird sich nun höher, wie alle Anders stellen, ein Tyrann werden!*

68   Stanford p. 220

69   Caeyers p. 359 *De aartshertog liet zich dat allemaal welgevallen omdat hij een onwankelbaar geloof had in de grootheid van Beethoven.*

70   Kopitz/Cadenbach pp. 355-356 *Zusammengefasster, energischer, inniger habe ich noch keinen Künstler gesehen. Ich begreife recht gut, wie er gegen die Welt wunderlich stehen muss.*

71   Kopitz/Cadenbach p. 359 *Beethoven habe ich in Teplitz kennengelernt. Sein Talent hat mich in Erstaunen gesetzt; allein er ist leider eine ganz ungebändigte Persönlichkeit, die zwar gar nicht unrecht hat, wenn sie die Welt detestabel findet, aber sie freilich dadurch weder für* *sich noch für andre genussreicher macht. Sehr zu entschuldigen ist er hingegen und sehr zu bedauern, da ihn sein Gehör verlässt, was vielleicht dem musikalischen Teil seines Wesens weniger als dem geselligen schadet. Er, der ohnehin lakonischer Natur ist, wird es nun doppelt durch diesen Mangel.*

72   Kopitz/Cadenbach p. 363 *An den Beethoven wollte er gar nicht heran. – Ich sagte ihm aber, ich könne ihm nicht helfen, und spielte ihm nun das erste Stück der C Moll-Symphonie vor. Das berührte ihn ganz seltsam. – Er sagte erst: 'das bewegt aber gar nichts; das macht nur Staunen; das ist grandios,' und dann brummte er so weiter, und fing nach langer Zeit wieder an: „das ist sehr groß, ganz toll, man möchte sich fürchten, das Haus fiele ein; und wenn das nun alle die Menschen zusammenspielen!'*

73   Kopitz/Cadenbach p. 200 *O, an den gestrigen Tag werde ich denken! In dem jungen Menschen steckt der Satan. Nie habe ich so spielen gehört! Er phantasierte auf ein von mir gegebenes Thema, wie ich selbst Mozart nie phantasieren gehört habe. Dann spielte er eigene Kompositionen, die im höchsten Grade wunderbar und großartig sind, und er bringt auf dem Klavier Schwierigkeiten und Effekte hervor, von denen wir uns nie etwas haben träumen lassen.*

74   Kopitz/Cadenbach p. 200 *Er ist ein kleiner, hässlicher, schwarz und störrisch aussehender junger Mann, ... und er heißt Beethoven.*

75   Coldicott p. 122

76   Letter to Peters (17 July 1823) *übrigens liegen ganz andere gelder für mich bereit u. man wartet gern, indem man rücksicht auf meine Kunst u. widerum meine schwächliche Gesundheit nimmt. – seyn sie versichert ich habe sie moralisch oder vielmehr merkantilisch u. musikalisch erkannt, nichts desto weniger werde ich wegen ihrem liegenden Gelde rücksicht nehmen, denn ich bin Mann in vollem verstande, ich brauche nicht Ehren hinzuzu sezen –*

77   Wolanek's letter to Beethoven (March 1825) *Da ich mit dem Einsetzen des Finale in Partitur zu Ostern erst fertig werden kann, und Sie selbes um diese Zeit nicht mehr benötigen können, so übersende ich nebst dem bereits angefangen die sämtlichen Stimmen zu Ihrer gefälligen Disposition.*
Dankbar bleibe ich für die erwiesene Ehre Ihrer mir zugekommenen Beschäftigung verpflichtet; was ferner das sonstige mishelle Betragen gegen mich betrifft, so kann ich belächelnd selbes nur als eine angenommene Gemüthsaufwallung ansehen: in der Töne Ideen Werth herrschen so viele Dissonanzen, sollten sie es nicht auch in der wirklichen?
Tröstend ist mir nur die feste Überzeugung, dass dem Mozart u Haydn, jenen gefeierten Künstlern, bei Ihnen, in der Eigenschaft als Kopisten, ein mir gleiches Schicksal zugeteilt würde;
Ich ersuche nur, mich mit jenen gemeinen Copiat ur Subjekt en nicht zu vermengen, die selbst bei sklavischer Behandlung sich glücklich preisen, ihre Exi stenz behaupten zu kennen.
Übrigens nehmen Sie die Versicherung, dass, auch nur um eines Körnleins Werth, ich nie Ursache habe, meines Betragens willen vor Ihnen erröthen zu müssen.
mit Hochachtung ergebner
Ferd. Wolanek

78   Letter to Wolanek (March 1825) *Dummer Eingebildeter Eselhafter Kerl! Mit einem solchen Lumpen-Kerl, der einem das Geld abstielt, wird man noch Komplimente machen, statt dessen zieht man ihn bei seinen Eselhaften Ohren. Schreib-Sudler! Dummer Kerl! Korrigieren sie ihre durch Unwissenheit, Übermut, Eigendünkel u. Dummheit gemachten Fehler, dies schickt sich besser, als mich belehren zu wollen denn das ist gerade, als wenn die Sau die Minerva lehren wollte. Beethoven!*

Mozart und Haydn erzeigen Sie die Ehre, ihrer nicht zu erwähnen. Es war schon gestern und noch früher beschlossen, Sie nicht mehr für mich schreiben zu machen.

79   Asperger p. 86 *Many autistic people lead solitary lives and do not marry and have children.*

80   Coldicott pp. 106-107

81   Wegeler/Ries p. 55 [...] *immer in Liebesverhältnissen* [...]

82   Forbes p. 232

83   Wegeler/Ries pp. 139-141 *Beethoven sah Frauenzimmer sehr gerne, besonders schöne jugendliche Gesichter, und gewöhnlich, wenn wir an einem etwas reizenden Mädchen vorbeigingen, drehte er sich um, sah es mit seinem Glase nochmals scharf an und lachte oder grinste, wenn er sich von mir bemerkt fand. Er war sehr häufig verliebt, aber meistens nur auf kurze Dauer. Da ich ihm einmal mit der Eroberung einer schönen Dame neckte, gestand er, die habe ihn am stärksten und längsten gefesselt – nämlich sieben volle Monate. –*
Eines Abends kam ich zu ihm nach Baden, um meine Lektionen fortzusetzen. Dort fand ich eine schöne, junge Dame bei ihm auf dem Sopha sitzen. Da es mir schien, als käme ich ungelegen, so wollte ich gleich mich entfernen, allein Beethoven hielt mich zurück und sagte: 'Spielen Sie nur einstweilen!' Er und die Dame blieben hinter mir sitzen. Ich hatte schon sehr lange gespielt, als Beethoven auf einmal rief: 'Ries! spielen Sie etwas Verliebtes!' Kurz nachher: 'etwas Melancholisches!' Dann: 'etwas Leidenschaftliches!' u. s. w. –
Aus dem, was ich hörte, könnte ich schließen, dass er wohl die Dame in etwas beleidigt haben müsse und es nun durch Launen gut machen wolle. Endlich sprang er auf und schrie: ,Das sind ja lauter Sachen von mir!' Ich hatte nämlich immer Sätze aus seinen eigenen Werken nur durch einige kurze Übergänge an einander gereiht, vorgetragen, was ihm aber Freude gemacht zu haben schien. Die Dame ging alsbald fort, und Beethoven wusste zu meinem großen Erstaunen nicht, wer sie war. Ich hörte nun, dass sie kurz vor mir hereingekommen sei, um Beethoven kennen zu lernen. Wir folgten ihr bald nach, um ihre Wohnung, und dadurch später ihren Stand zu erforschen. Von Weiten sahen wir sie noch (es war mondhell), allein plötzlich war sie verschwunden. Wir spazierten nachher unter mannigfaltigen Gesprächen wohl noch anderthalb Stunden in dem angrenzenden schönen Thal. Beim Weggehen sagte Beethoven jedoch: 'Ich muss herausfinden, wer sie ist, und Sie müssen helfen.' Lange Zeit nachher begegnete ich ihr in Wien und entdeckte nun, dass es die Geliebte eines ausländischen Prinzen war. Ich teilte meine Nachricht Beethoven mit, habe aber nie, weder von ihm, noch von sonst jemand etwas Weiteres über sie gehört.

84   Letter to Eleonore von Breuning (2 November 1793) *Verehrungswürdige Eleonore! meine theuerste Freundin! Erst nach dem ich nun hier in der Hauptstadt bald ein ganzes Jahr verlebt habe, erhalten sie von mir einen Brief, und doch waren sie gewiß in einem immerwährenden lebhaften Andenken bey mir. sehr oft unterhielt ich mich mit ihnen und ihrer lieben Familie, nur öfters mit der Ruhe nicht, die ich dabey gewünscht hätte. da war's, wo mir der fatale Zwist noch vorschwebte, wobey mir mein damaliges Betragen so verabscheuungswerth vorkam, aber es war geschehen; o wie viel gäbe ich dafür, wäre ich im Stande meine damalige mich so sehr entehrende, sonst meinem Charakter zuwider laufende Art zu handeln ganz aus meinem Leben tilgen zu können. freylich waren mancherley Umstände, die unß immer von einander entfernten, und wie ich vermuthe, war das Zuflüstern von den wechselweise gegen einander gehaltenen Reden von einem gegen den andern, Hauptsächlich dasjenige, was alle Übereinstimmung verhinderte. Jeder von unß glaubte hier, er spreche mit wahrer überzeugung, und doch war es nur angefachter Zorn, und wir waren beyde getaüscht. ihr guter und edler Charackter meine liebe Freundin bürgt mir zwar dafür, daß sie mir längst* *vergeben haben, aber man sagt, die aufrichtigste reue sey diese, wo man sein verbrechen selbst gestehet, dieses habe ich gewollt. – und lassen sie unß nun den Vorhang für diese ganze Geschichte ziehen, und nur noch die Lehre davon nehmen, daß, wenn Freunde in streit gerathen, es immer besser sey, keinen vermitteler dazu zu brauchen, sondern der Freund sich an den Freund unmittelbar wende.*

85   Wegeler/Ries p. 72 […] *eine Dame, welche von allen Personen weiblichen Geschlechts, die ich in einem ziemlich bewegten Leben, bis zum hohen Alter hinaus, kennen lernte, dem Ideal eines vollkommenen Frauenzimmers am nächsten stand.*

86   Letter to Wegeler (16 November 1801) *Etwas angenehmer lebe ich jetzt wieder, indem ich mich mehr unter Menschen gemacht. Du kannst es kaum glauben, wie öde, wie traurig ich mein Leben seit 2 Jahren zugebracht; wie ein Gespenst ist mir mein schwaches Gehör überall erschienen, und ich floh die Menschen, musste Misanthrop scheinen und bin's doch so wenig. – Diese Veränderung hat ein liebes, zauberisches Mädchen hervorgebracht, das mich liebt, und das ich liebe; es sind seit 2 Jahren wieder einige selige Augenblicke, und es ist das erste mal, dass ich fühle, dass heiraten glücklich machen könnte; leider ist sie nicht vom meinem Stande, - und jetzt – könnte ich nun freilich nicht heiraten; ich muss mich nun noch wacker herumtummeln.*

87   Kopitz/Cadenbach p. 268 *Man glaubte Engelschöre zu hören, welche den Eingang meines armes Kindes in die Welt des Lichtes feierten.*

88   Kopitz/Cadenbach p. 268 *Er war sehr reizbar, sehr aufbrausend, sehr empfindlich und dadurch oft ungerecht und misstrauisch gegen seine besten Freunde. Wer hätte aber der durch seine zunehmende Taubheit so unglückliche Mann gram sein können! Man muss seinen physischen und moralischen Leiden Rechnung tragen und ihm Alles vergeben. Auf diese Weise haben wir jahrelang in ungetrübter Freundschaft gelebt.*

89   Letter to Erdödy (8 March 1808) *Meine lieber Gräfin ich habe gefehlt, das ist wahr – verzeihen sie mir, Es ist gewiss nicht vorsätzliche Bosheit von mir, wenn ich ihnen wehe getan habe – erst seit gestern Abend weiß ich recht wie alles ist, und es tut mir sehr leid, dass ich so handelte – lesen sie ihr Billet kaltblütig, und urteilen sie selbst, ob ich das verdient habe, und ob sie damit nicht alles Sechsfach mir wiedergegeben haben, indem ich sie beleidigte ohne es zu wollen. Schicken sie mir noch heute mein Billet zurück, und schreiben mir nur mit einem Worte, dass sie wieder gut sind, ich leide unendlich dadurch, wenn sie dieses nicht tun, ich kann nichts tun, wenn das so fortdauern soll – ich erwarte ihre Verzeihung.*

90   Taken from Goethe's play *Egmont*.

91   Letter to Therese Malfatti (May 1810) *Sie erhalten hier, verehrte Therese, das Versprochene, und wären nicht die triftigsten Hindernisse gewesen, so erhielten Sie noch mehr, um Ihnen zu zeigen, dass ich immer mehr meinen Freunden leiste, als ich verspreche. – Ich hoffe, und zweifle nicht daran, dass Sie sich ebenso schön beschäftigen als angenehm unterhalten – letzteres doch nicht zu sehr, damit man auch noch unser gedenke. – Es wäre wohl zu viel gebaut auf Sie oder meinen Wert zu hoch angesetzt, wenn ich Ihnen zuschriebe: „Die Menschen sind nicht nur zusammen, wenn sie beisammen sind; auch der Entfernte, der Abgeschiedene lebt in uns". Wer wollte der flüchtigen, alles im Leben leicht behandelnden Therese so etwas zuschreiben? – Vergessen Sie doch ja nicht in Ansehung an Ihrer Beschäftigung das Klavier oder überhaupt die Musik im ganzen genommen. Sie haben so schönes Talent dazu; warum es nicht ganz kultivieren? Sie, die für alles Schöne und Gute so viel Gefühl haben, warum wollen Sie dieses nicht anwenden, um in einer so schönen Kunst auch das Vollkommenere zu erkennen, das selbst auf uns immer wieder zurückstrahlt? – Ich lebe sehr einsam und still, obschon* *hier oder da mich Lichter aufwecken möchten, so ist doch eine ausfüllbare Lücke, seit sie alle fort von hier sind, in mir entstanden, worüber selbst meine Kunst, die mir sonst so getreu ist, noch keinen Triumph hat erhalten können.*

92   Letter to Therese Malfatti (May 1810) *Leben Sie nun wohl, verehrte Therese! Ich wünsche Ihnen alles, was im Leben gut und schön ist. Erinnern Sie sich meiner und gern – vergessen Sie das Tolle – Seien Sie überzeugt, niemand kann Ihr Leben froher, glücklicher wissen wollen als ich, und selbst dann, wenn Sie gar keinen Anteil nehmen an Ihrem ergebensten Diener und Freund Beethoven.*
N.B. Es wäre wohl sehr hübsch von Ihnen, in einigen Zeilen mir zu sagen, worin ich Ihnen hier dienen kann.

93   Letter to Gleichenstein, June 1810 *Deine Nachricht stürzte mich aus den Regionen des höchsten Entzückens wieder tief herab – wozu denn der Zusatz, du wolltest mir es sagen lassen, wenn wieder Musik sei, bin ich denn gar nichts als dein Musikus oder der andern? – so ist es wenigstens auszulegen.*

94   Letter to Gleichenstein, June 1810 – *So sei es denn, für Dich, armer B., gibt es kein Glück von außen, Du mußt Dir Alles in Dir selbst erschaffen, nur in der idealen Welt findest Du Freunde. –*

95   Stephan von Breuning's letter to Franz Wegeler (11 August 1810) Kopitz/Cadenbach p.257 [...] *ich glaube, seine Heyraths Parthie hat sich zerschlagen* [...]

96   Letter to Bettina Brentano (February 1811) *nun lebwohl liebe liebe B. ich küsse dich auf deine Stirne, und drücke damit, wie mit einem Siegel, alle meine Gedanken für dich auf Schreiben Sie bald, bald, oft Ihrem Freund Beethoven*

97   Letter to Antonie Brentano-Birkenstock (6 February 1816) [...] *dass ich die Stunden, welche ich in ihrer beyderseitigen Gesellschaft zubrachte, als die mir unvergesslichsten mir gern zurückrufe* [...]

98   Kopitz/Cadenbach p. 257 *Vorgestern war Beethoven wieder mehrere Stunden in unserer Mitte. Dieser Abend hinterließ mir einen ungemein angenehmen Eindruck, welcher den Wunsch mit sich führt, mehrere ihm ähnliche zu erleben. Er zeigt sich uns, oder vielmehr wir sehen ihn immer mehr in jenem schönen Lichte, welches die wahrhaft Guten umgibt. Was er von seinem Freunde erzählte, von seiner vortrefflichen Mutter, sein Urteil über Männer, die sich mit ihm in eine Linie stellen, alles zeugt von einem ebenso gebildeten Herzen als Verstand. Überhaupt finde ich das Meiste was er spricht, wert aufgeschrieben zu werden, so richtig und gediegen ist es. Wenn ihm unsere Gesellschaft recht unentbehrlich werden könnte, so würde es mich recht glücklich machen!*

99   Kopitz/Cadenbach p. 322 *Daß Beethoven auf uns böse ist, ist etwas was mich die Zeit her recht sehr betrübte, obwohl die Art wie er es zeigte, das traurige Gefühl mehr in ein bitteres umschuf. Es ist wahr, daß der Vater nicht artig gegen ihn gehandelt hat, aber Menschen die ihm ihre Achtung und Liebe jederzeit so bewiesen haben wie wir, sollte er nicht mit beißendem Spott zurückweisen wollen. Er hat jenen Brief wohl in einer seiner menschenfeindlichen Launen geschrieben und ich verzeihe es gern.*

100   Kopitz/Cadenbach p. 327 [...] *als mich Beethovens Brief an den Vater, in welchem er eine so höchst kränkende Meinung von mir zeigt, im Innersten schmerzt, ja empörte.*[...] *Noch nie habe ich eine so kränkende Erfahrung gemacht und von einem Menschen, welchen ich so sehr hochschätzte, schmerzt sie desto mehr.*

101 Kopitz/Cadenbach p. 340 *Einmal kam ich mit Beethoven in sehr unangenehme Kon-flikte, weil er geglaubt hatte, ich gäbe ihm in seiner Handlungsweise Unrecht gegen seinen Neffen.*

102 Letter to Nanette Streicher (18 June 1818) *Beste Frau v. Streicher! Es war nicht möglich, ihnen eher zu schreiben auf ihr letztes. Ich hätte ihnen schon einige Täge zuvor als die Dienstbothen weggejagt wurden geschrieben, zauderte aber noch mit meinem Entschluß, bis ich gewahr wurde, daß besondere Frau D... Karl abhielte alles zu gestehn; ›Die Mutter sollte er doch schonen‹ sagte sie ihm; eben so wirkte die Peppi mit; natürlich wollten sie nicht entdeckt werden; beide haben schändlich mitgespielt, und sich brauchen lassen von der Frau v. Beethoven; beide empfingen Kaffee und Zucker von ihr, die Peppi Geld, die Alte vermuth-lich auch dasselbe; denn es unterliegt gar keinem Zweifel, daß sie bei der Mutter Karls selbst gewesen; sie sagte auch zu Karl daß, wenn ich sie aus dem Dienst jagte, sie gleich zu seiner Mutter gehen würde. Dies geschah bei Gelegenheit, als ich ihr ihr Betragen verwiesen, womit ich öfter Ursache hatte unzufrieden zu sein; die Peppi, welche öftere lauschte, was ich mit Karl sprach, schien versucht zu werden, die Wahrheit gestehen zu wollen, allein die Alte hielt ihr ihre Dummheit vor und zankte sie tüchtig aus – und so verstockte sie wieder, und suchte mich auf falsche Spuren zu bringen. – Die Geschichte dieser abscheulichen Verrätherei kann beinahe 6 Wochen gedauert haben, beide würden nicht so bei einem weniger großmüthigen Menschen davon gekommen sein. Die Peppi erhielt von mir 9 oder 10 fl. für Hembdentuch, die sie aufnahm, und ich ihr hernach schenkte, und erhielt statt 60 fl.: 70 fl.; sie hätte schon können sich diese elenden Bestechungen versagen. Bei der Alten, die sich überhaupt am schlechte sten benommen, mag wohl Haß mitgewirkt haben, da sie sich immer zurückgesetzt glaubte, (ohnerachtet sie mehr erhalten als sie verdient) denn selbst durch ihr hohnlächelndes Gesicht an einem Tage, als mich Karl umarmte, ahndete ich Verrätherei, und wie schändlich eine solche alte Frau, wie heimtückisch sie sein konnte. Stellen sie sich vor, 2 Täge vorher als ich hieher mich begab, ging K. ohne mein Wissen nachmittags zu seiner Mutter, und sowohl die Alte als P. wußten es ebenfalls. Aber hören sie den Triumpf einer greifen Verrätherin; als ich mit K. und ihr hieher fuhr, sprach ich mit K. über die Sache im Wagen, obschon ich noch nicht alles wußte, und indem ich Furcht äußerte, daß wir in Mödling nicht sicher würden sein, rief sie aus, ›ich sollte mich nur auf sie verlassen‹. O der Schändlichkeit! Nur 2 mal mit diesemmal ist mir in dem sonst ehrwürdigen Alter beim Menschen nur so etwas vorgekommen.*

103 Letter to Nanette Streicher (7 February 1817) *Ich bitte sie tausendmal um Verzeihung wegen gestern; es war eine Zusammenkunft wegen der Angelegenheit meines Neffen, [...] und bei dergleichen bin ich vielleicht immer in Gefahr den Kopf zu verlieren; so ging es auch gestern. Mögen sie sich nur nicht dadurch beleidigt finden [...]*

104 Letter to Josephine von Brunsvik (March/April 1805) *Wie ich sagte die Sache mit Lichnowsky ist nicht so arg meine Geliebte J. als man sie ihnen machte – Lichnowsky. hatte durch Zufall das Lied an die Hoffnung bei mir liegen sehen, ohne daß ich es bemerkte, und er auch nichts darüber sagte, er schloss aber hieraus, daß ich wohl nicht ganz ohne Neigung für sie sein würde, und als nun Zmeskall in der Angelegenheit von ihnen und Tante Guicci-ardi zu ihm kam, fragte er ihn, ob er nicht wüste, ob ich öfter zu ihnen gehe, Zmeskall sagte nicht ja und nicht nein, im Grunde konnte er auch nichts sagen, da ich seiner Wachsamkeit mich so sehr als möglich entzogen hatte – Lichnowsky sagte, er glaube bemerkt zu haben, daß ich nicht ohne Neigung für sie durch einen Zufall (das Lied), Wovon er aber wie er mich hoch und teuer versicherte Zmeskall nichts gesagt hatte. – und Zmeskall solle mit der Tante Guicciardi reden, daß sie mit ihnen spräche, daß sie mich mehr aufmunterten meine Oper zu vollenden, indem er glaube, daß das viel gutes Wirken könne, indem er sicher wüste, wie viel Achtung ich für sie hätte – das ist das ganze Factum – Zmeskall – vergrößerte es – und Tante Guicciardi – ebenfalls – unterdessen – können sie nun ruhig sein, indem Niemand als diese zwei Personen in Anschlag kommen – L. sagte selbst, daß er selbst zu sehr mit Delikatesse*

Bekannt sei, als daß er auch nur ein Wort gesagt hätte, wenn er für gewiss ein engeres Verhältnis vorausgesetzt hätte– im Gegenteil wünsche er nichts so sehr als daß ein solches Verhältnis zwischen ihnen und mir entstehen möge, wenn es möglich wäre, indem, so viel man ihm von ihrem Charakter berichtet habe, dieses nicht anders als Vorteilhaft für mich sein könne. – basta così – Es ist nun Wahr, ich bin nicht so tätig als ich hätte sein sollen – aber ein innerer Gram – hatte mich lang – meiner sonst gewöhnlichen Spannkraft beraubt, einige Zeit hindurch als das Gefühl der Liebe in mir für sie angebetete J. / zu keimen anfing, vermehrte sich dieser noch – sobald wir einmal wieder ungestört beisammen sind, dann sollen sie von meinen wirklichen Leiden und von dem Kampf mit mir selbst zwischen Tod und Leben, denn ich einige Zeit hindurch führte unterrichtet sein – Ein Ereignis machte mich lange Zeit an aller Glückseligkeit des Lebens hienieden zweifeln – nun ist es nicht halb mehr so arg, ich habe ihr Herz gewonnen, o ich weiß es gewiss, welchen Wert ich drauf zu legen habe, meine Tätigkeit wird sich wieder Vermehren, und – hier verspreche ich es ihnen hoch und teuer, in kurzer Zeit werde ich meiner und ihrer Würdiger da stehen – o mögen sie doch einigen Werth drauf legen, durch ihre Liebe meine Glückseligkeit zu gründen – zu Vermehren – o geliebte J., nicht der Hang zum andern Geschlechte zieht mich zu ihnen, nein nur sie ihr ganzes Ich mit allen ihren Eigenheiten – haben meine / Achtung – alle meine Gefühle – mein ganzes Empfindungsvermögen an sie gefesselt – als ich zu ihnen kam – war ich in der festen Entschlossenheit, auch nicht einen Funken Liebe in mir keimen zu lassen, sie haben mich aber überwunden – ob sie das wollten? – oder nicht wollten? – diese Frage könnte mir J. wohl einmal auflösen – Ach Himmel, was mögt ich ihnen noch alles sagen – wie ich an sie denke – was ich für sie fühle – aber wie schwach wie armselig diese Sprache – wenigstens die meinige – / Lange – Lange – Dauer – möge unsrer Liebe werden – sie ist so edel – so sehr auf wechselseitige Achtung und Freundschaft gegründet. – selbst die große Ähnlichkeit in so manchen Sachen, im Denken und empfinden – o sie lassen mich hoffen, dass ihr Herz lange – für mich schlagen werde – das meinige kann nur – aufhören – für sie zu schlagen – wenn – es gar nicht mehr schlägt – geliebte J.
leben sie Wohl – Ich hoffe aber auch– dass sie durch mich ein wenig glücklich werden – sonst wär ich ja – eigennützig

105 Letter to Josephine von Brunsvik (April/May 1805) *Es darf wohl keines Beweises – wie gern ich heute zu ihnen gekommen – aber – nur Überhäufung von Arbeiten – und noch dazu erst diese Nacht um halb 3 – nach hause gekommen – sie waren so Traurig gestern Liebe J. – kann ich denn gar nichts auf sie wirken – da sie ja doch so sehr auf mich wirken – mich so glücklich machen – überlassen sie sich doch ja so sehr nicht ihrem Hange zur Traurigkeit, wie wehe tut es mir sie so zu sehen – und umso mehr, wenn man nicht weiß, wie oder wo man helfen kann - hier ihr – ihr– Andante […]*

106 Josephine's letter (draft) to Beethoven (First quarter of 1805) *Mein Herz haben Sie schon längst, lieber Beethoven […] den größten beweis meiner Liebe – meine Achtung empfangen Sie, durch dieß Geständnis, durch daß Vertrauen! […] – Nicht mein Herz zerreißen - Nicht weiter in mich dringen – Ich liebe Sie unaussprechlich – wie ein frommer Geist den andern – Sind sie dieses Bündnis nicht fähig? – Andrer Liebe bin ich nicht für jetzt nicht empfänglich.*

107 Letter to Josephine von Brunsvik (20 September 1807) *Liebe, geliebte, einzige Josephine! – auch wieder nur einige Zeilen von ihnen – machen mir große Freude – Wie oft habe ich geliebte Josephine. mit mir selbst gekämpft, um das Verbot, welches ich mir auferlegte, nicht zu überschreiten – aber es ist vergebens, Tausend Stimmen flüstern mir immer zu, dass sie meine einzige Freundin meine einzige Geliebte sind – ich vermag es nicht mehr zu halten, was ich mir selbst auferlegt, o liebe Josephine, lassen sie uns unbekümmert auf jenem Wege wandeln, worauf wir oft so glücklich waren – Morgen oder übermorgen sehe ich sie, möge der Himmel mir eine ungestörte Stunde bescheren, wo ich mit ihnen bin, um einmal die lang'*

Entbehrte Unterredung zu haben, wo einmal wieder mein Herz und meine Seele ihnen wieder begegnen kann.

108   Letter to Josephine von Brunsvik (6/7 July 1812) *Am 6. Juli Morgens*
Mein Engel, mein alles, mein Ich! - Nur einige Worte heute, und zwar mit Bleistift (mit deinem); – erst bis morgen ist meine Wohnung sicher bestimmt, welcher Nichtswürdige Zeitverderb in d.g. – warum dieser tiefe Gram, wo die Notwendigkeit spricht – Kann unsre Liebe anders bestehen als durch Aufopferungen, durch nicht alles verlangen, kannst Du es ändern, dass Du nicht ganz mein, ich nicht ganz dein bin? – Ach Gott blick in die schöne Natur und beruhige Dein Gemüth über das müssende – die Liebe fordert alles und ganz mit recht, so ist es mir mit Dir, Dir mit mir – nur vergisst du so leicht, dass ich für mich und für Dich leben muss - wären wir ganz vereinigt, Du würdest dieses schmerzliche eben so wenig als ich empfinden – meine Reise war schrecklich - ich kam erst Morgens 4 Uhr gestern hier an, da es an Pferden mangelte, wählte die Post eine andere Reiseroute, aber welch schrecklicher Weg, auf der vorletzten Station warnte man mich bei Nacht zu fahren, machte mich einen Wald fürchten, aber das reizte mich nur – und ich hatte Unrecht, der wagen musste bei dem schrecklichen Wege brechen, grundlos, bloßer Landweg, ~~und die~~ ohne 2 solche Postillione, wie ich hatte, wäre ich liegen geblieben Unterwegs – Esterhazi hatte auf dem andern gewöhnlichen Wege hierhin dasselbe Schicksal mit 8 Pferden, was ich mit vier – jedoch hatte ich zum Teil wieder Vergnügen, wie immer, wenn ich was glücklich über-
stehe. – nun geschwind zum Inneren vom Äußern; wir werden uns wohl bald sehn, auch heute kann ich dir meine Bemerkungen nicht mittheilen, welche ich während dieser einigen Tage über mein Leben machte – wären unsre Herzen immer dicht an einander, ich machte wohl keine d.g. die Brust ist voll, Dir viel zu sagen – ach – es gibt Momente, wo ich finde, dass die Sprache noch gar nichts ist – erheitere dich – bleibe mein treuer, einziger Schatz, mein alles, wie ich Dir; das übrige müssen die Götter schicken, was für uns sein muss und sein soll. – Dein treuer Ludwig

---

Abends Montags am 6ten Juli.
Du leidest du mein teuerstes Wesen – eben jetzt nehme ich wahr, dass die Briefe in aller Frühe aufgegeben werden müssen. Montags – Donnerstags – die einzigen Tage wo die Post von hier nach Karlsbad geht – Du leidest – ach, wo ich bin, bist Du mit mir, mit mir und Dir werde ich machen, dass ich mit Dir leben kann, welches Leben!!! so!!! ohne dich – verfolgt von der Güte der Menschen hier und da, die ich meine – eben so wenig verdienen zu wollen, als sie zu verdienen – Demuth des Menschen gegen den Menschen – sie schmerzt mich – und wenn ich mich im Zusammenhang des Universums betrachte, was bin ich und was ist der – den man den Größten nennt – und doch – ist wieder hierin das Göttliche des Menschen – ich weine wenn ich denke dass du erst wahrscheinlich Sonnabends die erste Nachricht von mir erhältst – wie du mich auch liebst – stärker liebe ich dich doch – doch nie verberge dich vor mir – gute Nacht! – als Badender muss ich schlafen gehen – ~~o geh mit, geh mit~~ - ach Gott – so nah! so weit! ist es nicht ein wahres Himmelsgebäude unsre Liebe – aber auch so fest, wie die Veste des Himmels. –

---

guten Morgen am 7. Juli –
schon im Bette drängen sich die Ideen zu dir, meine Unsterbliche Geliebte, hier und da freudig, dann wieder traurig, vom Schicksale abwartend, ob es uns erhört – leben kann ich entweder nur ganz mit dir oder gar nicht, ja ich habe beschlossen in der Ferne so lange herum zu irren, bis ich in deine Arme fliegen kann, und mich ganz heimatlich bei dir nennen kann, meine Seele von dir umgeben ins Reich der Geister schicken kann – ja leider muss es sein – du wirst dich fassen, umso mehr da du meine Treue gegen dich kennst, nie eine andre kann mein Herz besitzen nie – nie – O Gott warum sich entfernen müssen, was man so liebt, und doch ist mein Leben in Wien so wie jetzt ein kümmerliches Leben – Deine Liebe macht mich zum

*glücklichsten und zum unglücklichsten zugleich – in meinen Jahren jetzt bedürfte ich einiger
Einförmigkeit Gleichheit des Lebens – kann diese bei unserm Verhältnisse bestehen? – Engel,
eben erfahre ich, dass die Post alle Tage abgeht – und ich muss daher schließen, damit Du
den Brief gleich erhältst – sei ruhig, nur durch Ruhiges beschauen unsres Daseins können wir
unsern Zweck zusammen zu leben erreichen – sei ruhig – liebe mich – heute – gestern – welche Sehnsucht mit Tränen nach dir – dir – dir – mein Leben – mein alles – leb wohl – o liebe
mich fort – verken[ne] nie das treuste Herz
deines Geliebten
L.
ewig Dein
ewig mein
ewig uns*

109   Caeyers p. 458 *Beethoven heeft dit belangrijke moment van onthechting en berusting
muzikaal gedocumenteerd in de liedcyclus* An die ferne Geliebte *(op. 98) die hij in april
1816 had beëindigd.*

110   Swafford p. 677

111   Caeyers pp.458-459 *Dit is meer dan een bericht aan de geliefde, het is een boodschap aan de wereld. Door deze gedichten te toonzetten én uit te geven, deed Beethoven
immers een publieke bekentenis die zowel de bevestiging van het bestaan als het afstand
nemen van zijn 'onsterfelijke geliefde' bevatte. Deze nostalgische hymne aan de verloren
liefde is echter vooral een loflied aan de kunst, het enige overgebleven communicatiemiddel
tot de geliefde[.]*

112   Swafford p. 677

113   Quoted from Klapproth p. 143

114   Swafford p. 755

115   Swafford p. 755

116   Klapproth p. 148

117   Coldicott p. 103

118   Swafford p. xiii

119   Caeyers p. 41 *Daarnaast krijgen wij de eerste getuigenissen over Beethovens ingewik-
kelde psyche en de neiging om in zichzelf gekeerd te zijn – andere tijdgenoten kleefden daar
zelfs al het etiket 'misantropie' op.*

120   Asperger p. 37

121   Gillberg p. 4 *People with Asperger syndrome – with their lack of flexibility and, often,
stunning egocentricity – have major problems coping with 'normal' life. At the same time,
many are 'free thinkers' and may be scientifically and aesthetically highly skilled people.*

122   Stanford p. 22

123   Asperger p. 77 *It has been my aim to show that the fundamental disorder of autistic* *individuals is the limitation of their social relationships. […] The nature of these children is revealed most clearly in their behavior towards other people*

124   Gillberg p. 30

125   Gillberg p. 32

126   Gillberg p. 30

127   Kopitz/Cadenbach pp. 569-570 *Er war schon als Kind in s[ich] gekehrt u. ernsthaft, d. gewöhl.[iche]n Kinderspiele waren nie s[ei]ne Unterhalt[un]g. […] d[a] er außer Musik nichts verstehe, was zum geselligem Leben gehöre, desh. sei er so verdrießl. unt. anderen Menschen, könne nicht mitsprechen u. ziehe s. zurück, d[a] man ihn für e. Misanthropen halte.*

128   Asperger p. 45 *We see here something that we have come across in almost all autistic individuals, a special interest which enables them to achieve quite extraordinary levels of performance in a certain area.*

129   Gillberg pp. 33-34 *Even when interests change, the style in which they are adhered to rarely does. Again, it has to be said that it is not the interest in itself, but rather the character of the person's relationship to the interest, that is the problem. The individual with Asperger syndrome so engrosses himself in the interest that it becomes tedious, indeed often painfully so, for other people. So much time, energy and thought are spent on it, that there is little or no time left for anything else.*

130   Stanford p. 135

131   Stanford pp. 135-136

132   Willey p. 122

133   Letter to Franz Wegeler (16 November 1801) *Für mich gibt's kein größeres Vergnügen als meine Kunst zu treiben en zu zeigen*

134   Kopitz/Cadenbach p. 19 *Wenn man zuweilen lange mit ihm spricht und auf eine Antwort wartet, so bricht er plötzlich in Töne aus, zieht sein Notenpapier hervor und schreibt.*

135   Kopitz/Cadenbach p. 1024 *Er lebt nur für seine Kunst und keine irdische Leidenschaft entstellt ihre Ausübung bei ihm, unglaublich fleißig und fruchtbar ist er.*

136   Kopitz/Cadenbach p. 754

137   Kopitz/Cadenbach p. 14 *Er starrte in das Notenblatt, trommelte, schrieb und vergaß ganz und gar auf den Nachbar. Endlich entfernte ich mich leise und er war so verloren, daß er es nicht bemerkte.*

138   Kopitz/Cadenbach p. 936 *Die Ereignisse der Außenwelt berühren ihn nur wenig, er ist ganz der Kunst eigen.*

139   Letter to Archduke Rudolph (23 July 1815) *Die üble Gewohnheit von Kindheit an, meine ersten Einfälle gleich niederschreiben zu müssen […] hat mir auch hier geschadet.*

140   Letter to Franz Wegeler (29 June 1801) *Ich lebe nur in meinen Noten, und ist das* *eine kaum da, so ist das andere schon angefangen. So wie ich jetzt schreibe, mache ich oft drei, vier Sachen zugleich.*

141 Letter to Ferdinand Ries (20 December 1822) *Denn Beethoven kann schreiben, Gott sei Dank, sonst freilich nichts in der Welt.*

142 Johann Andreas Streicher's letter to Carl Peters (5 March 1825) *Was soll ich aber zu dem Betragen Beethovens geben Sie sagen, oder wie soll ich ihn zu entschuldigen suchen? Ich kann es nur durch seine eigene Meynung thun, die er von sich selbst in meinem Hause geäußert hatte. „Alles was ich ausser der Musik thue, geräth schlecht und ist dumm" diß sind seine eigene Worte, die auch mit seinen Handlungen, so wie auch mit den Erfahrungen die seine Freunde mit ihm und durch ihn gemacht haben, vollkommen übereinstimmen.*

143 Wegeler/Ries p. 120 *Noch kann ich nicht begreifen, wie er es so lange in dieser höchst unbequemen Stellung hat aushalten können. Seine Begeisterung machte ihn für äußere Eindrücke unempfindlich.*

144 Wegeler/Ries pp. 118-119 *Bei einem ähnlichen Spaziergange, auf dem wir uns so verirrten, dass wir erst um acht Uhr nach Döbling, wo Beethoven wohnte, zurückkamen, hatte er den ganzen Weg über für sich gebrummt oder teilweise geheult, immer herauf und herunter, ohne bestimmte Noten zu singen. Auf meiner Frage, was es sei, sagte er, 'da ist mir ein Thema zum letzten Allegro der Sonate eingefallen' (in F moll Opus 57). Als wir ins Zimmer traten, lief er, ohne den Hut abzunehmen, ans Klavier. Ich setzte mich in eine Ecke, und er hatte mich bald vergessen. Nun tobte er wenigstens eine Stunde lang über das neue, so schön dastehende Finale in dieser Sonate. Endlich stand er auf, war erstaunt, mich noch zu sehen, und sagte: 'Heute kann ich Ihnen keine Lektion geben, ich muss noch arbeiten.'*

145 Asperger pp. 66-67

146 Gillberg p. 34

147 Derived from: Stanford p. 151

148 Willey p. 129

149 Stanford p. 152 *Aspies are capable of so much, but flexibility is not on the list. Aspies tend to thrive on predictability, a stable environment, and a visible, set schedule.*

150 Caeyers p. 220 *Beethoven organiseerde zijn werkdagen met veel discipline.*

151 Coldicott p. 130 *While he was in Vienna, as opposed to his long summer sojourns away from the city, his daily routine varied little.*

152 Schindler part II p. 192 & *Kopitz/Cadenbach p. 896*

153 Schindler part II p. 192

154 Gillberg p. 44

155 Coldicott p. 105

156 Schindler II pp. 192-193 & Breuning pp. 61-62

157 Schindler II p. 192: *unentbehrlichen Lebensbedürfnissen*

158 Asperger pp. 70-71

159 Asperger p. 71

160 Stanford p. 219

161 Gillberg p. 136

162 Attwood (2007) p. 219

163 Ian Stuart-Hamilton p. 193

164 Gillberg p. 35

165 Letter to Josephine von Brunsvik (6/7 July 1812) *Es gibt Momente, wo ich finde, dass die Sprache noch gar nichts ist.*

166 Letter to Josephine von Brunsvik (spring 1805) *Aber wie schwach wie armselig diese Sprache – wenigstens die meinige.*

167 Kopitz/Cadenbach p. 839 *Von Beethoven wurde ich äußert gut empfangen und war schon einigemal bei ihm. Er ist ein höchst sonderbarer Mann. Große Gedanken schweben in seiner Seele, die er aber nicht anders als durch Noten zu äußern vermag; Worte stehen ihm nicht zu Gebote.*

168 Kopitz/Cadenbach p. 828 *In solchen Momenten, da er, ganz erfüllt von dem Gegenstand, redete, erschien die Fülle der Ideen, die seinem Munde entströmten, wahrhaft wunderbar.*

169 Kopitz/Cadenbach pp. 970-972 *Beethoven sprach sehr gern und viel […] Nun sprach er in einem fort […] und da er ununterbrochen fort sprach*

170 Breuning p.1 *Er sprach fast ohne Unterbrechung*

171 Letter to Wegeler (29 July 1801) *Aber Schreiben, das weißt Du, war nie meine Sache: auch die besten Freunde haben jahrelang keine Briefe von mir erhalten.*

172 Zanden, Van der p. 7: *Corresponderen vond Beethoven lastig en tijdrovend. Het vergde concentratie en aandacht, die hij naast het vele componeren maar moeilijk kon opbrengen. Bovendien had hij moeite om – bij het corresponderen, maar ook bij andere vormen van communicatie – gangbare omgangsvormen in acht te nemen en conventies te eerbiedigen. Hij was in het algemeen niet erg voorkomend of diplomatiek in zijn uitlatingen, en zijn belangstelling voor zijn omgeving was tamelijk mager. Werd eenmaal tot een brief besloten, dan stond daarin meestal de boodschap centraal, met een minimum aan opsmuk.*

173 Asperger p. 82 *Another characteristic of autistic children is the absence of a sense of humour. […] When making puns, however, autistic people sometimes shine, and may even be highly creative. This can range from simple word-play and sound associations to precisely formulated, truly witty remarks.*

174 Gillberg p. 101 *Most people with Asperger syndrome have a type of humour that* *differs from that of people in general. Some appear to be totally devoid of humour. [...] Others love to play with words and statements made by famous people or to draw attention to the many absurdities of life.*

175   Kopitz/Cadenbach p. 216 [...] *voll von Witzen und Spott.*

176   Kopitz/Cadenbach p. 218 *Überall wusste er ein Wortspiel anzubringen.*

177   Kopitz/Cadenbach p. 24 [...] *wegen seinem wunderlichen Humor*

178   Kopitz/Cadenbach pp. 300, 314, 343, 344 [...] *seinen lustigen Wortspielen [...] und so war er voll Späße und Wortspiele [...] Zuweilen war er voll Scherz und Neckerei [...] Und so war er oft in heiterer Laune voll Wortspiele [...]*

179   Kopitz/Cadenbach p. 602 *Eigentümlich sind alle seine Äußerungen, immer gemischt mit satirischem Humor;*

180   Breuning p. 43 *Diese Vorliebe, Späße, selbst absonderliche Art, bei jeder möglichen Gelegenheit anzubringen, begegnet man sehr häufig bei Beethoven.*

181   Kopitz/Cadenbach p. 344

182   Letter to Hoffmeister & Kühnel in Leipzig (8 April 1802)

183   Letter to Peters (20 December 1822)

184   Letter to Goethe (8 February 1823)

185   Kopitz/Cadenbach p. 896

186   Letter to Braunhofer (13 May 1825)

187   Letter to Countess Erdödy (Summer 1815)

188   Letter to Countess Erdödy (19 September 1815)

189   Letter to Gleichenstein (April 1810)

190   Letter to nephew Karl (16 August 1823)

191   Forbes p. 771

192   Kopitz/Cadenbach p. 640

193   Kopitz/Cadenbach p. 279

194   WoO 191

195   WoO 180

196   Kopitz/Cadenbach p. 218

197   Letter to Nanette Streicher (27 July 1817)

198 Letter to Nanette Streicher (20 July 1817)

199 Letter to Anna Milder-Hauptmann (6 January 1816)

200 WoO 183

201 Breuning p. 74

202 Breuning p. 44

203 Kopitz/Cadenbach p. 897

204 Letter to Josephine von Brunsvik (6/7 July 1812)

205 Asperger p. 42

206 Gillberg p. 38

207 Breuning p. 1 *Sein Aussehen war kräftig, die Statur mittelgroß, sein Gang energisch, wie seine lebhaften Bewegungen; der Anzug so wenig elegant als eben bürgerlich, und doch lag ein Etwas in seiner Gesamtheit, das in keine Rangordnung passte.*

208 *sforzando*: to be played with strong initial attack; *piano*: to be played softly; *crescendo*: a gradual increase in loudness or intensity; *forte*: a passage that is loud and played with force

209 Kopitz/Cadenbach p. 931 *Soviel ich auch hatte davon erzählen hören, so überraschte es mich doch in hohem Grade. Beethoven hatte sich angewöhnt, dem Orchester die Ausdruckszeichen durch allerlei sonderbare Körperbewegungen anzudeuten. So oft ein Sforzando vorkam, riss er beide Arme, die er vorher auf der Brust kreuzte, mit Vehemenz auseinander. Bei dem Piano bückte er sich nieder und umso tiefer, je schwächer er es wollte. Trat dann ein Crescendo ein, so richtete er sich nach und nach wieder auf und sprang beim Eintritte des Forte hoch in die Höhe. Auch schrie er manchmal, um das Forte noch zu verstärken, mit hinein, ohne es zu wissen.*

210 Kopitz/Cadenbach pp. 39-40 *Er stand gleichsam auf einer einsamen Insel und dirigierte mit seltsamen Gebärden […] seiner dunkle dämonischen Harmonien Ausflug in die Welt der übrigen Menschen.*

211 Kopitz/Cadenbach pp. 893-894 *Überhaupt war es schwer, ja rein unmöglich, aus seinen Mienen Zeichen des Beifalls oder des Missbehagens zu entziffern: er blieb sich immer gleich, scheinbar kalt und ebenso verschlossen in seinen Urtheilen über Kunstgenossen; nur der Geist arbeitete rastlos im Innern, die animalische Hülle glich einem seelenlosen Marmor.*

212 Kopitz/Cadenbach p. 517 *In freundlichen Gespräch nahm er aber wieder einen gutmüthigen u milden Ausdruck an wenn ihn nehmlich das Gespräch angenehm berührte. – Jede Stimmung seiner Seele drückte sich augenblicklich in seinen Zügen gewaltsam aus.*

213 Kopitz/Cadenbach p. 755

214 Fischer p. 88 *Ludwig van Beethoven war am Morgen in seinem Schlafzimmer nach dem Hof zu und lag an der Fenster und hat sein Kopf in beide Hände gelegt und sah ernsthaft starr auf einen Flecken hin.*

215   Kopitz/Cadenbach p. 529 [...] *kleine, blinzende Augen* [...]

216   Kopitz/Cadenbach p. 427 [...] *mit leuchtenden Augen* [...]

217   Kopitz/Cadenbach p. 172 [...] *feurige Augen, die zwar klein, aber tief liegen, rund und voll ungeheuren Lebens sind.*

218   Kopitz/Cadenbach p. 517 *Sein Auge [war] blaugrau und höchst lebendig.*

219   Kopitz/Cadenbach p. 39 [...] *tiefsinnige, melancholische Augen,* [...]

220   Kopitz/Cadenbach p. 754

221   Kopitz/Cadenbach p. 640 *In diesem Augenblick trat Beethoven mit seinem gewöhnlichen finsteren Blick in den Laden.*

222   Kopitz/Cadenbach p. 1042 [...] *das Auge verkündigt unergründliche Tiefen der Empfindung* [...]

223   Kopitz/Cadenbach p. 602 [...] *mit schönen sprechenden Augen* [...]

224   Kopitz/Cadenbach p. 714 [...] *unruhige, leuchtende, ja bei fixirtem Blick fast Augen* [...] *im Ausdruck des Antlitzes, besonders des geist- und lebensvollen Auges, eine Mischung oder ein, zuweilen augenblicklicher Wechsel von herzlichster Gutmüthigkeit und von Scheu* [...]

225   Kopitz/Cadenbach p. 850 [...] *mit überirdisch begeistertem Auge* [...]

226   Kopitz/Cadenbach p. 14 [...] *sah mich mit einem durchdringenden, fast dämonischen Blicke an* [...]

227   Kopitz/Cadenbach p. 549 *Der dunkelglühende Blick des großen Meisters lag durchdringend auf mir.*

228   Kopitz/Cadenbach p. 798 [...] *die grossen durchdringende Augen* [...]

229   Kopitz/Cadenbach p. 53

230   Kopitz/Cadenbach p. 873 [...] *hat nicht große, aber tiefliegende, feuersprühende Augen* [...]

231   Kopitz/Cadenbach p. 979

232   Kopitz/Cadenbach pp. 969-970 *Sein großes tiefliegendes Stech-Auge, das zu blitzen schien und in der Seele des vor ihm stehenden Individuum sich Eingang zu versichern wusste* [...]

233   Kopitz/Cadenbach p. 371 [...] *dunklen stechenden Augen* [...]

234   Kopitz/Cadenbach pp. 278-279 *Bald darauf trat eine gedrungene Gestalt in Mittelgröße mit freundlicher Gebärde und liebevollem Blick heraus und nöthigte mich in sein Zimmer.*

235 Kopitz/Cadenbach p. 280 *Sein Augen- und Mienenspiel antwortete mir: Was verstehst Du, Tölpel, und alle ihr Klügler davon, die ihr meine Werke tadelt? Euch fehlt der Schwung, die kühnen Adlerflügel, um mir nachfolgen zu können.*

236 Kopitz/Cadenbach p. 681 [...] *mit einem solchen Blick der Güte, und zugleich des Leidens* [...]

237 Kopitz/Cadenbach p. 682 [...] *das Auge klein, blaßgrau, doch sprechend.* [...] *in seinen milden Augen* [...]

238 Kopitz/Cadenbach p. 561 [...] *namentlich übertraf der wunderbare, fast unheimlich fremdartige Glanz seiner Augen Alles in der Art* [...] *mit einem durchdringenden Blick fixirte, dann weiter ging. Nie werde ich dieses Menschenauge, in dessen leuchtenden Abgrund ich so nahe geblickt, vergessen!* [...] *denn er richtete einmal seine kleinen, wetterleuchtenden Augen halb befremdet, halb verächtlich auf mich.* [...]

239 Kopitz/Cadenbach p. 91 [...] *die Blicke aus scharfen, geistreichen Augen unstät entsendend* [...]

240 Kopitz/Cadenbach p. 927 *In seinem Augen lag etwas ungemein Lebendiges und Glänzendes* [...]

241 Kopitz/Cadenbach p. 746 *Aber was kein Kupferstecher ausdrücken kann, war die unerklärliche Traurigkeit in all seinen Zügen, - während unter den buschigen Augenbrauen, wie aus der Tiefe von Höhlen, Augen hervorblitzten, die, obwohl klein, einen zu durchbohren schienen.*

242 Gillberg p. 38

243 Kopitz/Cadenbach p. 515 *Beethoven sah sehr ernst aus, seine äußerst lebendigen Augen schwärmten meist mit einem etwas finsteren gedrückten Blick nach oben, den ich gesucht habe im Bilde wiederzugeben.*

244 Gillberg p. 61 *The majority of those with Asperger syndrome have motor incoordination or motor 'fluency' problems of various kinds.*

245 Gillberg p. 39

246 Kopitz/Cadenbach p. 200 „O" – *sagte Gelinek ganz niedergeschlagen, „an den gestrigen Tag werde ich denken! in dem jungen Menschen steckt der Satan. Nie habe ich so spielen gehört! Er fantasirte auf ein von mir gegebenes Thema, wie ich selbst Mozart nie fantasieren gehört habe. Dann spielte er eigene Compositionen die im höchsten Grade wunderbar u großartig sind u er bringt auf dem Clavier Schwierigkeiten u Effekte hervor, von denen wir uns nie etwas haben träumen lassen."*

247 Wegeler/Ries pp. 141-142 *Beethoven war in seinem Benehmen sehr linkisch und unbeholfen; seinen ungeschickten Bewegungen fehlte alle Anmut. Er nahm selten etwas in die Hand, das nicht fiel oder zerbrach. So warf er mehrmals sein Tintenfass in das neben dem Schreibpult stehende Klavier. Kein Möbel war bei ihm sicher, am wenigsten ein kostbares; alles wurde umgeworfen, beschmutzt und zerstört. Wie er es so weit brachte, sich selbst rasieren zu können, bleibt schwer zu begreifen, wenn man auch die häufigen Schnitte auf seinen Wangen dabei nicht in Betracht zog. – Nach dem Takte tanzen konnte er nie lernen.*

248   Gillberg p. 61

249   Breuning p. 65 *Wie Beethoven von einer ihm eigentümlichen Unbeholfenheit gewesen: die Schreibfedern sich zurechtzuschneiden, ebenso erwiesen sich seine mehr plumpen Finger auch wenig geeignet, die Bleistifte, ohne sie bald zu brechen, zuzuspitzen. Dies mag die Veranlassung gegeben haben, dass er es liebte, Bleistifte dicken Kalibers, ähnlich jenen, wie sie die Zimmerleute zu gebrauchen pflegen, sich anzuschaffen.*

250   Gillberg p. 39

251   Gillberg p. 60

252   Asperger p. 80

253   Temple Grandin (1995) p. 74

254   Attwood (2007) p. 275

255   Temple Grandin (1986) p. 20

256   Attwood (2007) pp. 276-278 & Stanford p. 183

257   Attwood (2007) p. 276

258   Caeyers p. 203 *Bovendien werd hij overgevoelig voor plots opduikende luide klanken en hard schreeuwende lieden.*

259   Letter to Wegeler (29 June 1801) *Manchmal auch hör' ich den Redenden, der leise spricht, kaum, ja die Töne wohl, aber die Worte nicht; und doch sobald jemand schreit, ist es mir unausstehlich.*

260   Kopitz/Cadenbach p. 1087 *Bedeutsam ist es jedoch, dass er vor der Erkrankung unübertrefflich zart- und feinhörig war und dass er auch jetzt noch allen Übellaut schmerzlich empfindet.*

261   Kopitz/Cadenbach p. 279 *'Auch ich', erzählte Beethoven, 'spielte in meiner Jugend viel die Orgel, aber meine Nerven vertrugen die Gewalt dieses Rieseninstrumentes nicht.*

262   Caeyers p. 371 *Onze verbeelding schiet tekort om Beethoven in dit plaatje te doen passen.[…] Ook de muzak die in de colonnades weerklonk werkte op zijn zenuwen. En het galmende geluid van de taterende menigte in de badruimtes moet hem pijn aan de oren hebben gedaan. Gewoon gepraat was hem al vaak te veel, laat staan echoënde smalltalk.*

263   Gillberg p. 68 *People with Asperger syndrome almost always have major strengths that may, wholly or partly, compensate for the major difficulties. Almost all the core features of the syndrome have 'positive' opposites. Good general IQ, perseverance, stubbornness and perfectionism are just a few of the strengths often shown by individuals with Asperger syndrome.*

264   Asperger p. 75

265   Caeyers p. 43 *Beethoven wilde dus wel leren, maar niet op commando, en hij heeft later zijn kennis en eruditie vooral op autodidactische wijze moeten verwerven.*

266 Kopitz/Cadenbach p. 500 *Sein Spiel unterscheidet sich auch so sehr von der gewöhnlichen Art das Klavier zu behandeln, dass es scheint, als habe er sich einen ganz eigenen Weg bahnen wollen, um zu dem Ziel der Vollendung zu kommen, an welchem er jezt steht.*

267 Kopitz/Cadenbach p. 666 *Es jammert mich oft recht herzinnig, wenn ich den grundbraven, trefflichen Mann finster und leidend erblicke, wiewohl ich auch wieder überzeugt bin, dass seine besten originellsten Werke nur in solcher eigensinnigen, tief missmutigen Stimmung hervorgebracht werden konnten.*

268 Kopitz/Cadenbach p. 754

269 Anton Schindler's letter to Ignaz Moscheles (24 March 1827) *Sein Eigensinn ist aber noch immer entsetzlich […]*

270 Wegeler/Ries p. 103 *Beethoven sei immer so eigensinnig und selbstwollend gewesen, dass er Manches durch harte Erfahrung habe lernen müssen, was er früher nie als Gegenstand eines Unterrichts habe annehmen wollen.*

271 Forbes p. 747

272 Gillberg p. 64

273 Caeyers pp. 220-221 *In tegenstelling tot het dagelijks leven, waarin hij een absolute sloddervos was, ging Beethoven bij het componeren zeer methodisch te werk*

274 See also Caeyers pp. 220-224; the terms *intuitive composer* and *constructive composer* are coined by Kurt Westphal.

275 Caeyers p. 360 *De uitgave van het Vijfde pianoconcert verschilde ook van de vorige door de precisie waarmee Beethoven alle uitvoeringsdetails heeft willen weergeven: de articulatietekens, het pedaalgebruik en de vele mogelijkheden van klank en expressie. Niets werd aan het toeval overgelaten.*

276 Swafford p. 715

277 Letter to Breitkopf & Härtel (23 August 1813) *Ich weiß, der Text ist äußerst schlecht, aber hat man sich einmal aus einem auch schlechten Text ein Ganzes gedacht, so ist es schwer, durch einzelne Änderungen zu vermeiden, dass eben dieses nicht gestört werde, und ist nun gar ein Wort allein, worin manchmal große Bedeutung gelegt, so muss es schon bleiben, und ein schlechter Autor ist dieser, der nicht so viel Gutes als möglich auch aus einem schlechten Text zu machen weiß oder sucht, und ist dieses der Fall, so werden Änderungen das Ganze gewiss nicht besser machen.*

278 Letter to Thomson (19 February 1813) *Ich bin nicht gewohnt meine Kompositionen zu überarbeiten. Ich habe das nie getan, da ich von der Wahrheit durchdrungen bin, dass jede teilweise Änderung den Charakter der ganzen Komposition verändert.* Beethoven's letter to Thomson is in French, so the original quote is: *Je ne suis pas accoutumé de retoucher mes compositions; Je ne l'ai jamais fait, penetré de la verité que tout changement partielle altere le Caractere de la composition.*

279 The opera only became popular in 1814, during the renewed popularity of Beethoven's music generally.

280   Gillberg p. 66 *Many with Asperger syndrome are impatient and tend to give up easily. Many others are extremely persistent. Others still combine impatience in some settings – usually those that are perceived as uninteresting or 'impossible' – with extreme tenacity and persistence in other situations – not least, of course, in areas of special narrow interests.*

281   Caeyers p. 212 *Net als de grote helden die hij bewonderde, moest Beethoven dus lijden om zichzelf te kunnen overstijgen, en grootse prestaties voor de mensheid te kunnen leveren.*

282   Letter to Wegeler (16 November 1801) [...] *aber mein Gehör ist gewiß um nichts noch gebessert, ich wage es nicht zu bestimmen, ob es nicht eher schwächer geworden?*

283   Letter to Kasper Karl and Johann Nikolaus van Beethoven (6 and 10 October 1802)
Für meine Brüder Carl und [Leerraum] Beethowen
O ihr Menschen die ihr mich für Feindseelig störisch oder Misantropisch haltet oder erkläret, wie unrecht thut ihr mir, ihr wißt nicht die geheime ursache von dem, was euch so scheinet, mein Herz und mein Sinn waren von Kindheit an für das zarte Gefühl des Wohlwollens, selbst große Handlungen zu verrichten dazu war ich immer aufgelegt, aber bedenket nur daß seit 6 Jahren ein heilloser Zustand mich befallen, durch unvernünftige Ärzte verschlimmert, von Jahr zu Jahr in der Hofnung gebessert zu werden, betrogen, endlich zu dem überblick eines **daurenden Übels** ~~das~~ *(dessen Heilung vieleicht Jahre dauren oder gar unmöglich ist) gezwungen, mit einem feurigen Lebhaften Temperamente gebohren selbst empfänglich für die Zerstreuungen der Gesellschaft, muste ich früh mich absondern, einsam mein Leben zubringen, wollte ich auch zuweilen mich einmal über alles das hinaussezen, o wie hart wurde ich dur[ch] die verdoppelte traurige Erfahrung meines schlechten Gehör's dann zurückgestoßen, und doch war's mir noch nicht möglich den Menschen zu sagen: sprecht lauter, schreyt, denn ich bin Taub, ach wie wär es möglich daß ich* ~~da~~ *die Schwäche* **eines Sinnes** *angeben sollte, der bey mir in einem Vollkommenern Grade als bey andern seyn sollte, einen Sinn denn ich einst in der grösten Vollkommenheit besaß, in einer Vollkommenheit, wie ihn wenige von meinem Fache gewiß haben noch gehabt haben – o ich kann es nicht, drum verzeiht, wenn ihr mich da zurückweichen sehen werdet, wo ich mich gerne unter euch mischte, doppelt Wehe thut mir mein unglück, indem ich dabey verkannt werden muß, für mich darf Erholung in Menschlicher Gesellschaft, feinere unterredungen, Wechselseitige Ergießungen nicht statt haben, ganz allein fast nur so viel als es die höchste Nothwendigkeit fodert, darf ich mich in Gesellschaft einlassen, wie ein Verbannter muß ich leben, nahe ich mich einer Gesellschaft, so überfällt mich eine heiße Ängstlichkeit, indem ich befürchte in Gefahr gesezt zu werden, meine[n] Zustand merken zu laßen*
so war es denn auch dieses halbe Jahr, was ich auf dem Lande zubrachte, von meinem Vernünftigen Arzte aufgefodert, so viel als möglich mein Gehör zu schonen, kamm er ~~mir~~ *fast meiner jezigen natürlichen Disposizion entgegen, obschon, Vom Triebe zur Gesellschaft manchmal hingerissen, ich mich dazu verleiten ließ, aber welche Demüthigung wenn jemand neben mir stund und von weitem eine Flöte hörte und* **ich nichts** *hörte, oder jemand den* **Hirten Singen** *hörte, und ich auch nichts hörte;*
solche Ereignisse brachten mich nahe an Verzweiflung, es fehlte wenig, und ich endigte selbst mein Leben – nur sie die **Kunst**, *sie hielt mich zurück, ach es dünkte mir unmöglich, die Welt eher zu verlassen, bis ich das alles hervorgebracht, wozu ich mich aufgelegt fühlte, und so fristete ich dieses elende Leben – wahrhaft elend, einen so reizbaren Körper, daß eine etwas schnelle Veränderung mich aus dem Besten Zustande in den schlechtesten versezen kann –* **Geduld** *– so heist es, Sie muß ich nun zur führerin wählen, ich habe es – daurend hoffe ich, soll mein Entschluß seyn, auszuharren, bis es den unerbittlichen Parzen gefällt, den Faden zu brechen, vieleicht geht's besser, vieleicht nicht, ich bin gefaßt*
– schon in meinem 28. Jahre gezwungen Philosoph zu werden, es ist nicht leicht, für den Künstler schwere[r] als für irgend jemand – Gottheit du siehst herab auf mein inneres, du kennst es, du weist, daß menschenliebe und neigung zum Wohlthun drin Hausen, o Men-

schen, wenn ihr einst dieses leset, so denkt, daß ihr mir unrecht gethan, und der unglückliche, er tröste sich, einen seines gleichen zu finden, der troz allen Hindernissen der Natur, doch noch alles gethan, was in seinem Vermögen stand, um in die Reihe würdiger Künstler und Menschen aufgenommen zu werden

– ihr meine Brüder Carl und [Leerraum], sobald ich Tod bin und Professor schmid lebt noch, so bittet ihn in meinem Namen, daß er meine Krankheit beschreibe, und dieses hier geschriebene Blatt füget ihr dieser meiner Krankengeschichte bey, zu damit wenigstens so viel als möglich die Welt nach meinem Tode mit mir versöhnt werde – zugleich erkläre ich euch beyde hier für meine die Erben des kleinen Vermögens, (wenn man es so nennen kann) von mir, theilt es redlich, und vertragt und helft euch einander, was ihr mir zuwider gethan, das wist ihr, war euch schon längst verziehen, dir Bruder Carl danke ich noch in's besondre für deine in dieser leztern spätern Zeit mir bewiesene Anhänglichkeit, Mein Wunsch ist, daß ich euch ein bessers sorgenvolleresloseres Leben, als mir, werde, emphelt euren nach Kindern Tugend, sie nur allein kann glücklich machen, nicht Geld, ich spreche aus Erfahrung, sie war es, die mich selbst im Elende gehoben, ihr Dank ich nebst meiner Kunst, daß ich durch keinen selbstmord mein Leben endigte

– lebt wohl und liebt euch; – allen Freunden danke ich, besonders fürst Lichnovski und P[r]ofessor schmidt – die Instrumente von fürst L.[ichnowsky] wünsche ich, daß sie doch mögen aufbewahrt werden bey einem von euch, doch entstehe deswegen kein Streit unter euch, sobald sie euch aber zu was nüzlicherm dienen können, so verkauft sie nur, wie froh bin ich, wenn ich auch noch unter meinem Grabe euch nüzen kann – so wär's geschehen - mit freuden eil ich dem Tode entgegen – kömmt er früher als ich Gelegenheit gehabt habe, noch alle meine Kunst-Fähigkeiten zu entfalten, so wird er mir troz meinem Harten Schicksaal doch noch zu frühe kommen, und ich würde ihn wohl später wünschen – doch auch dann bin ich zufrieden, befreyt er mich nicht von einem endlosen Leidenden Zustande? – Komm, wann du willst, ich gehe dir muthig entgegen – lebt wohl und Vergeßt mich nicht ganz im Tode, ich habe es um euch verdient, indem ich in meinem Leben oft an euch gedacht, euch glücklich zu machen, seyd es –

Ludwig van Beethowen

Heiglnstadt am 6ten october 1802

für meine Brüder Carl und [Leerraum] nach meinem Tode zu lesen und zu vollziehen – Heiglnstadt am 10ten oktober 1802 – so nehme ich den Abschied von dir – und zwar traurig – ja dir geliebte Hoffnung – die ich mit hieher nahm, wenigstens bis zu einem gewissen Punkte geheilet zu seyn – sie muß mich nun gänzlich verlassen, wie die blätter des Herbstes herabfallen, gewelkt sind, so ist – auch sie für mich dürr geworden, fast wie ich hieher kamm – gehe ich fort – selbst der Hohe Muth – der mich oft in den Schönen Sommertägen beseelte – er ist verschwunden – o Vorsehung – laß einmal einen reinen Tag der Freude mir erscheinen – so lange schon ist der wahren Freude inniger widerhall mir fremd – o wann – o Wann o Gottheit – kann ich im Tempel der Natur und der Menschen ihn wider fühlen – Nie? – nein – o es wäre zu hart

284   Asperger p. 89 *To our own amazement, we have seen that autistic individuals, as long as they are intellectually intact, can almost always achieve professional success, usually in highly specialised academic professions, often in very high positions, with a preference for abstract content. [...] There are also several musicians of considerable stature who were observed by us when children.*

285   Gillberg p. 51

286   Stanford p. 23 *I believe that someday we will wake up as a civilization and realize that the Aspie traits that now confuse us are part of the core of human progress. Geniuses throughout history who have been previously identified as highly eccentric are now being recognized as having AS and are being authoritatively diagnosed post-mortem. I believe that as we* *become more sophisticated in our perceptions, we will realize some of the brilliance behind the Aspie brain.*

287   Gillberg p. 6

288   Gillberg p. 6

289   Gillberg p. 6 - Gillberg writes "routines and <u>interests</u>;" my rephrasing is with his consent.

290   Gillberg p. 6

291   Gillberg p. 6

292   Gillberg p. 6

293   Gillberg p. 7

294   Roberts p. 41 (slightly altered)

295   Roberts p. 52

296   Aron p. 10

297   Aron pp. 10-11

298   Klemm p. 133 *fest überzeugt*

299   Klemm p. 134 [...] *seine künstlerische Hochbegabung, die extremen Stimmungs-schwankungen, die innige Naturverbundenheit, seine große Empfindsamkeit, sein – vor der Ertaubung – außergewöhnlich guter Hörsinn (worauf Beethoven in seinem „Heiligenstädter Testament" selbst anspielt), womöglich sogar einige seiner chronischen Erkrankungen.*

300   Klemm p. 58 *Dabei sind es die typischen Missgeschicke, die einem Hochsensiblen in Momenten nervlicher Anspannung unterlaufen – wie seine Schrittfehler beim Tanzen.*

301   Davies p. 260

302   Kopitz/Cadenbach p. 828 *In solchen Momenten, da er, ganz erfüllt von dem Gegenstand, redete, erschien die Fülle der Ideen, die seinem Munde entströmten, wahrhaft wunderbar.*

303   Asperger p. 74 *We have mentioned repeatedly that autism occurs at different levels of ability. The range encompasses all levels of ability from the highly original genius, through the weird eccentric who lives in a world of his own and achieves very little, down to the most severe contact-disturbed, automaton-like mentally retarded individual.*

304   During the time I did write these lines (March 2016), it turned out that Johan Cruijff had passed away. From the obituaries it became clear that a sportsman can also be seen as a genius.

305   *Stammbuch* inscription (29 October 1792) [...] *Mozart's Genius trauert noch und beweinet den Tod seines Zöglinges. Bey dem unerschöpflichem Hayden fand er Zuflucht, aber* *keine Beschäftigung; durch ihn wünscht er noch einmal mit jemanden vereinigt zu werden. Durch ununterbrochenen Fleiß erhalten Sie: Mozart's Geist aus Haydens Händen.*

306 It is striking that Waldstein writes about the Genius of Mozart, but not about the Genius of Haydn.

307 Forbes p. 375 adapted

308 Hoffmann (2006) pp. 52-54 *Sollte, wenn von der Musik als einer selbständigen Kunst die Rede ist, nicht immer nur die Instrumental-Musik gemeint sein, welche jede Hülfe, jede Beimischung einer andern Kunst (der Poesie) verschmähend des eigentümliche nur in ihr zu erkennende Wesen dieser Kunst rein ausspricht? – Sie ist die romantischte aller Künste, beinahe möchte man sagen, allein echt romantisch, denn nur das Unendliche ist ihr Vorwurf.*
[...]
So öffnet uns auch Beethoven's Instrumental-Musik *das Reich des Ungeheuern und Unermeslichen. Glühende Strahlen schießen durch dieses Reiches tiefe Nacht und wir werden Riesenschatten gewahr, die auf- und abwogen, enger und enger uns einschließen und uns ernichten, aber nicht den Schmerz der unendlichen Sehnsucht, in welcher jede Lust, die schnell in jauchzenden Tönen emporgestiegen, hinsinkt und untergeht, und nur in diesem Schmerz, die Liebe, Hoffnung, Freude, in sich verzehrend aber nicht zerstörend unsere Brust mit einem vollstimmigen Zusammenklange aller Leidenschaften zersprengen will, leben wir fort und sind entzückte Geisterseher!*
[...]
Beethovens Musik bewegt die Hebel der Furcht, des Schauers, des Entsetzens, des Schmerzes und erweckt eben jene unendliche Sehnsucht, welche das Wesen der Romantik ist. Er ist daher ein rein romantischer Komponist, und mag es nicht daher kommen, dass ihm Vokalmusik, die den Charakter des unbestimmten Sehnens nicht zulässt, sondern nur durch Worte bestimmte Affekte als in dem Reiche des Unendlichen empfunden darstellt, weniger gelingt.

309 Caeyers p. 76 *Helene Breuning kende dat soort erupties, wist die te duiden en besefte dat men moest kunnen leven met de schaduwzijde van Beethovens genialiteit om te kunnen profiteren van zijn lichtkant.*

310 Asperger p. 46

311 Asperger p. 89

312 Asperger p. 87 *In the less favorable cases, they roam the streets as 'originals,' grotesque and dilapidated, talking loudly to themselves or unconcernedly to passers-by as autistic individuals would. They are taunted by urchins and react to this with wild but ineffectual outbursts.*

313 Von Breuning pp. 63-64 *Beethovens äußere Erscheinung hatte, der ihm ganz eigentümliche Nonchalance in der Bekleidung wegen, auf der Straße etwas ungewöhnlich Auffälliges an sich. Meist in Gedanken vertieft und diese vor sich hin brummend, gestikulierte er, wenn er allein ging, nicht selten mit den Armen dazu. Ging er in Gesellschaft, so sprach er sehr lebhaft und laut [...] So kam es, dass die meisten der ihm Begegnenden sich nach ihm umwandten, und ihm nachriefen. Neffe Carl verschmähte deshalb mit ihm auszugehen, und hatte ihm auch geradezu einmal gesagt, dass er sich schäme, ihn seines ‚narrenhaften Aussehens' wegen auf der Straße zu begleiten, worüber er sehr gekränkt und verletzt uns gegenüber sich äußerte.*

314 Von Breuning p. 35 *Seine Abgezogenheit von der Außenwelt bekundet sich mitunter* *in wahrhaft außergewöhnlichen Eigentümlichkeiten. So z.B. lies er es sich nicht anfechten, fasst seiner sämtlichen Bekleidung sich zu entledigen und diese dann über dem Stocke auf der Achsel zu tragen, wenn er die Sommerhitze auf seinen Spaziergängen in einsamen Wäldern zu drückend fühlte. Namentlich soll er dies in den von ihm mit Vorliebe besuchten Waldungen zwischen Baden und Gaden sich erlaubt haben; so dass mein Vater wiederholt die Besorgnis aussprach, es könnten gelegentlich deshalb ihm Unannehmlichkeiten von Seiten ihm Begegnender widerfahren.*

315   Von Breuning p. 74 *Als wir nach Hause gingen, schoben mehrere Jungen in der Mitte der rechtsseitigen Allee vor der Schönbrunner Brücke Kegel mit einer kleinen Kugel, und diese traf Beethoven zufällig an den Fuß. Wähnend, es sei dies aus mutwilliger Absicht geschehen, ihn zu necken, wandte er sich unmittelbar heftig gegen sie, ausrufend: ,Wer hat Euch erlaubt hier zu spielen? Müsst Ihr gerade hier Euer Unwesen treiben?!', und wollte auf sie losstürzen, sie wegzutreiben. Mein Vater, die Rohheit des Gassenjungen fürchtend, beruhigte ihn aber bald wieder, und überdies hatte ihm das Streifen der Kugel nur flüchtigen Schmerz verursacht.*

316   Caeyers p.15 & p. 530 *stadsrariteit*

317   Asperger pp. 89-90 *We are convinced, then, that autistic people have their place in the organism of the social community. They fulfil their role well, perhaps better than anyone else could, and we are talking of people who as children had the greatest difficulties and caused untold worries to their care-givers.*

www.ingramcontent.com/pod-product-compliance
Lightning Source LLC
Chambersburg PA
CBHW081550280526
45788CB00011B/3425